MAO'S ARMY GOES TO SEA

MAO'S ARMY GOES TO SEA

THE ISLAND CAMPAIGNS AND THE FOUNDING OF CHINA'S NAVY

TOSHI YOSHIHARA

GEORGETOWN UNIVERSITY PRESS | WASHINGTON, DC

The publisher is not responsible for third-party websites or their content. URL links were active at time of publication.

Library of Congress Cataloging-in-Publication Data

Names: Yoshihara, Toshi, author.
Title: Mao's army goes to sea : the island campaigns and the founding of China's navy / Toshi Yoshihara.
Description: Washington, DC : Georgetown University Press, 2022. | Includes bibliographical references and index.
Identifiers: LCCN 2021062356 (print) | LCCN 2021062357 (ebook) | ISBN 9781647122812 (hardcover) | ISBN 9781647122829 (paperback) | ISBN 9781647122836 (ebook)
Subjects: LCSH: China. Zhongguo ren min jie fang jun. Hai jun. | China—History, Naval—20th century.
Classification: LCC DS739 .Y67 2022 (print) | LCC DS739 (ebook) | DDC 359.00951—dc23/eng/20220901
LC record available at https://lccn.loc.gov/2021062356
LC ebook record available at https://lccn.loc.gov/2021062357

♾ This paper meets the requirements of ANSI/NISO Z39.48-1992 (Permanence of Paper).

24 23   9 8 7 6 5 4 3

Printed in the United States of America

Cover design by Jeremy John Parker
Interior design by BookComp, Inc.

For Susan, Teresa, and Dorothy

CONTENTS

MAPS

ACKNOWLEDGMENTS

This was an unexpected book project. Since the late 1990s, I have been laser-focused on the present and the future of the Chinese navy. Its origins were, at best, an afterthought. For years, I had uncritically accepted the dismissive interpretations of Communist China's earliest years at sea. The conventional wisdom held that China's maritime thought was largely a Soviet derivative and that the founding naval leaders—army officers selected for their loyalty to the Chinese Communist Party—contributed little to the nautical enterprise. There was not much interesting or substantive to examine.

My view changed when I took an unanticipated detour through history. I began an intellectual journey after I stumbled across Chinese open sources about the short, sharp clash between China and South Vietnam over the Paracel Islands in 1974. The little-known Chinese victory in that naval battle, minor by Western standards, furnished China a foothold in the South China Sea. I was stunned by the availability of writings on the naval engagement and discovered that the literature provided rich materials on the operational success. I published an article documenting the Chinese perspectives of the campaign for the *Naval War College Review* in 2016. After dipping my toe in China's naval past, I became more intrigued about the Chinese navy's origins.

I looked further back in time and came across a large body of works on the Chinese navy's founding and Communist China's earliest offshore campaigns. Some writings were firsthand accounts by those who participated in the critical first months of China's seaward turn. The origin story, as the Chinese have retold it, is far richer than most in the West have presumed. Just as I saw parallels between the 1974 Paracels sea battle and present-day Chinese maritime behavior, I detected patterns in 1949 and 1950 that could have implications for Chinese sea power today. I became convinced that an understanding of China's prospects at sea in the twenty-first century requires an acquaintance with its maritime past. This book is the product of these leaps back in time.

I am indebted to many colleagues who made this book possible. I thank Thomas G. Mahnken, president and CEO of the Center for Strategic and Budgetary Assessments, for his unstinting support to the project from its inception to its publication. I am grateful for the terrific feedback on the book's earlier draft by Evan Montgomery, director of research and studies at the Center for Strategic and Budgetary Assessments; Ian Easton, senior director at the Project 2049 Institute; Grant Newsham, senior research fellow at the Japan Forum for Strategic Studies; John Schurtz, senior research associate at the Georgia Tech Research Institute; and Brig. Gen. Anthony Henderson, United States Marine Corps whose input was entirely his own and does not represent the views of the Department of Defense, Department of the Navy, or the United States Government. The study benefited from the constructive and learned commentaries by three anonymous reviewers. Special thanks go to Grace Kim, Josh Chang, and Peter Kouretsos for their diligent assistance throughout the course of the research project. Most of all, I thank my wife, Susan, and my two daughters, Teresa and Dorothy, for their love and encouragement.

MAP 0.1. The Offshore campaigns, 1949–1950

© Toshi Yoshihara

ONE

Introduction

This is the story of the People's Liberation Army's (PLA) first encounters with the seas. Drawing extensively from Chinese-language sources, *Mao's Army Goes to Sea* recounts the Chinese navy's founding and the earliest naval engagements and amphibious operations by Mao Zedong's forces to secure China's maritime periphery. The ensuing chapters detail how Mao's trusted lieutenants struggled to establish a new naval service and to fight at sea even as the wider Chinese Civil War on the mainland drew to its bitter end. The study further shows that the navy-building process, the pitched battles at sea, and the contested landings on offshore islands had a lasting influence on the Chinese military's institutions, outlook, strategy, doctrine, and force structure.

In April 1949, Chinese Communist forces crossed the Yangzi River, the last major obstacle to Mao's conquest of mainland China. As the PLA swept to victory across southern China amid collapsing Nationalist resistance, Mao's armies reached the long coastline facing the East and South China Seas. After making contact with the seas, they found that they had exchanged one set of operational challenges on land for a new kind of problem: the Nationalist threat at sea. To dislodge Nationalist defenders dug in on islands, some no more than a few nautical miles offshore, Communist forces had to learn to operate in an entirely new environment. Over the course of eighteen months from April 1949 to October 1950, Mao's subordinates scrambled to stand up a new navy from scratch while launching improvised amphibious operations to drive the Nationalists from offshore islands and ultimately from Taiwan.

AN ARMY GOES TO SEA

This is a remarkable but little-known story in the West. A revolutionary, agrarian-based army, a stranger to sea power, had to adapt to radically new circumstances. Lifelong army officers had to acquaint themselves with nautical affairs and naval tactics, while combat-hardened soldiers, many of whom had never seen the ocean, had to retrain for sea crossings and beach landings. Mao and his senior army commanders too had to puzzle through the unique institutional and material requirements of a new navy. They learned that the naval buildup was not merely a technological question. It had as much to do with cultivating human capital as with forging weaponry. The PLA, moreover, confronted an adversary that still commanded the air and the seas, while Communist forces had virtually no navy, no air force, and no modern industrial base to speak of.

And yet, in less than two years Mao and his commanders notched some significant successes even as they suffered one of the most disastrous defeats in the civil war. The establishment of the East China Navy, the predecessor of the Eastern Theater Navy or East Sea Fleet, served as an institutional laboratory for constructing the national navy, the People's Liberation Army Navy (PLAN). The Communists built a makeshift navy that drew its resources, in part, from former Chinese Nationalist Party (Kuomintang [KMT]) officers and sailors and from the civilian sector, including its fishermen and merchantmen and their boats. The naval leadership founded naval academies and established a system for grooming the next generation of seagoing officers and troops in lightning speed. By the fall of 1950, the Chinese navy had developed a long-term vision and a concrete buildup plan. But war on the Korean Peninsula and Mao's subsequent decision to intervene in the conflict abruptly changed Beijing's priorities and substantially curtailed the navy's program.

Running parallel to the PLAN's institutional development were a series of amphibious operations by Mao's forces to capture various offshore islands occupied by the Nationalists. The PLA conducted a remarkably diverse set of island-seizing campaigns. The objectives, the scale of the landings, and the physical terrain varied widely, and the strategic consequences of the battles were equally diverse. The field armies that had conquered large swaths of the mainland launched the cross-sea landings along China's southeastern and southern coasts. The Third Field Army covered operations along the coasts of Zhejiang and Fujian Provinces, while the Fourth Field Army was responsible for taking islands located off Guangdong Province.

In October 1949, the Third Field Army's abysmal failure to seize Jinmen, a small island garrison just off the coast of Fujian Province, derailed Mao's original invasion plans against Taiwan, marking the beginning of the cross-strait stalemate that persists to this day. The calamitous campaign that saw three regiments, numbering some nine thousand troops, wiped out within days deeply shook Mao and the high command. The defeat awakened the Communists to the harsh and unforgiving realities of naval combat and amphibious operations. The Jinmen catastrophe also served as a cautionary tale from which subsequent theater commanders drew important lessons. The operation still resonates deeply today: it is a classic case study in the PLA's historiography and professional military education. Chinese scholars and strategists continue to argue over its causes and its implications for a future war against Taiwan.

In early 1950, the Fourth Field Army launched the PLA's first large-scale amphibious operation against Hainan, an island comparable in size to Taiwan. In the assault against Hainan, the Communists landed some forty-five thousand troops, making the campaign one of the largest in postwar history. The captured island furnished China with a commanding position over the South China Sea. Today, the Yulin naval base on Hainan's southern tip is the locus of Chinese sea power in the region. The seizure of the Wanshan archipelago in the summer of 1950 was the first joint army-navy operation, which preceded the more famous triservice campaign against the Yijiangshan Islands in 1955. The various naval battles and island landings cleared the mouth of the Pearl River, securing the seaborne approaches to Guangzhou, a major economic and maritime hub. The Wanshan campaign is considered the Chinese navy's first combat operation and is integral to the naval service's historiography.

In short, this story is not strictly confined to the Chinese navy. Rather, this study adopts a broad view of sea power. As Geoffrey Till notes, sea power encompasses all implements of national power that can directly determine the course and outcome of maritime affairs, including "navies, coast guards, the marine or civil marine industries broadly defined and, where relevant, the contribution of land and air forces."[1] As this study shows, nonnaval instruments, including Mao's armies and China's civilian maritime sector, were indispensable to the Communists' earliest successes at sea.

This story also shows that the PLAN's origins are inseparable from the PLA's offshore operations in 1949 and 1950. As one Chinese National Defense University study explains, "During the early period of the navy's founding, the 'coastal defense' maritime thought had an obvious imprint of 'land combat.' The central missions in the struggle for maritime defense were clearing banditry at sea, breaking the naval blockade, and recovering the offshore islands. These missions substantively reflected the continued extension and expansion of the nation's military struggle on land toward the coastal direction. They were the new China's 'finishing touches' for seizing and establishing political power."[2]

In other words, Mao's armies went to sea to complete the final tasks of the civil war, and the navy's founding was in large measure a continuation of that effort. At the same time, those armies' earliest experiences at sea shaped the PLAN's outlook, strategy, and forces. Indeed, the PLA considers its armies' offshore operations the seedlings of Chinese naval doctrine. As a Chinese National Defense University study on naval campaigns asserts, "Shortly after the People's Navy's birth in April 1949, it was immediately thrown into combat to liberate enemy-occupied coastal islands and to shatter the enemy's maritime blockade. The naval combat experiences from liberating Hainan Island, the Wanshan Islands, and the Zhoushan archipelago established a certain foundation for the subsequent study of naval campaign theory."[3]

Given the centrality of ground forces, civilian shipping, and local seamen in these offshore campaigns, sea power, rather than the narrower concept of naval power, is the proper analytical lens with which to examine this period. These maritime events, spanning just eighteen months, produced a range of legacies that continue to sway China's outlook on nautical affairs. The offshore campaigns, including the abortive Jinmen operation, set the stage for the 1954 and 1958 Taiwan Strait Crises, key events in Cold War history. Jinmen remains out of China's grasp, and to many Chinese the island is a reminder of their nation's division. Bureaucracies set up for the Chinese navy in 1950 still constitute the core organizational structure of the naval service. Tellingly, the anniversary of the PLAN's founding marks the day the East China Navy formed in April 1949 rather than the day the national navy came into being a year later. Elements of Chinese naval doctrine that emphasize deception and mobility trace their origins to these earliest months of fighting.

A FORMATIVE EXPERIENCE

The navy-building process and the offshore engagements of late 1949 and early 1950 influenced critical debates about China's early maritime imperatives and naval strategy. The Chinese navy's founding and combat at sea were formative experiences that shaped the naval service's outlook and values, which remain relevant today. Indeed, the story of the Communists' first encounter with the seas provides the essential historical context to China's current rise as a sea power. Yet, this story remains largely unknown in the West. *Mao's Army Goes to Sea* seeks to fill this blank canvas and, in the process, illustrate the history's importance to the West's understanding of Chinese sea power and its future trajectory.

First, the PLA's naval buildup and early offshore campaigns demonstrate that the Chinese Communist Party (CCP) had to wrestle with nettlesome maritime challenges well before it seized power across China. The conquest of coastal China brought Mao's armies, which had operated for decades in mostly land-locked areas, to unfamiliar terrain. Mao's early encounter with—and responses to—the intensely nautical character of the Chinese littorals show that China's quest for sea power far predated the more energetic turn to the seas following Deng Xiaoping's reform and opening in the late 1970s. The Western literature typically attributes the emergence of a coherent and modern naval strategy to Liu Huaqing's intellectual contributions in the 1980s.[4] While this standard view is correct, it is also incomplete. It understates the role that earlier combat experiences and associated doctrinal debates played in the formulation of Chinese naval strategy in the post-Mao era.

Second, the story behind the navy's birth are key constituents of the PLAN's institutional identity. Chinese doctrinal writings describe the past sea battles, even if modest in scale by Western standards, as the PLAN's "glorious history."[5] Official accounts portray the navy's early combat experiences as defining moments. The historiography shows how the Chinese navy beat the odds, prevailing against technologically and materially superior adversaries. The PLA's naval leadership has advanced this historical interpretation repeatedly to inspire and motivate the officer corps and below. Indeed, the notion that the weak can prevail over the strong resonates deeply with the Chinese military to this day.[6] How the PLA understands its own past will almost certainly have implications for how it discerns present and future operational requirements.

Third, the Chinese navy's first planning conference in August 1950 had a lasting impact on the PLAN's doctrinal and force structure developments. Naval leaders insisted from the start that the PLA's fine traditions and its core values be the foundation of Chinese sea power. Contrary to conventional historical interpretations in the West, the PLA's generals were not unthinking automatons who borrowed concepts indiscriminately from the Soviet Union. For example, the PLAN's doctrine of "sabotage warfare at sea" emerged from the hard-earned experiences of coastal warfare that began in 1949. Drawing from their indigenous Maoist operational thought and learning from the savage force-on-force encounters with the Nationalists, the Communists refined their hit-and-run tactics and plans for disruptive assaults on enemy sea lines of communications. Notably, sabotage warfare at sea remains integral to the Chinese navy's current doctrine of offshore defense.[7]

It was in early 1950 when the PLAN's commander, Xiao Jinguang, set the service on course for a decades-long buildup of submarines, shore-based aircraft, and fast-attack craft. Xiao's vision for a light and quick-footed combat force designed for coastal operations against seaborne threats was later codified at an all-important meeting in the summer of 1950. This force, premised as it was on the PLA's long-standing preference for flexible and nimble tactics, dovetailed with the Communists' operational style. Here again, the naval leadership asserted the primacy of the PLA's traditions and insisted that material factors had to conform to China's unique strategic circumstances. This legacy is still visible in the Chinese naval force structure today. The PLAN's fleets of conventional submarines, shore-based aircraft, and coastal combatants are descendants of the forces that the naval leadership pursued in the early 1950s.

Fourth, the offshore campaigns gave birth to a distinctive Chinese way of naval warfare. Virtually all sea battles and landing operations during this time frame involved deception, surprise, night combat, close-in engagements, and preemptive strikes. Lacking the material wherewithal, Chinese Communist forces frequently pitted much smaller but nimbler combatants against larger, better-armed, and more modern enemy warships. To compensate for such disparities in mass and firepower, the Chinese navy relied on such unorthodox methods as surprise attacks to pull off a series of tactical successes. This small-ship ethos persists well into the twenty-first century.

Relatedly, a major feature of this Chinese way of naval warfare was the extensive use of paramilitary forces and civilian vessels and personnel. The application of the Maoist people's war concept at sea in late 1949 and early 1950 served as a force multiplier to conventional military power. In trials of strength against superior opponents, these irregular forces proved indispensable to success. The China Coast Guard and the Maritime Militia units that feature so prominently in current maritime coercion campaigns are just the most recent incarnation of the nonmilitary implements of Chinese sea power.[8]

Fifth, these early maritime operations and institution-building efforts tested the political leadership, the PLA's generalship, and civil-military relations, offering unique insights into the Communists' politico-military system. Mao was intimately involved in key bureaucratic and personnel decisions about the national navy. He was open to the inclusion of former Nationalist officers in building the navy. The Jinmen disaster shocked Mao. He urged his commanders to learn from the failure. In fact, Mao was so concerned that he became directly engaged in the planning, down to the tactical level, of the Hainan operation. This leadership style characterized his decisions and actions in subsequent conflicts and crises with fateful consequences for the Cold War and China's relationships with the Soviet Union and the United States.[9]

Some of China's most celebrated and renowned operational commanders were participants in this epochal period. Gen. Zhang Aiping, who served as commander of the East China Navy, provided the template for building the PLAN. Gen. Ye Fei directed the 1949 landing operation on Jinmen that ended in disaster. Lin Biao, who commanded the Fourth Field Army that successfully seized Hainan Island, worked closely with Mao on operational planning. Zhang, Ye, and Lin would go on to the highest levels of the party-army system. The offshore campaigns, moreover, reveal how CCP and PLA leaders dealt with uncertainty, risk, surprise, and operational successes and failures. They also show how PLA generals assessed the evolving warfighting environment, learned to fight in a new operational domain, recovered and drew lessons from mistakes, and adapted to unfamiliar combat conditions. Their leadership qualities or lack thereof remain examples for close study to the PLA today.

PAST IS PROLOGUE

It is the central contention of this study that these early operational and institutional experiences offer unique insights about the PLA and the Chinese navy. Chinese military writings about this period have consistently exhibited a deep historical consciousness and an intellectual openness to intimacy with the past. The literature suggests that the PLA is committed to understanding its own history and applying this understanding to its current strategic and operational thought. This remembered past reveals much about the PLA's core values, including its warfighting ethos, offensive mindset, and tactical preferences. Communist China's early naval history and the PLA's interpretation of this history thus opens a window onto the Chinese military's institutional identity, habits of thought, strategic traditions, and operational proclivities.

If past is prologue, then what the Chinese have learned from their own history may offer hints as to how they plan to act in the future. Given that the most likely sources of conflict for China today lie offshore, including Taiwan and the territorial disputes in the East and South China Seas, this history and its contemporary implications should be of great interest to stakeholders in maritime Asia. Drawing US policy makers and strategists closer to this past will help them better understand their principal rival in the twenty-first century.

By providing an account of this obscure yet critical moment in China's maritime history, this study will help policy makers and strategists better understand the origins of the Chinese navy and naval strategy, doctrine, and force structure; the profiles of early Chinese naval leadership; the lasting institutional legacies of the political battles in navy headquarters; the amphibious operations that have defined the PLA's institutional identity; and the contemporary Chinese interpretations of this maritime past and their influence on Chinese sea power. It is worth repeating that this study is not exclusively concerned with the Chinese navy. Rather, it is about how naval power and other instruments of sea power interacted to achieve China's aims in the maritime arena. This deeper historical understanding will help observers take better measure of the PLA today and its potential challenge to the United States and maritime Asia in the coming years.

It is worth briefly explaining the rationale for limiting the study's historical coverage to 1949 and 1950. To be sure, the PLA conducted important operations throughout the 1950s, including during the 1954 and 1958 Taiwan Strait crises and the 1955 Yijiangshan campaign. The PLA also defeated a Nationalist assault on Dongshan Island in a defensive battle in July 1953. But the first eighteen months of Communist China's encounters with the seas were a unique period. The critical institutional decisions and the major campaigns recounted in this study took place before the all-consuming war on the Korean Peninsula broke out in June 1950. Not surprisingly, offensive offshore campaigns ceased in the summer of 1950 as Mao turned to the crisis in Korea and the PLA ceased major operations at sea until 1954.

During those eighteen months the Communists were largely left to their own devices. While the Soviets provided assistance to the naval program during those earliest months, such foreign aid was still modest in scale. By contrast, the Chinese military that fought on the peninsula was a Russianizing force that would later refashion itself after the Soviet military in doctrine, outlook, and organization. Thus, a far more well-resourced, standardized, and Soviet-equipped PLA waged the campaigns of the mid to late 1950s. The post–Korean War military was qualitatively different from the sparse, hodgepodge force of 1949 and 1950. This study captures that moment before conflict on the peninsula transformed the PLA.

To recount this story, this study is structured as follows. Chapter 2 introduces the analytical aims of the study, the sources and methods behind the research, and the historical background to the Chinese navy's founding and its offshore campaigns. Chapter 3 retells the origins of the East China Navy and the critical role that Zhang Aiping, the navy's first commander, played in shaping the service's institutions. Chapter 4 continues the story of the East China Navy and its initial operations and documents the formal founding of the PLAN. Chapter 5 details the offshore operations by the Third Field Army, the organization responsible for the island campaigns along China's east coast, and describes the little-known Xiamen campaign and the famous Jinmen campaign that followed. Chapter 6 focuses on the Fourth Field Army's operations to take Hainan Island and the Wanshan archipelago, the target of the PLA's first open-water operation. Chapter 7 provides an integrated assessment of the Chinese navy's institutional building process and the offshore campaigns. Chapter 8 connects the past to the present and future by examining the institutional legacies from this critical period. Chapter 9 offers some concluding thoughts about areas for future research and the intersection of Chinese history and current US assessments of the PLAN.

NOTES

1. Geoffrey Till, *Seapower: A Guide of the Twenty-First Century*, 2nd ed. (London: Routledge, 2004), 21.
2. 霍小勇 主编 [Huo Xiaoyong, ed.], 军种战略学 [The Science of Service Strategies] (Beijing: National Defense University, 2008), 260.
3. 陈访友 主编 [Chen Fangyou, ed.], 海军战役学教程 [Course Materials on the Science of Naval Campaigns] (Beijing: National Defense University, 1991), 11.
4. You Ji, *The Armed Forces of China* (London: I. B. Tauris, 1999), 164; James R. Holmes and Toshi Yoshihara, *Chinese Naval Strategy in the 21st Century: The*

Turn to Mahan (London: Routledge, 2008), 27–39; and Nan Li, "The Evolution of China's Naval Strategy and Capabilities: From 'Near Coast' and 'Near Seas' to 'Far Seas,'" *Asian Security* 5, no. 2 (2009): 154–56.

5. 杜景臣 主编 [Du Jingchen, ed.], 中国海军军人手册 [Handbook for Officers and Enlisted of the Chinese PLA Navy] (Beijing: Haichao, 2012), 7–11. This handbook was issued by the PLAN Headquarters.

6. 尚金锁 吴子欣 陈立旭 主编 [Shang Jinsuo, Wu Zixin, and Chen Lixu, eds.], 毛泽东军事思想与高技术条件下局部战争 [Mao Zedong's Military Thought and Local Wars under High-Technology Conditions] (Beijing: Liberation Army Press, 2002), 50–57.

7. 中国海军百科全书编审委员会 [Editorial Committee of the Chinese Navy Encyclopedia], 中国海军百科全书 [Chinese Navy Encyclopedia] (Beijing: Haichao, 1999), 731.

8. The China Coast Guard is officially called the Chinese People's Armed Police Force Coast Guard Corps (中国人民武装警察部队海警总队) after a reorganization in 2018, and the Maritime Militia is formally known as the People's Armed Forces Maritime Militia (中国海上民兵).

9. For a sense of Mao's leadership style during the 1958 Taiwan Strait Crisis, see Chen Jian, *Mao's China and the Cold War* (Chapel Hill: University of North Carolina Press, 2001), 163–204.

T W O

An Overlooked History

The origin story of Communist China's seaward turn remains relatively obscure in the West. The existing Western literature provides cursory examinations of the PLAN's founding, while a handful of studies offer in-depth treatments of the initial offshore campaigns of 1949 and 1950. Moreover, the writings tend to denigrate the Communists' performance, introducing bias to assessments of this early period. For years, analysts have had to rely on a few well-respected but dated works, thereby limiting the academic and policy discourse.

The absence of a well-developed founding history, which reveals much about an institution's identity, reason for being, motivations, and worldview, has precluded a better understanding of Chinese sea power. The need to fill this gap has gained urgency as China's sustained investments in its maritime prowess in recent years have shifted the power balance across the Indo-Pacific. Thanks to the proliferation of publicly available Chinese-language sources over the past two decades, there is now a unique opportunity to offer a more complete account of Maoist China's turn to the seas. To set the stage for this backstory, the following describes the purpose, methodology, and historical background to the study.

ANALYTICAL AIMS

A firmer grasp of the Chinese navy's institutional origins and the island seizure campaigns will benefit PLA studies and offer policy-relevant insights for US policy makers, strategists, and planners alike. First, this study will draw attention to an underexamined period of China's naval history. Western historiography of the Chinese navy's founding and the PLA's early amphibious operations is a virtual blank canvas. Recent studies of the PLAN devote the bulk of their analysis on the present and the future of the naval service's goals, plans, strategy, operations, and force structure.[1] Bernard Cole's pathbreaking volume on the Chinese navy, for example, touches briefly on the service's beginnings.[2]

For decades, the go-to English-language books on the topic were the pioneering works by Bruce Swanson and David Muller. But they are outdated and incomplete, relying as they did on Western sources and suffering as they did from limited access to Chinese open sources.³ Bruce Elleman has rendered a signal service to the field by publishing a comprehensive history of the modern Chinese navy from the mid-nineteenth century to the present. However, he touches lightly on the period covered in the study in two short chapters.⁴ Histories that cover the Chinese Civil War or address the early warfighting experiences of the PLA provide glimpses of the military campaigns that took place along China's coast.⁵ The critical period that is at the nexus of the civil war's end, the PLAN's birth, and Communist China's initial encounters with maritime threats has been largely overlooked. This study seeks to bring this important but mostly neglected history into sharp focus.

As more recent writings demonstrate, there is renewed interest in the Chinese navy's past and the PLA's amphibious operations in the early Cold War. In his award-winning article, Dale Rielage, former director of intelligence for the US Pacific Fleet, makes a persuasive case that understanding the Chinese navy's past is essential to a fuller appraisal of the PLAN today. He argues that "the first three decades of the PLAN are central to their culture, structure, and self-image." He further warns of "the dangers of ignoring or dismissing the PLAN's past."⁶ Such an ahistorical mindset, he contends, might lead US policy makers and planners to misdiagnose the challenge of Chinese sea power.

Another excellent article by Brig. Gen. William Bowers and Christopher Yung advances a similar case for historical awareness. They observe that the Chinese military has closely studied its own history to understand the future of offensive amphibious operations. They recount the difficulties the Communists faced in preparing for and assembling the necessary forces for an invasion of Taiwan in late 1949 and early 1950. The lost opportunity to seize Taiwan and the bitter lessons from that failure, they believe, continue to inform the PLA's thinking about twenty-first-century amphibious warfare.⁷

Yet, these important works employ sources that are dated, some decades old. Rielage references David Muller's 1983 book no less than five times in a short article. Similarly, Bowers and Yung cite a chapter by He Di in a 2003 edited volume seven times and a 1987 article by Jon Huebner. While these citations in no way diminish the analytical contributions that Rielage, Bowers, and Yung make to the field, they show that the English-language literature of the PLA in the early Cold War years has aged. There is thus a need to add a fresh and updated perspective on this topic of growing importance.

Second, this study provides an overdue corrective to the prevailing view about the Chinese navy's early years. The Western conventional wisdom holds that China had minimal if any exposure to the demands of maritime policy and naval strategy until the 1980s, the Chinese possessed few if any original ideas about naval doctrine and uncritically accepted concepts borrowed from their Soviet ally in the 1950s, and the first naval leaders—who were trained as army officers and rose through the ranks waging insurgencies and ground campaigns—lacked the intellectual wherewithal to adapt to the nautical environment. The conventional wisdom is largely dismissive of China's naval project during its founding period.[8] This current study shows that these findings overly deprecate the PLA's independent agency and contends that the Chinese leadership's determination to go to sea was more resolute than previously understood. Chinese statesmen and commanders at the time were also more creative, imaginative, and pragmatic than Western observers have assumed.

Third, this study adds value to the field by paying close attention to the operational level of war. It adheres strictly to Carl von Clausewitz's definition of "engagement" as the central organizing principle of the case studies on the PLA's island campaigns. As Clausewitz observes, "Tactics teaches the use of armed forces in the engagement; strategy, the use of engagements for the objects of the war."[9] In other words, a significant element of the study is about fighting between opposing armed forces. While high politics, diplomacy, and geopolitics are important contextual elements of the narrative, this study focuses tightly on the PLA's combat experiences.

The analytical goal is to draw insights from the intersection of strategy, operations, and tactics. This study shows how Mao and his subordinates had to learn quickly, stand up new organizations, develop best practices, choose the right leaders, and build suitable tools as they came up against the Nationalists in an unfamiliar warfighting domain. It recounts how the Communists thought about and responded to these formidable challenges at the operational level and how they assessed, reassessed, and adapted to the nautical environment. In addition, the study demonstrates that quality of intellect is essential to evaluating the PLA's warfighting performance.

Finally, this is not a history for history's sake. This study argues that the offshore campaigns—and the PLA's interpretation and understanding of them—form a core element of the Chinese military's institutional memory and identity. This history is a metaphorical mirror that shows how the PLA sees itself. The narrative, told and retold over past decades, has been a source of esprit de corps and tactical élan. While this past may not predict future doctrine and force modernization, it points to the values and attitudes that the Chinese officer corps likely holds about certain operational and tactical concepts. Indeed, this storyline has not lost its cogency even as the PLAN directs its sights on blue-water missions far from mainland shores. At a minimum, this historical understanding will provide an analytical baseline with which to study Chinese sea power. The extent that China's future naval strategy will deviate from this offshore tradition will reveal both the scope and the possible institutional limits of Beijing's maritime ambitions.

SOURCES AND METHODS

This study provides a history of the Chinese navy's understudied founding and the earliest offshore campaigns. As noted above, Communist China's initial encounters with maritime threats have been at best a footnote in Western historiography. The recent availability of Chinese-language literature now makes it possible to reconstruct this poorly understood period of China's naval history. Indeed, the open sources furnish surprising and hitherto unknown operational details down to the regimental and battalion levels. There is now a unique opportunity to tell a more faithful story of Communist China's first encounters with the seas.

Several trends explain this new openness in the People's Republic of China. Growing popular and academic interest in sea power, due in no small part to official encouragement, incentivized writings on Chinese naval affairs. Equally important, the PLA has a good story to tell. After all, the offshore campaigns were an important step in the Communists' road to victory. These operations and the PLA's narratives about them inspire pride. The PLA also sees genuine value in drawing lessons from its past. As this study shows, official military histories are forthright about mistakes and failures, which serve as useful cautionary tales for current and future planners. Consequently, general studies on maritime issues, memoirs and biographies of naval leaders, official histories of the PLA, and secondary accounts of the Chinese navy—based on recently opened archives in China—are now widely available. This wealth of information sheds new light on an obscure yet critical moment in the making of Chinese sea power.

Chinese open sources offer details about the critical decisions behind the founding of the East China Navy and later the PLAN. They appraise offshore campaigns that raged from the closing months of the Chinese Civil War to mid-1950. These maritime operations, many of which preceded the formal establishment of the Chinese navy, were seminal and defining experiences. Indeed, the initial quest to secure China's maritime periphery was arguably the PLA's most combat intensive period in the nautical direction. These sea battles and amphibious operations along the Chinese coast have had an outsize impact on China's long-term security and strategy.

This study draws upon the PLA's war history (战史) series published by the Liberation Army Press. The volumes on the Third Field Army and the Fourth Field Army, which concluded the civil war with a series of offshore operations along the Chinese coast, are central to chapters 5 and 6, respectively. In addition, this study uses a six-volume study on the PLA's military history (军史) published by the Academy of Military Science Press. Organized chronologically, the history encompasses the PLA's institutional evolution and campaigns from 1927 to the late 1970s. This study also mines a seven-volume series on the PLA's history published by Qingdao Press. To supplement these histories, this study consults graduate-level course materials on the PLA's war history published by the Academy of Military Science Press. These military histories together serve as the baseline for assessing the PLA's own interpretation of its past campaigns.

This study also examines biographies and memoirs of key decision makers, including Mao Zedong, the theater commanders, and the local commanders. These works include a memoir by Gen. Ye Fei, commander of the landing operations on Jinmen in 1949; a memoir and three biographies of Gen. Xiao Jinguang, the commander of the PLAN; a memoir by Gen. Liu Huaqing, the commander of the PLAN in the 1980s; and two biographies of Gen. Zhang Aiping that specifically detail his role as the commander of the East China Navy. Other related works cover Mao's maritime policy decisions, support for the Chinese navy, and relationships with the PLAN's commanders and the history of the CCP's thinking on maritime defense. Of interest are the memoirs and biographies of those who participated in or led the offshore campaigns, which frequently express candid—and thus invaluable—views of both operational successes and failures.

This study references more than twenty books on island warfare and amphibious operations, many of which cover the Jinmen, Zhoushan, Hainan, Wanshan, and other offshore campaigns. They include a three-volume study on island warfare by Gen. Zhu Wenquan, the former commander of the Nanjing Military Area Command; a dozen commercially available books that examine the offshore campaigns of the 1950s; and five internally circulated (军内, or *junnei*) PLA studies on island warfare, island blockade campaigns, and island landing operations. The internal studies, some of which adopt the case study approach to assess the amphibious campaigns, presumably offer unvarnished views of the past. These works provide the operational and tactical details of this study.

The research also benefited from books on the Chinese navy. These include a two-volume official encyclopedia of the naval service; the PLAN's official handbook for officers and enlisted personnel; two official histories of the Chinese navy published in the 1980s (Xiao Jinguang and Liu Huaqing sat on the editorial boards of each book, respectively); a history of naval campaigns published by Haichao Press, the PLAN's publishing house; and four commercially available books on the early years of the Chinese navy based on recently released government archives. As noted above, the study uses the volume on the PLAN's history published by Qingdao Press. These sources reveal how the Chinese navy, as an institution, interprets its own past and applies that past to present circumstances.

Finally, this book gleans insights from periodicals ranging from authoritative PLA journals to general-interest naval magazines. The History Department of the Academy of Military Science publishes *Military History*, a bimonthly journal that provides occasional coverage of China's offshore campaigns. *Military History Research*, a bimonthly journal from the PLA's Nanjing Political College, is another valuable source for researching past operations. The current study consults well-connected naval outlets, including *Navy Today* (formerly *Modern Navy*), *Modern Ships*, *Naval and Merchant Ships*, and *Shipborne Weapons*. *Renmin Haijun*, the PLAN's official newspaper, is another useful resource. These periodicals carry retrospective analyses of major Chinese naval campaigns.

Drawing from these open sources, this study explores the Chinese navy's founding and major offshore campaigns in standard case study format. Chapters 3 and 4 follow the birth of the East China Navy and its operations and the founding of the PLAN largely in a chronological narrative. Chapters 5 and 6 examine the operations of the Third Field Army and the Fourth Field Army, respectively. For each offshore campaign, the chapters examine the strategic intent of the battle, the course of the engagement including a blow-by-blow account of tactical combat, and the outcomes and larger consequences of the campaign. As noted above, this study is in part a campaign history that examines events at the operational level of war. Thus, the study pays close attention to unit-level actions at sea and on land.

A CAVEAT ON PLA WRITINGS

Any study that relies heavily on Chinese open sources must wrestle with the objectivity, ulterior motives, authenticity, and authoritativeness of the writings. It is important to identify possible biases and analytical pitfalls that distort the narratives. The histories of the Chinese Civil War can be particularly problematic. After all, the stories are about a prolonged bitter struggle against an archnemesis over which the Communists prevailed. These accounts are essential elements of the foundational myths surrounding the victory of the CCP and the establishment of the People's Republic of China. Not surprisingly, then, the PLA literature surveyed in this study frequently features hagiography and exhibits triumphalism. There is a discernible tendency to romanticize the past. Some of the histories play up and perhaps exaggerate the heroism and virtues of Communist forces while demonizing the Nationalist adversary. Others overstate the Communists' apparent magnanimity toward the defeated Nationalists. It is therefore important not to take at face value the PLA literature. This study is alert to such biases in the literature and identifies those that may have a significant bearing on the historiography's integrity.

To adjudicate such partiality, this study selectively verifies the Communists' histories by employing Republic of China (ROC) and US sources to corroborate or contradict the PLA writings. The ROC's professional military journals regularly publish articles on the Chinese Civil War, including the offshore campaigns featured in this study. Such contemporary works offer important analysis and perspectives that can either confirm or dispute the Communist version of events. Archival materials from declassified US Central Intelligence Agency (CIA) reports offer additional evidence to compare against Communist accounts. This methodology requires careful judgments about which episodes or elements of the PLA narratives to cross-check against other sources. As appropriate, this study cites these third-party materials in instances when Communist accounts of strategic import diverge significantly or converge.

At the same time, it is important to reemphasize the value of the PLA's literature even when there is some hagiography and triumphalism. As noted above, officialdom encouraged the growth of these histories to promote discourse on naval and maritime affairs. In other words, the PLA may have instrumentalized its past to promote its own agenda. A central tenet of this study is that this "usable past" is analytically valuable. The PLA's sometimes exaggerated and triumphalist narratives about its combat history still matter because they are the stories that the PLA retells to itself. They open a window into the PLA's corporate identity. The narratives, even if highly romanticized, reveal much about the core beliefs, institutional values, and warfighting qualities that the Chinese military holds in high esteem. The PLA's self-image offers important clues about how it might think and act in future conflicts, thereby furnishing policy-relevant findings to practitioners in Washington, DC, and across Asian capitals today. It is thus important to follow these narratives even if they do not meet Western standards of historiography.

It is also important not to lend undue weight to hagiography and triumphalism, treating them as if they are omnipresent in the writings. There is an overriding imperative for the PLA writings to be forthright about Mao's armies in 1949 and 1950. After all, the writings on the offshore campaigns are parables about Taiwan, the PLA's highest priority. How the PLA might perform in a crisis or in war over Taiwan is of utmost importance. The challenges that Mao's field armies faced in conducting amphibious operations against well-defended islands will be as relevant in a prospective Taiwan scenario as they were in 1949 and 1950. In short, there are close analytical linkages between the operational histories and the PLA's real-world military problems associated with Taiwan. It is therefore in the PLA's self-interest to engage in a dispassionate appraisal of its own performance and to extract meaningful lessons from its past combat experiences. Moreover, as noted above, this study cites internally circulated books that critically assess past campaigns to mine relevant lessons for current and future PLA leaders. These works, designed to inform operational planning and doctrine, have every incentive to avoid misleading triumphalism and hagiography.

Finally, not all hagiographies and triumphalism are equally harmful to the reliability of the Communist narratives. Embellishments of individual acts of heroism might add flair to the story, but they do not fundamentally undermine the broader strategic and operational lessons that could be derived from the PLA's official histories. Conversely, misrepresentations of events related to strategic decision-making and to the overall conduct of the campaigns would clearly be analytically problematic. Most instances of triumphalism and hagiography belong in the former category. More importantly, this study identifies areas where hagiography and triumphalism could potentially distort the historical, strategic, and operational picture.

STRATEGIC, OPERATIONAL, AND ORGANIZATIONAL BACKGROUND

To set the stage for the case studies, the following provides a brief explanation of how this history fits within the broader organizational evolution of the PLA and the larger Chinese Civil War. From 1927 to 1949 the Communists' military forces, the armed wing of the CCP, underwent several name changes to reflect new circumstances during each phase of the revolutionary struggle.[10] In the first phase, from 1928 to 1937, the CCP led the Red Army. During this time Mao headed an element of the Red Army's Fourth Army in the Jinggang Mountains of Jiangxi Province, a hill-country hinterland. When imperial Japan began its all-out invasion of China in 1937, the CCP formed a united front with the Nationalists and reorganized its forces into the Eighth Route Army in the northwest and the New Fourth Army in the south.

At the end of the Second Sino-Japanese War in 1945 the Communists, anticipating a renewed civil war, prepared to face off with the Nationalists. To win this conflict, which broke out into full-scale fighting in June 1946, the CCP transformed the Eighth Route Army and the New Fourth Army into warfighting organizations for large-scale mobile conventional campaigns. As the Communists gained ground and momentum and shifted toward a strategic counteroffensive in late 1948, the CCP again reorganized its military, renaming all forces under its command the Chinese People's Liberation Army.

From this reorganization emerged four field armies, with each responsible for a major geographic region in early 1949. The First, Second, Third, and Fourth Field Armies were formed for northwest, central, east, and northeast China, respectively. Each field army (野战军, or *yezhanjun*) comprised two to four armies (兵团, or *bingtuan*), with each of those armies commanding two to four corps (军, or *jun*).[11] Below the corps level the army's tactical units were organized, in descending order, into the division, the regiment, the battalion, the company, the platoon, and the squad. These terms are used to depict the unit-level actions in this study.[12]

The offshore campaigns marked the end of the Chinese Civil War. The most decisive and bloody battles had already taken place during the Liao-Shen campaign in northeast China, the Ping-Jin campaign in the Beijing-Tianjin area, and the Huai-Hai campaign north of the Yangzi River. The scale of these engagements was staggering. During the Huai-Hai campaign over 1.8 million troops faced off across a two hundred–kilometer front.[13] Over the course of these three campaigns, from September 1948 to January 1949, the Communists killed, wounded, or captured more than 1.5 million Nationalist troops, wiping out Generalissimo Chiang Kai-shek's best troops.[14] During the Liao-Shen campaign alone, the KMT lost nearly 400,000 soldiers.[15] In less than four months, Communist offensives shattered the enemy. With these campaigns, northeast China, most of northern China, and the Central Plain north of the Yangzi fell to Mao's forces. Most of the Nationalist forces documented in this study were remnants of the army that had escaped destruction or capture. They were demoralized from previous defeats. Worse, they were pushed out of their home provinces and were defending territories that were culturally and linguistically foreign to them.

Mao's massive victories opened the way to southern China. After crossing the Yangzi River, the watery barrier that separated northern and southern China, the four field armies fanned out to conquer the rest of China. The Yangzi crossing, the seizure of Nanjing, the seat of the Nationalist government, and the subsequent campaigns, including the offshore operations, fall within the Chinese Civil War's final phase of "strategic pursuit [战略追击]" that began in February 1949 and ended in June 1950.[16] The four phases that preceded strategic pursuit from September 1945 to January 1949 were: strategic transition (战略过度), strategic defense (战略防御), strategic attack (战略进攻), and strategic battles of decision (战略决战).

During the strategic pursuit phase, the First Field Army under Peng Dehuai pushed northwest to reach as far as Xinjiang while the Second Field Army under Liu Bocheng moved southwest to seize Yunnan, Sichuan, and Tibet. The Third Field Army under Chen Yi rolled into the eastern coastal provinces of Zhejiang and Fujian, while the Fourth Field Army under Lin Biao dashed south through Hunan to occupy Guangdong and Guangxi. The Third and Fourth Field Armies, after reaching the East and South China Seas, respectively, became the principal warfighting organizations responsible for wresting control of the offshore islands from the Nationalists. These two field armies are at the center of the drama in chapters 5 and 6, respectively.

In this conclusive stage of the civil war, the four field armies collectively waged thirty-three major campaigns. Among them, six were considered strategically important: the cross-river campaign, the Heng-Bao [Hengyang-Baoqing] campaign in Hunan, the Liangyang [Yangjiang-Yangchun] campaign in Guangdong, the Zhang-Xia [Zhangzhou-Xiamen] campaign in Fujian, the Hainan Island campaign, and the Lanzhou campaign in Gansu.[17] Notably, four of the offshore operations covered in this study belong to these six critical campaigns. The Zhang-Xia campaign included the Pingtan, Xiamen, and Jinmen amphibious assaults by the Third Field Army, while the Hainan Island campaign by the Fourth Field Army ranked among the weightiest in the strategic pursuit phase.

Institutionally, the Chinese navy's origins were inseparable from the PLA's field armies.[18] The East China Navy's leadership and staff were drawn from the Third Field Army. The East China Navy then became the basis for the East Sea Fleet. The Fourth Field Army contributed its leaders and staff to form the PLAN. Later, the Fourth Field Army provided the manpower to administer Qingdao naval base, which in turn became the foundation for the North Sea Fleet. In addition, the Fourth Field Army helped establish a riverine defense command in Guangzhou that functioned as the incubator for the South Sea Fleet. In this sense, it is accurate to depict Mao's turn to the seas as an institutional process of transforming an army into a navy. As this study shows, this process would have a lasting impact on the Chinese navy's values, outlook, and operational proclivities.

Finally, the offshore campaigns were inextricably tied to Mao's ultimate prize: Taiwan. The urgency with which local commanders executed their operations at sea must be understood in this context of sharply heightened expectations of a final showdown with Chiang. In mid-June 1949, Mao began to issue directives to his subordinate commanders of the Third Field Army about preparations for conquering Taiwan.[19] The Central Military Commission then ordered the Third Field Army to assume responsibilities for the expected campaign against the island.

There was debate at the time about the approach and sequence of actions to take Taiwan. One school advocated an "island-by-island attack [逐岛攻击]" that would wage a progressive campaign to seize all offshore terrain along China's coast before a final attack on Taiwan. Another view held that the PLA could replicate the US military's island-hopping strategy during the Pacific War when American forces bypassed and isolated Japanese island garrisons. In a similar fashion, the Chinese military would seize Xiamen and then use the island as a launch pad for the invasion of Taiwan while setting aside the Nationalists' other island holdings until after Taiwan fell.[20]

The Central Military Commission chose the former option. Mao and his lieutenants reasoned that the PLA lacked naval power and airpower to bypass the other offshore islands. Unprotected at sea and from the air, transports transiting the strait would risk interdiction by Nationalist air and naval forces based on the outlying islands near the mainland. Moreover, a methodical campaign against the offshore garrisons would destroy elements of the KMT's military power that could otherwise be withdrawn and concentrated on Taiwan. The island outposts' proximity to the mainland considerably brightened the odds of success for a force utterly lacking familiarity with amphibious operations. The PLA could use its superior night-fighting skills over short distances to negate the adversary's dominance of the skies and seas. And an incremental approach furnished the troops with opportunities to learn and train for new skills while accumulating much-needed combat experiences.[21]

The amphibious operations that began in September 1949 and ended in the summer of 1950 were all conducted with an eye toward Taiwan. Taiwan cast a long shadow over the high-level deliberations on each major operation. Mao and his commanders observed closely as each campaign unfolded to discern lessons and implications for the final invasion plan. The successes and failures against the offshore islands influenced the Communists' calculus about the probability of victory and the force requirements to ensure victory against the Nationalists. In sum, the offshore campaigns served as a proof of concept for defeating Chiang's armies on Taiwan. It is against this backdrop that Mao's China turned seaward.

NOTES

1. Bernard D. Cole, *The Great Wall at Sea: China's Navy in the Twenty-First Century*, 2nd ed. (Annapolis, MD: Naval Institute Press, 2010); James C. Bussert and Bruce A. Elleman, *The People's Liberation Army Navy* (Annapolis, MD: Naval Institute Press, 2011); Philip C. Saunders, Christopher Yung, Michael Swaine, and Andrew N. Yang, eds., *The Chinese Navy: Expanding Capabilities, Evolving Roles* (Washington, DC: National Defense University Press, 2012); Yves-Heng Lim, *China's Naval Power: An Offensive Realist Approach* (Surrey, UK: Ashgate, 2014); Andrew S. Erickson, ed., *Chinese Naval Shipbuilding: An Ambitious and Uncertain Course* (Annapolis, MD: Naval Institute Press, 2017); Toshi Yoshihara and James R. Holmes, *Red Star over the Pacific: China's Rise and the Challenge to U.S. Maritime Strategy*, 2nd ed. (Annapolis, MD: Naval Institute Press, 2019); and Michael A. McDevitt, *China as a Twenty-First-Century Naval Power: Theory, Practice, and Implications* (Annapolis, MD: Naval Institute Press, 2020).
2. Cole, *The Great Wall at Sea*, 16–20.
3. Bruce Swanson, *The Eighth Voyage of the Dragon: A History of China's Quest for Seapower* (Annapolis, MD: Naval Institute Press, 1982); and David G. Muller, *China as a Maritime Power* (Boulder, CO: Westview, 1983).
4. Bruce Elleman, *A History of the Modern Chinese Navy* (London: Routledge, 2021).
5. Edward L. Dreyer, *China at War, 1901–1949* (London: Longman, 1995); Odd Arne Westad, *Decisive Encounters: The Chinese Civil War, 1946–1950* (Stanford,

CA: Stanford University Press, 2003); Mark A. Ryan, David M. Finkelstein, and Michael A. McDevitt, eds., *Chinese Warfighting: The PLA Experience since 1949* (Armonk, NY: M. E. Sharpe, 2003); Xiaobing Li, *A History of the Modern Chinese Army* (Lexington: University of Kentucky Press, 2007); and Bruce Elleman, *Taiwan Straits: Crisis in Asia and the Role of the U.S. Navy* (Lanham, MD: Rowman and Littlefield, 2015).

6. Dale C. Rielage, "The Chinese Navy's Missing Years," *Naval History* 32, no. 6 (November–December 2018), 18–25, https://www.usni.org/magazines/naval -history-magazine/2018/december/chinese-navys-missing-years.

7. William Bowers and Christopher D. Yung, "China Has the Learned the Value of Amphibious Operations," *U.S. Naval Institute Proceedings* 144, no. 11 (November 2018), 24–28, https://www.usni.org/magazines/proceedings/2018/november /china-has-learned-value-amphibious-operations.

8. Bernard D. Cole, "More Red Than Expert: Chinese Sea Power during the Cold War," in *China Goes to Sea: Maritime Transformation in Comparative Historical Perspective*, ed. Andrew S. Erickson, Lyle J. Goldstein, and Carnes Lord, 320–40 (Annapolis, MD: Naval Institute Press, 2009); and Bernard D. Cole, "The People's Liberation Army Navy after Half a Century: Lessons Learned in Beijing," in *The Lessons of History: The Chinese People's Liberation Army at 75*, ed. Laurie Burkitt, Andrew Scobell, and Larry M. Wortzel, 157–91 (Carlisle, PA: Strategic Studies Institute, Army War College, 2003).

9. Carl von Clausewitz, *On War*, ed. and trans. Michael Howard and Peter Paret (Princeton, NJ: Princeton University Press, 1984), 128.

10. For the evolution of the Communist forces from 1927 to 1949, see Li, *A History of the Modern Chinese Army*, 45–78.

11. There are inconsistencies among Western sources on the naming conventions for the PLA's army organizations during this period. *Bingtuan* has been referred to as "army corps," "army group," and "group army." *Jun* has been called "army" and "corps" or has been left untranslated. To avoid confusion, this study refers to *bingtuan* as "army" and to *jun* as "corps." He Di refers to *bingtuan* as "army corps." Xiaobing Li and Ronald Spector refer to *bingtuan* as "army group" and to *jun* as "army." Shuguang Zhang calls *bingtuan* "group army." Jon Huebner refers to *jun* as "army." Miles Yu refers to *bingtuan* as "army" and to *jun* as "corps." See He Di, "The Last Campaign to Unify China: The CCP's Unrealized Plan to Liberate Taiwan, 1949–1950," in *Chinese Warfighting*, ed. Ryan et al., 78; Li, *A History of the Modern Chinese Army*, 76; Ronald Spector, "The Battle That Saved Taiwan," *Quarterly Journal of Military History* 25, no. 1 (Autumn 2012): 10; Shuguang Zhang, "'Preparedness Eliminates Mishaps': The CCP's Security Concerns in 1949–1950 and the Origins of Sino-American Confrontation," *Journal of American–East Asian Relations* 1, no. 1 (Spring 1992): 50; Jon W. Huebner, "The Abortive Liberation of Taiwan," *China Quarterly*, no. 110 (June 1987): 263; and Miles Maochun Yu, "The Battle of Quemoy: The Amphibious Assault That Held the Postwar Military Balance in the Taiwan Strait," *Naval War College Review* 69, no. 2 (Spring 2016): 94. In an earlier study on the field army system, William Whitson refers to *jun* as "corps." See William Whitson, "The Field Army in Chinese Communist Military Politics," *China Quarterly*, no. 37 (March 1969): 7. A Royal United Services Institute article examining the PLA's past organizational structures leaves all terms untranslated. See "History of the PLA's Ground Force Organizational Structure and Military

Regions," RUSI, June 17, 2004, https://rusi.org/explore-our-research/publications /commentary/history-plas-ground-force-organisational-structure-and-military -regions. The Office of Naval Intelligence similarly leaves the term *jun* untranslated in reference to the current PLAN. See Office of Naval Intelligence, *China's Navy 2007* (Suitland, MD: Office of Naval Intelligence, 2007), 2.

12. As a reference, the following provides the tactical organizational components of the contemporary PLA in ascending order: 10 personnel form a squad (班, or *ban*), three to four squads form a platoon (排, or *pai*) numbering about 40 personnel, three to four platoons form a company (连, or *lian*) numbering between 120 and 150 personnel, three to five companies form a battalion (营, or *ying*) numbering between 200 and 700 personnel, three battalions form a regiment (团, or *tuan*) numbering between 1,000 and 2,500 personnel, three regiments form a division (师, or *shi*) numbering between 8,000 and 10,000 personnel (prior to restructuring in early 2000s, three to four regiments formed a division numbering between 10,000 and 12,000 personnel), and at least four divisions and several regiments form a group army (集团军, or *jituanjun*), the rough equivalent of a corps or *jun* referenced in this study, numbering between 30,000 and 50,000 personnel. For a detailed analysis of the PLA's tactical organization prior to the 2015 reforms, see Dennis J. Blasko, *The Chinese Army Today: Tradition and Transformation for the 21st Century*, 2nd ed. (London: Routledge, 2012), 43–51. The PLA's organization in the 1970s was roughly similar: twelve troops formed a squad, three squads formed a platoon of 37 troops, three platoons formed a company of 160 troops, three companies formed a battalion of 800 troops, three battalions formed a regiment of 3,000 troops, three regiments formed a division of 12,000 troops, and three divisions formed a corps of 50,000 troops. See Harvey W. Nelsen, *The Chinese Military System: An Organizational Study of the Chinese People's Liberation Army* (Boulder, CO: Westview, 1977), 4. Note that Nelsen refers to *jun* as "corps."

13. Westad, *Decisive Encounters*, 199.

14. Li, *A History of the Modern Chinese Army*, 75.

15. Westad, *Decisive Encounters*, 197.

16. 王厚卿 主编 [Wang Houqing, ed.], 战役发展史 [The History of Campaign Development] (Beijing: National Defense University Press, 2008), 543.

17. Wang, 547–52.

18. In June 1950, the Central Military Commission ordered the transition of the field armies into regional military commands. The Third Field Army was reorganized to establish the East China Command. Its tactical units that occupied six provinces marked the geographic scope of the regional command, which included the coastal provinces of Zhejiang and Fujian. Li, *A History of the Modern Chinese Army*, 133–34.

19. He Di, "The Last Campaign to Unify China," 73–74. He Di offers one of the best English-language accounts of the CCP's thinking and plans to conquer Taiwan from June 1949 to the outbreak of the Korean War in June 1950.

20. 中国人民解放军军史编写组 [Editorial Team of the Chinese People's Liberation Army's Military History], 中国人民解放军军史 第四卷 [Military History of the Chinese People's Liberation Army, Vol. 4] (Beijing: Academy of Military Science, 2011), 112.

21. Editorial Team of the Chinese People's Liberation Army's Military History, 112–13.

THREE

The East China Navy

Mao Zedong and his subordinates began to plan for a new navy after the decisive battlefield victories over their Nationalists rivals in early 1949. They recognized at the outset that the final phases of the civil war would require naval power to finish off their opponent and to secure their conquest. The record of events shows how a revolutionary group, once it seized power, learned to wield a new instrument of state by creating an entirely new institution of a new service in a new domain. Communist leaders, utterly lacking in experience with nautical affairs, struggled to come to grips with the institutional, human, ideological, and material dimensions of sea power.

This is also a story about the Chinese Civil War's aftermath and how the victor dealt with its defeated foe. The remnants of the Nationalist navy who had defected or surrendered to the Communists or chose not to flee to Taiwan possessed a reservoir of expertise. In its quest for sea power, the CCP found that collaboration with its former enemy was a necessity, however distasteful it might have been for revolutionary leaders. The Nationalists therefore played a role in the navy's founding. The PLAN's early history thus draws attention to the complex mix of indigenous, foreign, and hybrid influences that the Communist cadre, Soviet advisers, and Western-trained Nationalists, respectively, exerted on the naval service's doctrine and outlook.

Throughout this narrative Zhang Aiping, the first to assume command of China's new navy, is featured prominently in this little-known drama. Zhang's leadership qualities, many of which are universal in nature, enabled him to overcome a mind-boggling set of challenges inherent to any start-up enterprise.

BORN IN WAR

The Communist leadership decided to build its navy at a decisive point in the Chinese Civil War, which was nearing its final stages after nearly three years of vicious fighting. In a resolution titled "The Current Situation and the Party's Missions in 1949" issued on January 8, 1949, the Politburo determined that "between 1949 and 1950, we should strive to establish a usable air force and a navy that can defend our rivers and coasts. This possibility exists."[1] The previous two months had been calamitous for the Nationalists. It suffered three massive military defeats in the Liao-Shen (Liaoning-Shenyang), Ping-Jin (Beijing-Tianjin), and Huai-Hai (Huai River–Haizhou) campaigns, losing Manchuria, northern China, and 1.5 million troops in succession.[2] Reeling from this debacle, Nationalist forces fell back to the Yangzi River to defend Nanjing, Shanghai, and Hangzhou even as major elements of the KMT evacuated to the island redoubt of Taiwan. These catastrophes opened the way for the Communists to cross the Yangzi and conquer southern China. As Edward Dreyer notes, "That the outcome of the Huai-Hai Campaign meant the fall of Nationalist China was clear to all concerned."[3]

To compound the growing disaster, defections to the Communists, a problem that had long plagued the Nationalists, spread to the Republic of China Navy (ROCN) at this critical juncture. According to S. C. M. Paine, "From 1 June 1946 to 31 January 1949, the Nationalists lost nearly 5 million soldiers, three quarters of whom defected to the Communists."[4] The bleeding would continue for the rest of the civil war. In February 1949, crews of the frigate *Huangan* and the cruiser *Chongqing* mutinied in sequence. The latter, the flagship and pride of the Nationalist navy, was a particularly devastating blow to morale.[5] Buoyed by the turn of events and hoping to encourage more defections, Mao Zedong and Zhu De, the commander in chief of Communist forces, sent a congratulatory telegram in late March to the *Chongqing*'s officers and sailors: "The Chinese people must build their own powerful national defense. Besides the army, we must build our own air force and navy. And, you will soon be the pioneers of joining the naval buildup"[6] It was a clear signal that the Communists envisioned a future role for the mutineers in postrevolution China.[7]

Unambiguous signs of collapsing Nationalist resistance and the continuing mutinies at sea added momentum to the earlier decision to establish a navy. Between February and December 1949, sixteen mutinies and a surrender turned over ninety-seven warships and 3,800 personnel to the Communists. In less than a year, the ROCN hemorrhaged more than a fifth of its fighting ships and about a tenth of its total manpower.[8] Moreover, the CCP recognized that the Nationalist retreat to Taiwan would extend the battlefield to the maritime sphere, making the planned naval buildup ever more urgent.

Preparations for the cross-river campaign along the Yangzi further illustrated the importance of naval power. At least on paper, the KMT's navy commanded the waterway. Over 120 warships and more than 230 military aircraft were positioned to interdict enemy river crossings. By contrast, the Communists lacked the capacity to contest Nationalist control of the Yangzi, protect troop transports, and provide gunfire support to the amphibious assaults.[9] This sharp asymmetry in power conferred a major advantage to the Nationalists.

The CCP understood that to prevail in offshore combat during the next phase of the civil war, it must first acquire sea power.

These factors together set in motion a scramble to pull together a new service from scratch. Yet, the internal strife on the mainland was far from over, and large swaths of southern China remained out of Communist hands. The CCP gambled that the tide had turned irreversibly in its favor and that resources could be spared to build a new navy. That responsibility fell on the shoulders of Zhang Aiping, a thirty-nine-year-old army officer.

HUMBLE BEGINNINGS

Zhang Aiping, best known in the West for his leadership roles in the 1955 Yijiangshan offshore campaign and China's nuclear and missile programs in the 1960s, joined the revolution at the tender age of fifteen. After surviving Chiang Kai-shek's anticommunist purges, Zhang participated in Shanghai's underground movement and helped mobilize the Red Army. He later joined his comrades in the Jiangxi soviet, where he escaped the Nationalists' fifth encirclement and suppression campaign to go on the epic Long March. During the war against the Japanese, Zhang rose through the ranks in a base area in Anhui Province. By late 1945 as the Communists and the Nationalists maneuvered to resume the civil war, he was promoted to deputy commander of the Central China Military Region.

When the CCP decided to build a navy, Zhang was a committee member of the Third Field Army, the East China Field Army's successor. Three years before he had suffered serious injuries in a car accident. It was not until early 1949, after extensive medical treatment in the Soviet Union and recovery in Dalian, that he was healthy enough to return to duty. By this time, the Communists were poised to cross the Yangzi River for a massive offensive to seize southern China.

On March 25, Zhang arrived at the General Frontline Committee of the Central Military Commission in Sunjiawei, Anhui Province, to receive his orders. Having missed several years of the civil war, he eagerly anticipated an active role in the planning and execution of the campaign. Instead, Chen Yi, the Third Field Army's commander, sprung an entirely new order on Zhang. The Central Military Commission had decided to assign Zhang and other support elements of the Third Field Army the task of building up a navy.

The Third Field Army's follow-on operations in southern China positioned it well to perform this job. The field army was expected to press forward along China's southeast coast as well as conquer the offshore islands and Taiwan. After crossing the Yangzi, the army would first take Nanjing, the Nationalist capital, and then move downriver to Zhenjiang and drive east to Shanghai. The army would then pursue retreating KMT forces into Fujian Province, taking the coastal cities of Fuzhou and Xiamen.

China's east coast was the epicenter of what was left of the Nationalist navy, including personnel and ships. Moreover, many of the most productive shipping industries and infrastructure, such as the Jiangnan Shipyard in Shanghai, were in the Third Field Army's area of operations. The CCP fully anticipated absorbing the remnants of its archrival's sea power. The Third Field Army was thus to assume responsibilities for establishing control over China's eastern seaboard, an inherently maritime theater, and to begin building a navy.

Zhang was wary of accepting the new task, not least because it threatened to keep him out of the upcoming cross-river campaign. He demurred and reportedly professed to Chen that his middle school education and his minimal swimming skills disqualified him for the job.[10] Zhang also recognized that a navy demanded highly technical skills for which his army background had little application. Chen had anticipated his subordinate's concerns and sought to reassure Zhang. Chen emphasized the prospective navy's importance to the CCP's larger plans to seize the rest of China, especially the mainland's offshore islands. Chen further noted that Mao had personally endorsed the decision to entrust Zhang with this important task.

More importantly, Chen had selected Zhang for his organizational acumen and his quick learning. Chen recalled that in 1941 Zhang was ordered to pacify the bandit-infested Hongze Lake area in Jiangsu Province, which endangered the region's Communist base areas. Despite limited resources and experience, Chen reminded him, Zhang still managed to organize a small fighting force composed of wooden sailing boats. The flotilla effectively suppressed the banditry.[11] Similar riverine-type forces operated in Shandong, Jiangsu, Zhejiang, Fujian, and Guangdong Provinces. Former members of these unconventional units, nicknamed "local navy [土海军]" to convey their irregular nature, would later join the new navy.[12] While this success story bore little resemblance to the difficulties ahead, it nevertheless illustrated the managerial and leadership skills that Zhang possessed to improvise and adapt to new stressful conditions. Those skills would soon pay off.

Zhang reluctantly accepted his orders and headed to Baimamiao in Jiangsu Province, the command headquarters of the Third Field Army. There he linked up with Su Yu, the deputy commander of the Third Field Army, whom Zhang had served alongside of in the New Fourth Army during the fight against the Japanese. Su promised to transfer elements of his forces to support Zhang's work, including training, security, and coastal defense units and administrative staff. Of course, the assault across the Yangzi had to take top priority, and there was a limit to how much the Third Field Army could spare in manpower.

In the meantime, Zhang did his best to learn on the job. Without any experience or relevant education to guide his thinking, he purportedly turned to a Soviet novel on the Battle of Tsushima, the climactic naval clash during the 1904–5 Russo-Japanese War, from which to draw inspiration.[13] He also scrounged for officers in the Third Field Army to assist him. The deputy chief of staff of the 28th Army's 84th Division, Li Jin, was among the first to join the new team. Another founding member was Huang Shengtian, an operations officer of the Third Field Army with extensive intelligence about the ROCN.[14] In one instance, Zhang had to strong-arm Zhang Weiqing, a logistics officer, to join his effort. Zhang would later be reassigned to the navy's logistics department to handle the infusion of former Nationalist ships and other assets.

After Communist forces crossed the Yangzi largely unopposed on April 21, 1949, events unfolded swiftly. Nanjing fell two days later. That same day Zhang convened a meeting with his skeletal thirteen-member staff. He was under orders from the Central Military Commission to establish the headquarters of the East China Military Region Navy (or East China Navy). The unassuming gathering marked the founding of the PLAN.

Zhang first declared the birth of the PLAN before his subordinates. He then described the challenges ahead. KMT forces were retreating to the offshore islands and Taiwan. Moreover, the enemy had blockaded the mouths of the Yangzi and Pearl Rivers, inflicting economic harm on Shanghai and Guangzhou, respectively. Without a navy, Zhang reasoned, China's coastal areas would remain insecure, and the task of taking Taiwan would go unfulfilled. Concurrently, Nationalist naval officers who had mutinied or defected were scattered in such places as Nanjing and Zhenjiang. This pool of talent would likely be a critical constituent of the East China Navy and would need to be actively recruited to join the new venture.

The following day Zhang and his crew headed to Jiangyin, a KMT fortress that had fallen to mutiny on the south side of the Yangzi just northwest of Shanghai. The stronghold served as a hub for handling former Nationalist personnel, ships, and equipment along the eight hundred–kilometer stretch of the Yangzi River from Jiangsu to Jiangxi Province. Within two days of his arrival, the promised personnel transfers from the Third Field Army began to arrive, and Zhang's organization quickly swelled to some eight hundred people.

On April 28 Zhang delivered a major speech titled "Strive to Build and Develop the People's Navy of New China." He first announced the establishment of the navy's leadership organs, including the party committee, command headquarters, and the political department. As the navy's commander, he would serve concurrently as the party committee's secretary, ensuring the party's absolute control over the navy. Zhang further ordered the formation of a coastal defense regiment and the East China Military Region's first naval flotilla.

Zhang then declared that the immediate task was "to build a navy with some escort and transport capacity that can, in coordination with the army and air force, liberate the offshore islands of the southeast coast and Taiwan and finally liberate all of China."[15] The sense of urgency was real enough: CCP leaders had ordered the creation of a combat-capable navy that would take part in Taiwan's liberation alongside its sister services by the end of 1949. On May 4, the Central Military Commission formally recognized Zhang as commander and political commissar of the East China Navy.

BRINGING THE ENEMY IN FROM THE COLD

As Zhang organized, Nationalist resistance crumbled at a rapid pace. On April 25, the Second Squadron operating on the Yangzi River near Nanjing mutinied. The loss of thirty surface combatants and over 1,200 officers and sailors stunned and devastated the KMT's naval leadership. This collapse in authority was an opportunity for the Communists to win over ex-Nationalist officers and men. It also represented an experiment for how the Communists would accept and integrate their former enemies into the PLAN. The first test was to bring around the Second Squadron's commander, Rear Adm. Lin Zun, a seasoned senior officer who understandably hesitated to turn over his fleet to his onetime adversaries.

Lin cut an impressive figure. He came from a navy family. His father had been an officer of the Beiyang Fleet and had participated in the Sino-Japanese War half a century before. Lin, a graduate of the Yantai Naval Academy, studied at the Royal Naval College in Greenwich. He rose through the ranks to include a stint as the assistant naval attaché in Washington, DC.[16] Following Japan's defeat in 1945, Admiral Lin led an expedition as fleet commander to recover the Paracel Islands and the Spratly Islands in 1946 and established Taiping Island as a forward base in the heart of the South China Sea.[17] Before Nanjing fell, Adm. Gui Yongqing, the ROCN's commander in chief, ordered Lin to bring the Second Squadron downriver to Shanghai. Before fleeing the capital, Gui further pressed Lin to deny the Communists access to the navy's pool of manpower.

Zhang recognized immediately that Lin would be an asset to his navy. Moreover, the uncertainties surrounding the intentions and loyalty of an admiral in control of a powerful fleet were surely unsettling to the Communists. To open a channel of communications, Zhang appointed Li Jin, a founding member of the new navy, to reach out to Lin. Zhang advised Li to approach the admiral with utmost care, respect Lin and his officers, and persuade him to join the Communist cause. In addition, Zhang instructed Li to convey to the Nationalist flag officer that the Communists were looking to the future and were not interested in retribution. To reassure Admiral Lin, Zhang further ordered Li to restore monthly rations and pay to the mutineers.[18]

After Li encountered a cool reception, Zhang hurried to Nanjing to speak directly with Lin, but suspicion and differences over the Second Squadron's fate stalled the talks. To break the logjam, Zhang called upon Liu Bocheng, the legendary commander of the Second Field Army and the temporary mayor of Nanjing, to broker the negotiations. Liu's reputation carried substantial weight. In a meeting with Lin and his staff, Liu spoke with emotion about the need for unity and asserted, perhaps with a hint of threat in his voice, that the mutineers had to make a clear choice.[19] His exhortations finally convinced the admiral to hand over the Second Squadron. The Central Military Commission quickly rewarded Lin for his acquiescence, promoting him to deputy commander of the East China Navy. Lin would later go on to serve as the deputy commander of the East Sea Fleet and as the director of military studies at the Academy of Military Affairs.

In another example of Zhang's efforts to recruit Nationalist personnel, he turned to Sun Keji, the director of the navy's political department, for advice. Sun was well acquainted with Communist double agents who had infiltrated and worked at the highest levels of the KMT regime. One of them was Rear Adm. Jin Sheng, director of administration in the ROCN's headquarters. In 1948 Jin defected to the Communist underground movement, providing valuable inside information about the Nationalists. When the KMT began to flee to Taiwan, Jin convinced many of his colleagues to stay on the mainland. Zhang recognized Jin's value as a source of navy contacts and, with Sun's help, convinced Jin to serve as a recruiter. Jin's network paid off handsomely, bringing out of hiding such high-level leaders as Rear Adm. Zeng Guosheng, the former director of the machinery bureau, Vice Adm. Zeng Yiding, and Rear Adm. Zhou Yingcong.[20]

In search of technical expertise, Zhang understood that he had to rise above the past. One of Adm. Jin Sheng's top recruits was Capt. Xu Shipu, deputy director of the Nationalist navy's administrative office. While Xu's previous work in the inner circles of the KMT made him politically toxic, Jin believed that his educational background and operational experiences would be invaluable to the navy.[21] From 1943 to 1946, Xu engaged in advanced studies at Swarthmore College and at the US Naval Academy.[22] In 1947, he commanded the 4,000-ton Achelous-class landing craft repair ship and brought it across the Pacific to China under Lend-Lease. Defying orders to retreat to Taiwan, Xu went into hiding. Jin vouched for Xu and persuaded Zhang to welcome the captain. In recognition of Jin's ability to tap his connections, he was later promoted to deputy director of the navy's research committee.

In addition to high-ranking officers boasting intimate knowledge of naval affairs, the larger infrastructure, force structure, and personnel of the ROCN began to fall into Communist hands. In early May 1949 the East China Navy stationed the newly formed First Flotilla in Zhenjiang, where it began to process ex-Nationalist naval officers and men and accept the turnover of abandoned KMT warships in the area. The flotilla took control of some forty ships, including gunboats, patrol boats, and landing craft. In preparation for the takeover of Shanghai, Zhang established an administrative body in Suzhou to expropriate left-behind naval assets.

On May 27, Shanghai fell. Zhang immediately brought his team there to set up headquarters. Within a month, the East China Navy inherited from the Nationalists a host of naval institutions, factories, shipyards, machinery, warehouses, and hospitals in the Shanghai area.[23] One of Zhang's first acts was to issue a proclamation in the local paper that was part amnesty and part recruitment of ex-ROCN personnel in the area.[24] Zhang then established registration centers in Qingdao and Shanghai to accept the services of former Nationalists. Thousands came out of hiding to register. Similar centers would later be opened in Fuzhou, Xiamen, and Guangzhou to draw on the talents of the former enemy.

By mid-June, the East China Navy oversaw all naval affairs in towns along the Yangzi as far upriver as Jiujiang, nearly nine hundred kilometers from Shanghai, and supervised the navy's assets in coastal cities stretching north-south from Qingdao to Xiamen. Zhang took control of some thirty shore facilities, including major shipyards in Shanghai and Qingdao, as well as over twenty ships and fifty small craft. Some seven thousand people, including two thousand ex-Nationalists, worked for him. In August Zhang established the command headquarters, the political department, and the logistics department, the three main administrative bodies of the East China Navy. He further urged the Central Military Commission to establish a national institution to unify and lead all elements of China's navy as soon as possible.

BUILDING A HODGEPODGE FLEET

As the East China Navy continued to absorb the remnant ROCN, Zhang turned his attention to the material conditions of the fleet. His navy was in a decrepit state. Only nine vessels could be counted as fighting ships. The rest were medium- to small-sized craft. Not only were the ships old, some dating to the pre-Republican era, but they were also poorly maintained under the Nationalists. Most ships were assigned to riverine duties and lacked seaworthiness. The countries of origin for the eighty or so ships under his command numbered more than ten. The dizzying array of propulsion systems that powered the fleet made a nightmare out of maintenance, repairs, and supply.

To further complicate matters, as the KMT fled to Taiwan, Admiral Gui, the ROCN's commander in chief, ordered his subordinates to destroy or sabotage ships stranded on the mainland. The Republic of China Air Force also regularly bombed the left-behind fleet and shore facilities. Indeed, air units struck six ships of the Second Squadron after its mutiny, reducing its combat capabilities. Subsequent air raids severely damaged the Jiangnan Shipyard in Shanghai while maiming or killing shipyard workers. Lacking the power to contest the KMT's command of the air, the Communists dispersed, hid, or camouflaged their ships while strengthening their air defenses. At the same time, shipyard workers changed their shifts to nighttime, when the Nationalists ceased their bombing runs.

To salvage what little he had, Zhang formed an inspection and repair committee. He charged Rear Adm. Zeng Guosheng, the Nationalist officer recruited by Admiral Jin, with the task of overseeing the group's work. A graduate of Wusong Naval Academy, Zeng served as a surface warfare officer. Like his Nationalist colleagues, he had studied abroad in Japan, Germany, and the United Kingdom, where he specialized in ship construction and torpedo technology. He spent his career in shipbuilding and by 1945 had been promoted to chief of the machinery bureau in navy headquarters and commanded the Shanghai naval shipyard.[25] As chair of the new committee, he faced a daunting task. Zeng calculated that the East China Navy needed twenty to twenty-four seagoing combatants to rival Nationalist sea power based in Taiwan and the offshore islands, a fleet size well beyond the immediate reach of the Communists. After some consultations with Zhang, Zeng pursued multiple lines of approach to add heft to the fleet and right the naval balance.

Admiral Zeng first conducted a systematic survey to compile a record of all ships, both naval and civilian, in the Shanghai area and selected repairable ships that could be quickly pressed into service. His crew towed in abandoned and captured frigates in the Huangpu River and in Jiangyin for major overhauls and modifications. He even requested the Central Military Commission to transfer a frigate from Qingdao. With permission from Chen Yi, then the mayor of Shanghai, Zeng procured six merchant and fishing vessels from a variety of civilian agencies, including the Shanghai Fisheries Corporation, that could be converted for military use. He even dispatched a member of the logistics department to Hong Kong to acquire merchant ships.[26] Zeng then established a local salvage company to recover four scuttled warships along the Yangzi River for rehabilitation.

To give the nascent navy more weight, Zeng bought or transferred eight tank landing ships and six troop transports from Qingdao and Shanghai. He also purchased several hundred Soviet naval guns and requisitioned nearly a thousand artillery pieces from the army.[27] Zeng then installed the cannons and howitzers aboard the ships, placing nearly eight hundred pieces of artillery on 134 vessels.[28] Within three months he delivered 16 armed civilian vessels and repaired warships. By May 1950 up to 150 ships were ready for service. According to another study, the East China Navy accumulated 183 warships from the Nationalist navy, 169 civilian vessels, 6 salvaged ships, and 48 used vessels purchased through Hong Kong, displacing totals of 43,000, 64,000, 1,715, and 25,000 tons, respectively.[29] For his unorthodox workarounds, Zeng was rewarded with a promotion to deputy commander of the logistics department and as director of the technical bureau.

Zeng faced another problem: the severe lack of spare parts. He estimated that five to six ships would need to be cannibalized just to keep one ship operational. This was clearly unsustainable. At the time, local cities and factories suffered the same shortages, while the West had already embargoed the Communists, cutting off foreign supply. To investigate the matter further, Zeng interviewed shipyard workers for possible solutions. He discovered that many workers had engaged in acts of civil disobedience by hiding equipment, instruments, gauges, metals, and tools when the Nationalists forcibly removed and shipped machinery to Taiwan as they evacuated Shanghai. It was possible that the navy might be able recall the goods that the workers had stashed away.

Zeng turned to Wang Rongbing, chief engineer at the Jiangnan Shipyard, to corroborate this new intelligence. Wang had been at the shipyard since 1946. He too was a well-educated Nationalist officer. A graduate of the Mawei Naval Academy in Fujian Province, Wang had studied internal combustion at the Manchester College of Arts and Technology and at Cornell University. He confirmed that the workers had risked their lives defying the Nationalists. But it was unclear where the goods were hidden. It was then decided that the navy would publicly call for "patriotic donations." Zhang hosted a mass rally to encourage the return of the hidden tools and equipment. Wang was the first to act, providing enormous amounts of technical data. Within days, donations began to pour in. Wang would be awarded a citation for setting an example. He would go on to become a famous naval engineer, leading the effort to build China's first-generation submarine and the first indigenous oceangoing cargo ship displacing over ten thousand tons.

Marking the first anniversary of the navy's founding on April 23, 1950, the East China Navy held a naming ceremony of its new fleet to commemorate the important milestone. The eclectic collection of warships and armed civilian vessels lined up along the Yangzi River's south bank at Caoxie Gorge in Nanjing. Lin Zun, deputy commander of the navy, served as the master of ceremonies. At the event he announced the Central Military Commission's orders to stand up the East China Navy's new fleets. They included two escort flotillas comprising six combatants each, an amphibious flotilla made up of fourteen vessels, and a minesweeping squadron of five boats.[30] Zhang conferred new names on each ship. Frigates were named after provincial capitals, gunboats carried the names of famous cities during the revolutionary era, and large landing craft were given names of base areas in the revolution.[31] These naming conventions remain to this day.

THE STORY BEHIND THE NAVY'S FLAGSHIP

The convoluted origins of the PLAN's first flagship, *Nanchang*, most clearly illustrate the Communists' desperate material state. China's lead ship began its nearly four-decade service as an oceangoing gunboat for the Imperial Japanese Navy. Built by Osaka Iron Works and commissioned in 1941, the *Uji* was assigned to the Imperial Japanese Navy's China Base Fleet. Outfitted as a flagship and designed to cruise inland waters and open seas, the boat boasted 120mm naval guns, antiaircraft artillery, an antisubmarine warfare suite, long-range communications gear, and radar. Operating out of Shanghai, the *Uji* spent its first years patrolling the Yangzi River and was later conscripted to escort convoys across the East China Sea during the Pacific War.

After Japan's surrender, the *Uji* was turned over to the Nationalist navy as a prize of war and renamed *Changzhi* in September 1945. At the time of transfer, the vessel was among the most heavily armed and modern in the fleet. The *Changzhi* was immediately put to use in the Chinese Civil War. Based in Qingdao as the flagship of the KMT's First Squadron, the ship led blockade operations against Communist-held areas along the Shandong Peninsula. As the tide turned and Nationalist resistance collapsed in northern China, the *Changzhi* evacuated trapped KMT troops along the coast and shuttled between the mainland and Taiwan during the Nationalist retreat to the island.[32]

The fall of Shanghai in May 1949 forced the Nationalist navy to fall back to the Dinghai naval base on Zhoushan Island located just east of Ningbo. To choke off Shanghai's riverine trade now in Communist hands, the ROCN assigned the *Changzhi* to blockade duty. The boat targeted shipping near Wusongkou, the outlet of the Huangpu River, a Yangzi tributary and Shanghai's major economic artery. On September 19, 1949, while the *Changzhi* anchored near Daji Island at the intersection of Hangzhou Bay and the mouth of the Yangzi River, a mutiny broke out aboard the ship. In the preceding months a Communist cell had infiltrated the boat, and by the time of the uprising as many as forty crew members had joined the cause.[33] The Communists surprised the Nationalist officers, killed the commanding officer and the executive officer, and quickly commandeered *Changzhi*.

The mutineers then steered the boat to the Bund, the famous Shanghai waterfront, where the deputy commander of the East China Navy's logistics department and former Nationalist flag officer, Zeng Guosheng, warmly received the turncoats. Fearing Nationalist retaliation, the navy's party committee ordered the boat to move inland along the Yangzi. Word of the mutiny quickly reached the KMT, and air raids to deny the Communist use of the *Changzhi* began almost as soon as the vessel reached Nanjing, some 270 kilometers from the coast. Despite efforts to camouflage the vessel and to keep on the move between Nanjing and Zhenjiang, the boat came under relentless ROC Air Force attacks. Recognizing that they could not win the cat-and-mouse game, the Communists decided to abandon their prize for the time being. They stripped the *Changzhi* of all vital equipment and scuttled the gunboat at Yanziji just north of Nanjing.[34]

In early 1950 after the Communists had adequately secured the airspace over the mainland, Zhang decided to salvage the *Changzhi*. With the help of Soviet advisers, the gunboat was raised intact and towed to the Jiangnan Shipyard in Shanghai for major repairs and restoration in February 1950. Two months later on the anniversary of the East China Navy's founding, the boat was rechristened *Nanchang* and assigned as the flagship of the newly established Sixth Squadron. By July 1950 the *Nanchang* was ready for service in the PLAN, and it would later be reequipped with Soviet naval guns and equipment.

The flagship would go on to participate in the 1953 Dongji Island campaign, the 1955 Yijiangshan campaign, and major naval exercises off the Liaodong Peninsula and the Chuanshan Peninsula at the eastern tip of Zhejiang Province in 1955 and 1959, respectively.[35] Perhaps most important, the *Nanchang* became the public face of the Chinese surface fleet, receiving visits by top CCP leaders. Between 1950 and 1953, Chen Yi, Liu Shaoqi, Peng Dehuai, and Mao Zedong took their turns inspecting the vessel.

Nanchang's first commanding officer, Guo Chengsen, followed a similarly circuitous path to his leadership post in the East China Navy. A graduate of the KMT's Fuzhou Naval Academy, Guo was one of eighty young officers sent to the United States and the United Kingdom in 1943 for further training and education. These rising stars were expected to form the nucleus of the postwar ROCN. Guo and twenty others enrolled at the Royal Naval College and subsequently underwent tactical training at Portsmouth Naval Base. They were then assigned to British fighting ships in the European theater of operations. Ensign Guo served as a watch officer aboard the heavy cruiser HMS *Kent*, witnessing several major engagements against the German navy.[36]

Upon his return to China in May 1946, Guo joined the Qingdao Naval Academy as an instructor. The Nationalist navy then reassigned Lieutenant Guo to serve as the *Changzhi*'s executive officer. Guo's foreign studies, wartime experiences, and English-language skills made him a highly prized commodity. Although the circumstances of his conversion remain unclear, Guo became a coconspirator in the *Changzhi* mutiny and used his positional authority to recruit Communist sympathizers. When the Nationalist naval command learned of his identity, the Communist underground spirited Guo away to safety. He went into hiding in Shanghai until the city fell to the Communists. While he missed the revolt, he undoubtedly played an important role in organizing the secret cells aboard the ship.

After the Communists scuttled the *Changzhi*, the East China Navy sent Guo to the Nanjing Naval Academy to help coordinate the salvage operation and train new crew members. Zhang repeatedly visited Guo to check on the progress of the ship's restoration. Zhang then promoted Guo to command what would become the *Nanchang* and even selected Guo to be a probationary member of the CCP, an unusual appointment on behalf of a former Nationalist officer. As commanding officer of the *Nanchang*, Guo would participate in major offshore campaigns in the early 1950s and would later run the navigation bureaus of the Sixth Squadron and of navy headquarters. In 1955 he would be transferred to Dalian Naval Academy, where he would spend a thirty-year career teaching navigation.

The stories of the *Nanchang* and Guo Chengsen provide a glimpse into the staggering technological and personnel challenges facing the new navy. The Communists inherited both the hardware and the software from their archrival. They had to settle for a thirdhand naval vessel that was at best a secondary combatant by the Imperial Japanese Navy's standards. The Communists had to draw from the experiences of a relatively young naval officer to command their first flagship. The Chinese navy had little choice but to scrounge for scraps. At the same time, the efforts to preserve and restore the gunboat demonstrated the tenacity and determination with which the Communists pursued the naval buildup. Zhang's can-do spirit and pragmatism contributed to the incremental progress in the naval buildup.

BUILDING HUMAN CAPITAL

Beyond the physical condition of the fleet, Zhang had to wrestle with the human dimension of naval power. The initial difficulties with winning over Adm. Lin Zun, commander of the KMT's Second Squadron, and the concerns over the political reliability of Capt. Xu Shipu illustrated the challenges of reconciling with former adversaries. To obtain the cooperation of Nationalist leaders, the CCP had to engage in artful persuasion. At the same time, the CCP had to demonstrate that the Communist cadre had something meaningful to offer in this joint venture.

In a gesture of reconciliation, the CCP leadership agreed to meet Zhang and his former KMT subordinates, including Lin Zun, Jin Sheng, Zeng Guosheng, and Xu Shiping, in August 1949. Reflecting the importance that top leaders attached to this meeting, Zhu De, Liu Shaoqi, Nie Rongzhen, and Zhou Enlai received Zhang's delegation. The visit culminated in a two-hour meeting with Mao Zedong in Zhongnanhai, the leadership compound in central Beijing. At the gathering Mao made clear his intent: "The navy we are building is a navy for the people. The people's navy is a component of the Liberation Army under the leadership of the Chinese Communist Party. It must inherit and carry forward the fine traditions of the Liberation Army, strive in unity, and defend our seacoast."[37]

Mao went on to declare that the ex-Nationalist naval officers were national treasures to the country. He acknowledged that there was much that his comrades needed to learn from them. At the same time, Mao insisted that his army possessed fine pedigrees in ideology and combat experience worthy of emulation. He concluded that "new and old comrades alike must unite, learn from each other, and strive together to build the People's Navy."[38] By asserting that unity and mutual learning would enable each side to draw the best qualities out of the other, Mao sent an unmistakable signal that the Communist leadership was ready to work with its past enemy. After the meeting he wrote an inscription commemorating the event: "We must build a navy. This navy must be able to protect our seacoast and effectively defend against possible imperialist invasion."[39] The inscription captured his vision for the future direction of the naval service.

While the meeting may have put to rest lingering concerns about the CCP's sincerity, Zhang was still left with the practical challenges of integrating former KMT personnel and the Communist cadre. To him, there were two problems. On the one hand, most of his personnel were drawn from the army. Their agricultural background, poor education, and low levels of technical knowledge were ill-suited to the demands of navy building. On the other hand, the ex-KMT naval officers and sailors possessed the right skills and knowledge but were inadequately indoctrinated in the CCP's ideology. Zhang bluntly described these two types of people as "cripples [跛子]."[40]

To close the gap between those lacking technical education and those insufficiently revolutionary, he established the navy's research committee and the naval academy. The research committee, set up within the navy headquarters, comprised seventeen high-ranking former KMT officers. Zhang appointed Adm. Zeng Yiding, the former chief of staff of the Nationalist navy, as director. To confer more authority on Zeng, Zhang promoted him to serve as deputy commander of the navy's logistics department. The committee functioned as the navy's internal think tank tasked with addressing major policy questions and also served as a clearinghouse that would enable the flow of ideas and concepts across the service. Zhang intended to empower the ex-Nationalists with institutional authority while adding intellectual fire-power to the new enterprise.

Zhang then founded a naval school on the grounds of the former ROCN headquarters in Nanjing and appointed himself the superintendent and politi-cal commissar of the school. He organized the academy into five regiments and one battalion.[41] The first three regiments provided political education to former KMT junior officers, while the fourth regiment took in newly admitted young intellectuals and educated urbanites. The single battalion was devoted to the political education of former Nationalist senior officers. In the fifth regiment, ex-KMT officers served as faculty assigned to teach basic technical curriculum to the army's cadre.[42] Zhang clearly intended the institution to cross-fertilize ideas, traditions, and know-how between the Communist and former Nation-alist camps. About 3,800 students attended when the school opened its doors in September 1949.

In preparation for the cross-strait invasion of Taiwan, the East China Navy organized two squadrons modeled along the naval academy's organizational structure. The school's fifth regiment served as the personnel pipeline for the First Squadron, while the graduates of the first regiment fed into the Second Squadron. Each squadron consisted of eight to ten surface combatants headed by a regiment commander, a regiment deputy commander, and corresponding political commissars. About two-thirds of the crew were army cadre, who had undergone minimal training and education, while the other third were former Nationalists.[43]

Despite concerns about political reliability, Zhang hired Capt. Xu Shipu to head the academy's technical department, but the educational challenge was enormous. The demand for qualified manpower far outstripped the supply of adequately trained and educated personnel. To compound this mismatch in supply and demand, the highly technical nature of building, maintaining, and operating a navy required substantial and sustained investment in human cap-ital. Zhang recognized that software was as important as hardware. According to Xu, the ROCN's officers possessed at minimum a high school education and at least six to nine years of additional training and education. But Zhang's start-up navy had neither the time nor the resources to afford such a luxury.

Xu thus proposed interim measures to keep pace with the personnel needs of the fleet. He was no stranger to such improvised methods. In 1945, Xu oversaw the accelerated shore training of his men in the United States as he prepared to accept the transfer of eight American warships to the ROCN. Two years later, he replicated the same techniques in Qingdao before taking command of the landing craft repair ship awaiting him in New Orleans. Based on this prior experience, Xu believed that no more than six months would be needed to place minimally trained personnel aboard ships.[44] The crew would have to learn at shore facilities and on the job. Under the circumstances, Zhang had little choice but to accept such shortcuts.[45]

Other problems associated with assimilation continued to plague the navy. Mutual distrust between the Communists and the ex-Nationalists simmered beneath the veneer of cooperation. Members on both sides had blood on their hands in the bitterly fought civil war. Cultural and class differences among the veterans sharpened the divide. The urban-based and better-educated former Nationalists looked down on their Communist counterparts, while the revolutionary cadre sneered at their former adversary's lack of ideological zeal. Given these deeply embedded biases and even outright enmity, Zhang had to pay attention to personnel policies, both big and small, to ensure that the KMT officers and men had a stake in the new navy's future.

Tellingly, Zhang had to adjudicate exactly what to call the ex-Nationalists. Some veterans of the revolution referred disparagingly to their former enemies as "those Nationalists" or "those people," sowing division and depressing morale. Zhang quickly moved to end such minor indignities that threatened esprit de corps. After some consideration, he proposed the term "original navy personnel [原海军人员]" to encompass all those who served in earlier regimes, including the Qing Empire, the KMT, and even the puppet governments that collaborated with the hated Japanese. Those drawn from the army and the Communist cadre would be called "new navy personnel [新海军人员]."[46] The rank and file enthusiastically accepted the neutral sounding phrases.

Zhang also found to his dismay that his cadre refused to share classified documents with former KMT staff, including high-ranking members of the navy's research committee. Such gatekeeping threatened to hinder much of the important intellectual and staff work ahead. Zhang's subordinates doubted the political reliability of the ex-Nationalists and, fearing leaks, cut off access to sources. Zhang immediately reprimanded them, ordering them to release all files unquestioningly. Now that the "original navy personnel" had joined the revolutionary cadre, he reasoned, it was imperative to trust them as comrades.

Zhang further insisted on maintaining the quality of life to which the ex-Nationalists were accustomed. Despite economic hardship, the commander diverted higher-quality staple foods, such as white rice and refined noodles, to the ex-KMT personnel, while the cadre ate unpolished rice and noodles made from whole grains. Zhang continued to pay the Nationalists monthly stipends and offered white rice as in-kind compensation when cash was unavailable. These policies were politically risky, since socioeconomic equity was the revolution's essential rationale. Moreover, the resulting inequalities were sure to stoke jealousies and complaints among the cadre. But to Zhang, the cost of keeping his precious human capital well fed, well paid, and motivated was a fair price to pay.[47]

Zhang had to intervene directly in a major dispute that broke out between the two factions at Zhenjiang, the home of East China Navy's First Squadron. Differences in family background, life experiences, education levels, political views, and cultural upbringing manifested themselves in social frictions big and small as the Communists and former Nationalists worked together and mingled daily. Ex-Nationalists groused about unfamiliar rules and regulations that governed their new lives, while the cadre pushed back against what they perceived as illegitimate complaints by the defeated bourgeoisie. By the early summer of 1949, only months after the squadron's formation, tensions boiled over. Overreacting to the infighting, the squadron's political department organized a self-criticism session. The move was a big mistake. The meeting degenerated into sharp exchanges of recriminations, ending with the cadre threatening to lock up the ex-Nationalists. As a result, several ex-KMT personnel deserted their posts, while others engaged in small acts of sabotage in protest.

Word of the incident soon reached Zhang, and he rushed to Zhenjiang. He directed his ire at his Communist colleagues in the belief that the blame rested primarily with the cadre. Had the revolutionaries responded to the Nationalist complaints with poise, then the arguments would not have escalated to the point of rupturing the delicate, budding relationship. He contended that reactionary thoughts and prejudices among the ex-KMT personnel were deeply ingrained. It would thus take time, patience, education, and suasion to nudge the former Nationalists to their side. Zhang exhorted his cadre to approach their counterparts with a spirit of confidence, cooperation, and unity. He broke up a fight that might have escalated and avoided a fallout that could have irreparably damaged the trust-building process. To Zhang, the mission rather than pride or emotions had to take top priority.

ZHANG AIPING'S CONTRIBUTIONS

It is difficult to understate the enormity of the challenge that Zhang confronted when he assumed command of the East China Navy in April 1949. He had to cope with severe shortfalls in matériel and human capital necessary to stand up a naval service. Yet, Zhang managed to establish the rudiments of a navy in about a year. The key leadership quality that enabled him to advance as far as he did was pragmatism. His willingness to adjudicate ideological differences and see beyond the past with his former enemies was crucial to his endeavor's start. As this chapter makes clear, the former Nationalist naval officers and sailors played a part in virtually every aspect of the regional navy's founding, ranging from the provision of technical expertise, training and education, and shipyard work to the manning of warships. As chapter 4 shows, Zhang's start-up project served as an important template for the formal establishment of the national navy, the PLAN.

NOTES

1. 黄胜天 魏慈航 朱晓辉 [Huang Shengtian, Wei Cihang, and Zhu Xiaohui], "华东军区海军的创建" [The Founding of the East China Military Region Navy], 军事历史研究 [Military History Research] 30, no. 1 (January 2016): 116. Huang Shengtian was a young operations staff officer when the East China Military Region Navy was founded. He would later serve as the deputy chief of staff of China's East Sea Fleet. The content of the article was narrated orally by Huang Shengtian, and the transcribed text was edited by Wei Cihang and Zhu Xiaohui.
2. S. C. M. Paine, *The Wars for Asia: 1911–1949* (Cambridge: Cambridge University Press, 2012), 258.
3. Edward L. Dreyer, *China at War, 1901–1949* (London: Longman, 1995), 345.
4. Paine, *The Wars for Asia, 1911–1949*, 258.
5. The *Chongqing* was a former British light cruiser, HMS *Aurora*. Britain sold the ship to the Nationalists in compensation for Chinese shipping losses during World War II. Displacing over 5,000 tons, the *Chongqing* was the largest and most powerful warship in the ROCN. To keep the prize out of enemy hands, Nationalist aircraft sank the cruiser in March 1949 in Dagu Harbor, Tianjin. For details of the mutiny, see 吴杰章 苏小东 程志发 [Wu Jiezhang, Su Xiaodong, and Cheng Zhifa], 中国近代海军史 [China's Modern Naval History] (Beijing: PLA Press, 1989), 426–30. Bruce Elleman offers an in-depth account of the *Chongqing* mutiny and its influence on the PLAN's founding. See Bruce Elleman, *A History of the Modern Chinese Navy* (London: Routledge, 2021), 133–45.
6. 吴殿卿 [Wu Dianqing], 蓝色档案—新中国海军大事纪实 [Blue Files—A Documentary of the Main Events of New China's Navy] (Taiyuan, Shanxi: Shanxi People's Press, 2015), 26–27.
7. The commanding officer of the *Chongqing*, Rear Adm. Deng Zhaoxiang (邓兆祥), would go on to an illustrious career in the PLAN. Deng would later be promoted to deputy commander of the North Sea Fleet and the deputy commander of the PLAN. See 冯晓红 [Feng Xiaohong], "毛泽东与邓兆祥少将" [Mao Zedong and Rear Admiral Deng Zhaoxiang], 文史精华 [Selected Works of Literature and History], no. 11 (2009): 4–10.
8. 吴殿卿 [Wu Dianqing], "毛泽东关心中国海军建设纪实" [A Documentary of Mao Zedong's Interest in the Chinese Navy's Buildup], 当代海军 [Modern Navy], no. 3 (1999): 5.
9. 张晓林 班海滨 [Zhang Xiaolin and Ban Haibin], "渡江战役与人民海军的创建" [The Cross-River Campaign and the Founding of the People's Navy], 军事历史研究 [Military History Research], no. 2 (1989): 20.
10. 陆其明 [Lu Qiming], 组建第一支人民海军部队的创始人 [The Founder of the People's Navy's First Fleet] (Beijing: Haichao, 2006), 8.
11. 胡士弘 [Hu Shihong], 张爱萍与新中国海军 [Zhang Aiping and the New Chinese Navy] (Beijing: Renmin, 2015), 18–20.
12. 史滇生 [Shi Diansheng], 世界海军军事概论 [Survey of World Naval Affairs] (Beijing: Haichao, 2003), 433.

13. Lu, *The Founder of the People's Navy's First Fleet*, 11; and Hu, *Zhang Aiping and the New Chinese Navy*, 42. The Soviet novel is likely by Aleksei Novikoff-Priboy and is titled *Tsushima*, published in 1933. See the translation by Eden and Cedar Paul, *Tsushima* (London: Aberdeen University Press, 1936). Two translations of the book were available in China in the 1930s. Translated by 梅雨 (Mei Yu), the books were published by Yinqing Publisher in Shanghai in 1937 and by Xinzhi Publisher in Shanghai in 1946. See www.worldcat.org.

14. 陆儒德 [Lu Rude], 江海客: 毛泽东 [A Maritime Advocate: Mao Zedong] (Beijing: Ocean Publisher, 2009), 190.

15. Huang et al., "The Founding of the East China Military Region Navy," 118.

16. Lu, *A Maritime Advocate*, 172.

17. Hu, *Zhang Aiping and the New Chinese Navy*, 55.

18. Lu, *The Founder of the People's Navy's First Fleet*, 25.

19. Lu, *The Founder of the People's Navy's First Fleet*, 31.

20. Hu, *Zhang Aiping and the New Chinese Navy*, 51.

21. A former subordinate of Admiral Jin, Xu Shipu worked as a plans officer for Chen Cheng (陈诚), the former commander in chief of the ROCN, and was very close to Adm. Gui Yongqing.

22. Hu, *Zhang Aiping and the New Chinese Navy*, 111.

23. Huang et al., "The Founding of the East China Military Region Navy," 119.

24. For the full text of the proclamation published in Shanghai's newspaper *Dagong-bao* [大公报], see 黄传会 周欲行 [Huang Chuanhui and Zhou Yuxing], 中国海军 [The Chinese Navy] (Beijing: China Publishing Group, 2019), 28–29. See also Wu, *Blue Files*, 32–34.

25. Lu, *A Maritime Advocate*, 196.

26. 吴殿卿 [Wu Dianqing], "人民海军装备建设史话:香港买船" [History of People's Navy's Equipment Buildup: Ship Purchase in Hong Kong], 铁军 [*Iron Army*], no. 1 (2013): 36–37. The periodical is published by the Research Association for the New Fourth Army and Central China Base Area. The "Iron Army" refers to the CCP's first armed group, and its successors all boast storied operational histories. Today, the 127th Division of the 54th Group Army carries the title "Iron Army."

27. 徐平 [Xu Ping], "共和国永远不会忘记—记张爱萍将军" [The Republic Will Never Forget—In Remembrance of General Zhang Aiping], 人民海军 [People's Navy], December 14, 2011, 3. Xu Ping was deputy dean of what was formerly the Navy Political Academy in Dalian. He witnessed conversations between Zhang and Zeng when he worked in the logistics command of the East China Navy.

28. Huang et al., "The Founding of the East China Military Region Navy," 123.

29. 当代中国丛书编辑部 [Editorial Department of the Contemporary China Book Series], 中国人民解放军 (下) [People's Liberation Army (Volume 2)] (Beijing: Contemporary China Publisher, 1994), 32.

30. Huang and Zhou, *The Chinese Navy*, 64–65.

31. Huang et al., "The Founding of the East China Military Region Navy," 124.

32. 吴殿卿 [Wu Dianqing], "新中国海军第一代指挥 '南昌' 号" [The New Chinese Navy's First Commander of *Nanchang*], 党史博览 [General Review of the Communist Party of China], no. 9 (2008): 45.

33. 吕俊军 [Lu Junjun], "一艘军舰与三个时代 回顾 '南昌' 舰和他的前身" [One Warship and Three Eras: A Retrospective of *Nanchang* and Its Previous Lives], 现代舰船 [Modern Ships], no. 10 (2004): 39.

34. 郭晔旻 [Guo Huamin], "'长治'号传奇" [The Legend of *Changzhi*], 舰载武器 [Shipborne Weapons], no. 9 (2010): 44.

35. Lu, "One Warship and Three Eras," 40.

36. 刘永路 陆儒德 [Liu Yonglu and Lu Rude], "鏖战大西洋的中国海军军官" [Chinese Naval Officers in the Fierce Battles of the Atlantic], 当代海军 [Modern Ships], no. 3 (1995): 31.

37. Lu, *A Maritime Advocate*, 205.

38. 慕安 [Mu An], "毛泽东与林则徐的侄孙林遵少将" [Mao Zedong and Lin Zexu's Nephew, Rear Admiral Lin Zun], 党史博览 [General Review of the Communist Party of China], no. 9 (2007): 10.

39. 吴殿卿 [Wu Dianqing], "毛泽东: 一定要建立强大海军" [Mao Zedong: Must Build a Powerful Navy], 党史博览 [General Review of the Communist Party of China], no. 4 (2009): 5.

40. Huang et al., "The Founding of the East China Military Region Navy," 121.

41. Chinese sources refer to *dadui* (大队) and *zhongdui* (中队) as the organizational structures of the naval academy. There are no consistent translations for these two terms. They refer most accurately to the organizational grade level of the PLAN. *Dadui* typically refers to a regiment leader-grade organization, while *zhongdui* typically refers to a battalion leader-grade organization. *Dadui* is usually translated as "squadron." This study uses the term "squadron" in reference to *dadui* to describe the organization of surface forces. See Office of Naval Intelligence, *China's Navy 2007* (Suitland, MD: Office of Naval Intelligence, 2007), 4–5.

42. Huang et al., "The Founding of the East China Military Region Navy," 121.

43. Shi, *Survey of World Naval Affairs*, 437–38.

44. Lu, *The Founder of the People's Navy's First Fleet*, 59.

45. See 王彦 [Wang Yan], "忆三野第35军改编到华东海军" [Reminiscing the Reorganization of the Third Field Army's 35th Corps into the East China Navy], 当代海军 [Modern Navy], no. 3 (1999): 58. The author, a member of a mountain artillery unit of the Third Field Army later transferred to the East China Navy, took a five-month crash course at the East China Naval Academy before being dispatched to the Seventh Squadron in Shanghai.

46. Lu, *The Founder of the People's Navy's First Fleet*, 39.

47. Hu, *Zhang Aiping and the New Chinese Navy*, 118–22.

FOUR

The People's Navy

As soon as the East China Navy was ready for action, it conducted its initial operations in mid-1950. The campaigns were modest in scale and sophistication by comparison to modern Western standards. But they served as a proof of concept for how the Chinese navy would wage war at sea. The East China Navy tested and validated tactical ideas in combat, premised on prevailing against a stronger opponent. Many of those same ideas found expression in other offshore campaigns documented in this study.

In early 1950, work began in earnest to stand up a national navy and to build on the East China Navy's progress. The formal founding of the PLAN under its first commander, Xiao Jinguang, required hard thinking about the service's place within China's defense establishment as well as its roles and missions. Xiao studied and replicated Zhang Aiping's experiments with the East China Navy and pursued a pragmatic approach to the former Nationalist naval personnel, who were deemed vital to the project. Xiao and his subordinates established the institutional framework for the service, created educational centers, set forth a force structure, and developed a buildup plan that would collectively have a lasting influence on the PLAN.

FIGHTING WHILE BUILDING

As Zhang Aiping sought to establish the institutional and material foundations of the new service, he had to contend with pressing security and operational challenges, a predicament described as "fighting while building [边打边建]."[1] One of his first missions was to contend with bandits and left-behind Nationalists, a constant threat to law and order and internal security. In August 1949 Zhang received orders from the Third Field Army, to which he still belonged, to eradicate banditry in Lake Taihu. Located on the borders of Jiangsu and Zhejiang Provinces west of Shanghai, the 2,200 square kilometers of water had been infested with outlaws for millennia. The First Coastal Defense Column based in Zhenjiang was called into action no more than three months after its establishment. The column's leaders selected a mix of Communist fighters (some former members of the *tuhaijun*) and ex-Nationalists, totaling two hundred men, and assembled thirteen gunboats, patrol boats, and landing craft to form a gunboat squadron for the mission.[2] The squadron chased the bandits ashore, where ground forces waited to round them up.

Even more problematic were the mines the ROCN sowed along the entrance to the Yangzi River as they fled to Taiwan. The blockade had choked off seaborne trade, delivering a heavy blow to Shanghai's economy. The economic impact was so severe that Zhou Enlai, Chen Yi (then the mayor of Shanghai), and Su Yu (the deputy commander of the Nanjing Military Region) all urged Zhang to act with utmost speed to clear the minefield. Zhang turned again to Zeng Guosheng, the resourceful deputy commander of the logistics department, for help. After learning from Zeng about the complexities of mine countermeasures, Zhang selected 150 students at the Nanjing Naval Academy to take a crash course on minesweeping. Zeng, in the meantime, went to work to convert and reequip small craft into minesweepers.

In April 1950, the East China Navy established its first minesweeping squadron. Within two months, the navy dispatched a task force of ten 25-ton landing craft on its first minesweeping mission. Soviet advisers were on hand to offer guidance. The first attempt was an utter failure. The small boats were unable to navigate and maintain their positions against the rapid currents, the thin sweep wires snapped when they snagged the mines' tether cables, and the crew lacked the skills and experience to prosecute the mission. After two months of fruitless sweeps, Zhang aborted the mission and regrouped.

In the meantime, merchant vessels were hitting mines and sinking at the mouth of the Yangzi, creating a major hazard. Zhang pressed to close the Yangzi to maritime traffic until the river was cleared of mines, but the economic pressures to risk the loss of shipping were too great. Shanghai's depressed economy desperately needed to keep seaborne commerce and the fisheries industry going. After some debate, Zhang and the local leaders in Shanghai reached an agreement to partially close sections of the Yangzi. In the meantime, Zhang conscripted four much larger infantry landing craft, displacing 380 tons, to serve as minesweepers. The navy equipped the ships with Soviet-supplied sweep wires while crews underwent intensive training. By mid-September, the new minesweeping task force was ready for a second try. Zhang's new measures worked. Within a month, the mouth of the Yangzi was cleared of mines.[3]

INITIAL OFFSHORE OPERATIONS (JUNE 15–JULY 8, 1950)

As the East China Navy engaged in mine clearing, it had to pay attention to other pressing offshore threats. In May 1950, the Nationalists evacuated 120,000 troops from the Zhoushan Island without a fight after the fall of Hainan

Island (see chapter 5). The retreat removed the biggest physical obstacle near Hangzhou Bay just south of Shanghai, China's most important economic hub, and also opened the way for the Communists to pry loose enemy control of the remaining offshore islands in the area. Zhang pivoted to three clusters of islands—the Qiqu Islands, the Shengsi Islands, and the Ma'an Islands—strategically located athwart the sea lines of communication that connected Shanghai, Ningbo, and Zhoushan. Running west to east from Qiqu to Ma'an, the archipelago stretches about forty nautical miles into the East China Sea. The Nationalist forces there were well positioned to disrupt commercial shipping, fishing, and naval transits in the area. The Communists also feared that saboteurs might use the islands to infiltrate the mainland.

To rid the area of this potential danger, Zhang developed a campaign plan suited to the navy's straitened circumstances. The Nationalist adversary still had control of the air and the seas and possessed technologically superior weaponry that delivered more lethal firepower than its Communist counterpart. Zhang thus formulated a slogan that captured the essence of his military guidance. He called on his forces to "attack island-by-island, attack the weak then the strong, attack the small then the big [逐岛进攻, 先弱后强, 先小后大]."[4] The motto meant that the PLA would sequentially seize the island chain. The strategy would prioritize the enemy's weakest or most vulnerable positions as the first targets and would progressively escalate military efforts against larger and more capable adversary units.

Zhang divided the campaign into successive phases. His forces would first take Tanxushan Island in Hangzhou Bay, an islet just off the south bank of Shanghai. Then, using Tanxushan as a launch pad, Zhang would move east to take Dayangshan and Xiaoyangshan Islands, the main features of the Qiqu cluster. Finally, he would employ his main forces to attack and occupy Shengsi and other islands farther east. By gradually chipping away at the KMT's holdings, he hoped that the rest of the enemy positions would become less tenable and ultimately collapse. For the employment of his forces, Zhang planned to dispatch small craft that enabled the units to rapidly disperse from threats and to quickly concentrate against opportunities. The crew would be well versed in close-in engagements, applying guerrilla tactics to sea combat. Zhang was very consciously drawing experiences from the PLA's operational traditions in land warfare to the naval domain. Moreover, because the Nationalists still dominated the air, the maneuverable small craft had a better chance of surviving airborne attacks.

On June 15, 1950, the East China Navy organized a flotilla composed of four landing ships carrying an infantry battalion and twelve gunboats to conduct the amphibious assault on Tanxushan. After a relatively uneventful transit the troops landed on the island unopposed, and without firing a shot, Zhang's forces captured fifty enemy personnel and some light weapons. The island's sei-zure apparently alarmed the KMT leadership. By taking Tanxushan, the most westerly outpost, the Communists in effect blinded and deafened the National-ist forces occupying the other islands farther east. Moreover, the Communists had surprised the Nationalists with the ability to conduct coastal operations, albeit with small forces at short distances from shore.

In early July, Zhang rode the momentum of victory and pressed his attack. The East China Navy organized a squadron comprising two landing ships and four gunboats for the follow-on assault. On July 6, the vessels departed Shang-hai and on the next day, after some difficulties in transit, delivered troops onto Dayangshan Island and Xiaoyangshan Island, which were lightly defended. On July 8, the ships headed east and engaged in a short artillery duel with a garrison on Shengshan Island, the eastern edge of the Ma'an archipelago. The troops conducted a landing under contested conditions but quickly overran the defenders, marking the end of the campaign.[5] The rapid island seizures spread panic across other KMT-held islands.

PISHAN CAMPAIGN (JULY 9–12, 1950)

The East China Navy then swiftly turned its attention to a cluster of islands enclosing Taizhou Bay off Zhejiang Province, some 130 nautical miles south of Shanghai. Like the situation in Hangzhou Bay, KMT forces had dug in on the islands, posing a persistent offshore threat to Taizhou, a major city, and to seaborne traffic along the coast. The Nationalist-held Dachen Island was one of the largest and most heavily defended features in the area. Located about 21 nautical miles southeast of Taizhou with no intermediate islands between Dachen and the mainland, the Communists would have to conduct a direct crossing against the island redoubt. This was a far more ambitious undertaking than the previous campaign near Shanghai.

The naval command assembled a squadron, including about ten wooden sailing boats, and dispatched it to Haimen Port in Taizhou, where it would carry the 186th Regiment of the 21st Corps. The army-navy command planned a surprise attack against the island. The boats would first sneak their way to Langjishan, located directly across from Dachen. The squadron would then await the opportune moment to surprise the Nationalist garrison on the island and would have to make a single transit across thirteen nautical miles of water. The plan was a far more direct and risky approach than Zhang's earlier military guidance.

On July 9, the ships transited undetected to Langjishan and slipped into Jin-qing Harbor. The flotilla hid and awaited orders. The following day two Com-munist gunboats on the lookout, No. 3 and No. 103, detected a Nationalist warship approaching Langjishan on regular patrols. No. 103 returned to Jin-qing Harbor to alert the rest of the flotilla, but the overly eager captain of No. 3 launched a premature and unauthorized attack on its own. The engagement was entirely lopsided. No. 3 was a 25-ton boat, while the incoming KMT vessel was well over 300 tons and was armed with superior guns. Outgunned and outsized, No. 3 was sunk in the skirmish, leaving three survivors out of a crew of seventeen. The encounter forewarned the Nationalist defenders of an impending attack against Dachen while exposing the Communist position at Langjishan to a counteroffensive. The Nationalists began to draw forces from nearby islands, the Yijiangshan Islands and Pishan, to reinforce the garrison on Dachen. Deprived of the element of surprise, the Communist army and navy headquarters ordered a retreat to Haimen. The decision likely spared the amphibious forces a disaster.

However, the army-navy team was unwilling to give up the initiative and was concerned that morale might tumble if the team did not abide by the tactical principle of continuity in pressing an attack. The joint command thus proposed an alternative course of action that would avoid a frontal assault against the island stronghold. Instead, the local commanders decided to attack another Nationalist holding on Dachen's perimeter. They reasoned that seizing less well-defended terrain near Dachen would still advance the Communists' objectives without incurring undue risk. The planners debated between Yijiangshan Islands and Pishan, which had been weakened as the Nationalists siphoned forces from them to shore up Dachen. The former was not as well defended, but it was only seven nautical miles north of Dachen from which the Nationalists could quickly dispatch help. While the latter was better defended, it was an isolated outpost, some thirty-seven nautical miles south of Dachen, and Nationalist reinforcements might take longer to reach it. Thus, the Communists decided to attack Pishan.

The joint army-navy command described its operational guidance as "feint toward Dachen, tie down enemy warships, direct main attack against Pishan [佯攻大陈, 牵制住敌舰, 主攻披山]."[6] The campaign planners envisioned a long-range night raid that would concentrate superior forces against the enemy. The assault forces would await high tide to rush forces on the island and conduct a rapid, deep attack that would overwhelm and quickly annihilate the defenders.[7] The planners recognized that effective escort during transit and a well-executed landing were essential to operational success. They also relied heavily on locals to learn more about the operational environment. They hired an experienced resident sea captain intimately familiar with the nautical conditions and the performance of the motorized junks to provide advice. Expecting difficulties with resupply, the troops brought extra ammunition and weaponry with them.

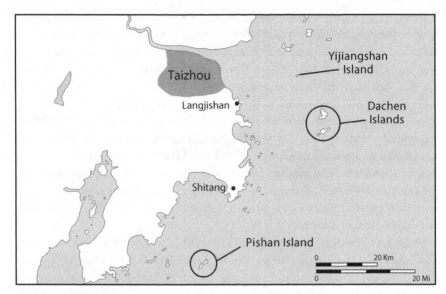

MAP 4.1. Pishan Island campaign, July 1950

© Toshi Yoshihara

At this juncture, Chinese sources offer two different accounts of the battle. In one version, the plan was to split the squadron into two prongs. The lead escort would fight off any Nationalist pickets screening Pishan, while the follow-on escort would protect the left flank of the vessels carrying the soldiers. Both escorts would provide fire support during the landings and guard the approaches to the island after the troops had been put ashore. Thirty motorized junks would split up and carry the assault force, composed of two infantry battalions, to two landing sites. As the flotilla approached Pishan, the junks would race past the lead escort and quickly unload the infantry units.

On July 11, 1950, the flotilla set sail and reached Shitang, about ten nautical miles north of Pishan, in late evening that day. The ships refueled while the troops reviewed their plans. The task force then headed toward Pishan, nearing the island in the early morning of July 12 just as high tide provided suitable conditions for the landings. However, a Nationalist gunboat, *Xinbaoshun*, detected the incoming Communist forces and began opening fire. As planned, the lead escort immediately responded by surrounding the patrol boat, shielding the vulnerable junks. The *Xinbaoshun*, a much larger vessel, offered stiff resistance. Unable to drive off the enemy, a Communist gunboat rammed the Nationalist ship astern, sinking it. Alerted to the danger, Nationalist defenders on the island fired on the nearing junks. The escorts turned their guns on the island to suppress enemy fire. In the meantime, many Communist troops leapt into the water and waded ashore. Once the two battalions seized and secured their respective beachheads, they maneuvered to surround enemy positions and cut off escape routes. After thirty minutes of intense fighting, the Communists had largely controlled the island.[8]

Another account, while conforming to the timing of the assault, differed on the encounter with the enemy. According to this version of events, one task force, composed of a gunboat, two amphibious assault vessels, and thirty empty motorized junks, made a feint toward Dachen Island to confuse and tie down Nationalist forces there. Meanwhile, four gunboats, two amphibious ships, and thirty junks carrying two infantry battalions headed for Pishan.[9] At dawn on July 12, the flotillas neared the island and began the landing operation. The stratagem worked, catching the Nationalists entirely off guard. Many defenders on ships and ashore were apparently still asleep when the attack came.

As the motorized junks put the assault troops ashore, the gunboats approached four KMT warships—former imperial Japanese fishing boats converted for military use—anchored off the island. The 25-ton boats snuck up to the 150-ton Nationalist vessels armed with larger guns. Despite the vast asymmetry in size and firepower, the Communists exploited the element of surprise and were able to open fire on the unsuspecting Nationalists at very close range. In the confusion, the KMT side believed that it faced a much larger and more capable force and scrambled to escape.

Two ships managed to elude the Communist pursuit while the other two found themselves in a melee. In one close-in encounter, the Communists killed the commanding officer of the *Jingzhong-1* and boarded the enemy vessel to accept surrender. In another intense engagement, a Communist vessel exchanged small-arms fire with the *Xinbaoshun* within fifteen meters of each other. As the duel continued, another Communist gunboat rammed the enemy ship. Its bow ruptured the hull astern, causing serious flooding. The Communist crew members then threw explosives and grenades aboard the *Xinbaoshun*, causing severe damage that eventually spelled its doom. One study describes the skirmish as "using the unorthodox to achieve victory [以奇取胜]."[10]

By early morning the battles at sea and ashore were over, but low tide stranded all the junks on Pishan's shores. Given the island's proximity to other KMT offshore holdings and to naval traffic, the battalions on Pishan and the escorts took up defensive positions in anticipation of an enemy counterattack while they waited for the tide to return. The riposte never came. When high tide finally arrived in the afternoon, the Communists quickly boarded the troops, the Nationalist prisoners, and supplies and slipped back to the mainland. The raid was a major success. At sea, the Communists sank one ship, captured one surface combatant and other smaller boats, killed or maimed more than 50 enemy crew, and captured some 60 officers and men. The infantry that landed on Pishan killed over 100 enemy troops and captured some 480 officers and soldiers, including the commanding officer of the island garrison.

SHORE-BASED INFRASTRUCTURE DEVELOPMENT

As these summer campaigns unfolded, the outbreak of the Korean War and the subsequent American intervention—including the Truman administration's decision to interpose the Seventh Fleet between China and Taiwan—significantly heightened tensions along the Chinese coast. The strategic maritime zone of east China, stretching from Qingdao in Shandong Province to Xiamen in Fujian Province, was potentially vulnerable to hostile American and Nationalist forces. After consulting his research committee, Zhang Aiping proposed a defense posture designed to "stop the enemy beyond the coastal frontier [阻敌于海岸前沿陆地之外]."[11] No longer would the Communists meet enemy forces on the mainland; they would interdict the opponent before it reached China's coast. To implement this plan, he envisioned the establishment of naval bases and air bases, coastal defense fortifications and coastal defense artillery positions, and fast-attack torpedo boats and other combat craft to conduct limited offshore operations, protect the army's maritime flanks, and actively cooperate with ground forces.

Zhang secured approval from the East China Military Region to fund the buildup of major naval bases in Zhoushan and Fuzhou. Zhang also set up coast guard squadrons organized around gunboats and coastal defense zones in Wusong, Zhoushan, Taizhou, and Wenzhou to protect local fishermen and coastal trade. Under a tight deadline set forth by the Central Military Commission, Zhang pushed through the construction of a runway at Zhuangqiao airbase in Ningbo within three months. He personally led an inspection team to survey possible sites for coastal batteries. His team, traveling aboard an amphibious assault ship, visited river mouths, harbors, bays, islands, beaches, and uninhabited rocks near the Hangzhou Bay area. During the planning process, differences between Zhang's team and the Soviet advisers emerged. Based on their experiences during World War II, the Soviets insisted on a particular type of entrenchment for the guns. Zhang overruled them, arguing that the unique geographical conformation of China's eastern coast was unsuited to their concept.[12] Within six months, the East China Navy formed fourteen coastal artillery positions.

After less than two years, Zhang had established a foundation for the new navy. He oversaw transitions ranging from personnel to material conditions to warfighting. The stress of the hard work, however, had proved harmful to his health, exacerbating illnesses tracing back to his car accident in 1946. As early as August 1949 when he led the former KMT naval delegation to Beijing, Zhang requested a transfer to a less taxing job. He finally got his wish on February 15, 1951, when he was appointed commander of the Zhejiang Military Region and of the 7th Corps. The following year, he became chief of staff of the East China Military Region. In 1954, he was promoted to deputy chief of staff of the PLA.[13] Zhang's accomplishments as the first navy commander had clearly positioned him well for future leadership posts.

ESTABLISHING A NATIONAL NAVY

While the East China Navy found its footing, the Communist leadership set to work on establishing national institutions and regional commands for the fledging navy, frequently taking cues from precedents set by Zhang Aiping and his lieutenants. Zhang had repeatedly pleaded with the top leadership to establish national institutions around which to organize the Chinese navy. An early indication of high-level support for a national navy came on September 21, 1949, during the Chinese People's Political Consultative Conference, a multiparty meeting convened to establish a new state under Communist control. At the convention, Mao Zedong delivered a speech titled "The Chinese People Have Stood Up!" He spoke explicitly about building a navy and an air force:. "Our national defense will be consolidated and no imperialist powers will ever again be allowed to invade our land. Our people's armed forces must be maintained and developed with the heroic and steeled People's Liberation Army as the foundation. We will have not only a powerful army but also a powerful air force and a powerful navy."[14]

Three months later, the Central Military Commission issued an order to transfer Xiao Jinguang, the Fourth Field Army's 12th Corps commander and political commissar and concurrently the commander of the Hunan Military Region, to lead the navy. Xiao, a Long March veteran, was a lifelong army officer with no training or background in naval affairs. When Mao approached Xiao about the assignment to head the navy in October 1949, Xiao protested at first. He confided to Mao that he was a landlubber (旱鸭子) and was prone to severe seasickness. According to one account, Mao responded lightheartedly that he was asking Xiao to command the navy, not to go to sea with the navy.[15]

On January 13, 1950, Mao, who was in Moscow, instructed the Central Military Commission to formally appoint Xiao as navy commander. Two days later, the commission issued an order that elevated Xiao to his new position and placed the Dalian Naval Academy, the East China Navy headquarters, and all personnel and ships across China under Xiao's command.[16] Until then, Zhang's East China Navy belonged under the command of the East China Military Region. The decision was in part informed by Mao's discussions and negotiations with Soviet leaders, including those representing the navy.[17] Xiao's educational background may have aided Mao's decision: Xiao studied for three years at Leningrad's Tolmachev Military-Political Academy in the 1920s. Xiao arrived in Beijing in mid-February to assume his new duties after settling his affairs in Hunan. Elements of the 12th Corps, including parts of its logistics department based in the Hunan Military Region, followed Xiao to Beijing to fill the ranks of the naval service. In all, about two thousand staff members arrived in the capital.

It was clear that Xiao's political masters had made few concrete decisions and had delegated to him the task of determining the navy's future direction. The newly minted commander immediately confronted basic questions about the very character of the naval service. Was it going to be a strategic decision-making institution or merely an administrative department subsumed within the Central Military Commission or the PLA's General Staff Department? In other words, was it going to be an independent service or a combat arm of the army? Where would the navy institution call home? Should it be head-quartered in Beijing or somewhere near the seas or near a naval port, such as Tianjin and Qingdao?

There was considerable debate over these fundamental questions. Initially, the majority view within the Central Military Commission and the General Staff Department held that the navy should fall under the administrative purview of the General Staff Department. Xiao and his staff conducted their own extensive research, examining the latest information on the institutional structures of the US and Soviet navies.[18] After looking into the matter, Xiao concluded that the navy must be an independent organization and that the service had to be headquartered in Beijing, near the epicenter of political power. He reasoned that all the great powers possessed an independent naval service headquartered in their national capitals. As a great power with various maritime interests, China too must follow in the footsteps of other major seafaring nations. The navy had to fulfill many missions, its equipment needs were numerous, and it intersected with many other national priorities, including diplomacy, transportation, fisheries, and science.[19] The navy therefore had to call Beijing home to interact with its many agency counterparts. Xiao clearly held a long-term view of Chinese sea power.

After extensive consultations with his own staff, Xiao met with Nie Rong-zhen, acting chief of staff of the General Staff Department, to explain his position. Nie in turn reported directly to Mao, who was still in Moscow. Mao concurred with Xiao's judgment. Upon his return from the Soviet Union, Mao met with Xiao in March and approved the navy commander's vision: the establishment of an independent service headquartered in Beijing.

In mid-April, PLAN headquarters formally entered service.[20] To commemorate the milestone, Xiao convened an inaugural conference for his staff. At the gathering, he delivered a two-hour speech that conveyed his vision for the new service. He outlined his guidance for navy building, drawing from Mao's inscription dedicated to the visiting ex-Nationalist naval leaders in August 1949 (see chapter 3). The inscription read "We must build a navy. This navy must be able to protect our seacoast and effectively defend against possible imperialist invasion." After reciting Mao's exhortation, Xiao described the navy's purpose and mission. The PLAN's primary goal was to conduct coastal defense. Consistent with the PLA's long-standing doctrine of active defense, the Chinese navy would serve strategically defensive goals but would conduct offensive operations and tactics to fulfill those aims.[21]

The naval service, Xiao continued, would exploit China's superior geographic conditions to compensate for its material weaknesses. He likened the Chinese mainland to an aircraft carrier from which the PLAN could project power to influence events over nearby seas.[22] China's coastal artillery batteries were akin to a warship's main guns, the primary weapon for defending the motherland from seaborne threats. Therefore, Xiao reasoned, the naval buildup would be modest in scale and ambition. There was little need for large combatants. Rather, the PLAN would construct small craft, including torpedo boats and minesweepers, that would operate near the coastline. The navy would also need to develop naval bases to support this light and nimble force.

Xiao then identified the most immediate priorities for the naval service. First, it needed to establish the navy's basing infrastructure as well as build up capabilities to support joint army-navy amphibious operations. Second, the Chinese navy needed to cultivate naval thought by bringing into play the PLA's fine traditions within its ranks. The navy needed to encourage former Nationalists and Communist army cadre alike to embrace the new service.[23] Third, the navy needed to stand up educational and training institutions to enhance the knowledge base and raise the technical proficiency of its officers and sailors.[24] All three tasks would consume Xiao's attention and energies in the years to follow.

In terms of personnel makeup, the PLAN was an army-dominated organization. In addition to the 12th Corps under Xiao's command, the Second, Third, and Fourth Field Armies transferred their own units to fill the navy's ranks. From 1950 to 1955 five army-level units, eleven division-level units, and twenty-eight corps-level units joined the PLAN. Many of the units had participated in the famous Liao-Shen, Ping-Jin, Huai-Hai, Jinan, Shanghai, and Hainan campaigns. In the personnel selection process, the Central Military Commission emphasized younger, better-educated, and more cosmopolitan staff and cadre. By the end of 1955, among the 188,000 naval personnel, about 60 percent hailed from the army. The rest included transfers from the air force, the intelligentsia from the civilian population, and the former Nationalist ranks.[25]

Institutionally, the navy had no model or experience from which to draw. Consequently, it replicated the organizational structure of the army. According to Xiao, it was originally a temporary measure.[26] The PLAN's four main leadership bodies were the headquarters, the Political Department, the Logistics Department, and the Health Department. The main functions of each department were as follows:

- PLAN headquarters: Administration, operations, intelligence, communications, and training.
- Political Department: Organization, propaganda, operational security, culture, and youths.
- Logistics Department: Finance, quartermaster, transportation, barracks, machinery, and engineering.
- Health Department: Medical administration, education, security, and supplies.

Imitating the Soviets, the navy later added the Staff Management Department, which was equal in stature to the Political Department. Reflecting the navy's dependence on foreign assistance, Soviet advisers arrived as soon as the PLAN headquarters stood up and were assigned to virtually every department, unit, and school and at every level of command.[27] The naval leadership described its reliance on the Soviets as an "invite in [请进来]" approach. The first group of 90 advisers arrived in October 1949, six months before PLAN's formal establishment. The second batch, numbering 621 members, joined in December 1950.[28] From then, the Soviet presence would be felt throughout the navy for a decade. Between 1949 and 1960, nearly 3,400 consultants and experts passed through the PLAN's various institutions from the highest levels of command to the navy's academies.

Operationally, there were few warfighting assets and troops under Xiao's command. At the time, only the East China Navy oversaw the movement and use of naval units and reported directly to the PLAN. As Xiao lamented at the time, he was an "empty-handed [两手空空]" naval commander.[29] In 1950, rudimentary regional naval organizations were just beginning to take shape in Guangzhou to the south and in Qingdao to the north. These local commands followed in the East China Navy's footsteps, relying on personnel from existing army organizations to fill billets.

In Guangzhou, the Communists established the Guangdong Military Region Riverine Defense Command under Hong Xuezhi in December 1949. The command drew its personnel from the Fourth Field Army's 15th Army. Troops were transferred from the 44th Corps, the 173rd Division of the 58th Corps, and other supply, training, and artillery units from the Fourth Field Army. Tellingly,

Xiao Jinguang saw the command's offshore operations as intimately connected to his naval project. On the eve of the Hainan invasion (see chapter 6), Xiao wrote to Hong to explain the campaign's place in the navy's larger plans:

> While the Guangdong Riverine Defense Command has only started to orga-nize itself and is still not quite powerful, it can still become the nucleus of the South China Fleet by sorting out and reforming its existing foundation. Whether it is the execution of the upcoming Hainan liberation campaign or whether it is the future development of the South China Fleet, they will all play a major role. As such, the main mission at present is to concentrate all power to participate in the Hainan campaign.[30]

The Riverine Defense Command later oversaw the Wanshan campaign in the summer of 1950 (see chapter 6) and then served as the nucleus of the South Central China Military Region Navy, which the Fourth Field Army founded in December 1950.

In the north, the East China Navy initially supervised the Qingdao naval port, which was run by elements of the 12th Army and the logistical units of the Fourth Field Army. Owing to administrative difficulties arising from the physical distance between the regional navy headquarters and Qingdao, the Central Military Commission and the PLAN headquarters assumed direct command of the base. In September 1950, the 11th Army of the Second Field Army transferred some 6,200 members of its staff from its headquarters and other departments to Qingdao.[31] The East China Navy, the South Central China Navy, and the Qingdao naval base would serve as the institutional progenitors of the East Sea Fleet (established in 1955), the South Sea Fleet (established in 1955), and the North Sea Fleet (established in 1960), respectively. In other words, the regional naval commands that define the PLAN's operational fleets today can be traced directly to the field armies that had helped the Commu-nists win the civil war.

INTELLECTUAL UNDERPINNINGS

Like Zhang Aiping, Xiao recognized that he faced severe shortfalls in human capital and, also like Zhang, turned to his former enemies for help. Soon after he assumed his new duties, Xiao learned of Zhang's formation of a research committee comprising former senior members of the Nationalist navy. Xiao agreed with Zhang's approach. In April, the PLAN commander ordered the transfer of twelve members from the East China Navy's research committee to Beijing, including Vice Adm. Zeng Yiding, the committee's director. These offi-cers would form the nucleus of the PLAN's own research committee, providing advice to the navy's party committee and navy headquarters and participating directly in the decision-making process.[32]

Xiao learned from Zeng that there were still many former KMT navy personnel scattered across the country who feared Communist retribution. Following in Zhang's footsteps again, Xiao initiated a nationwide recruitment drive to register the ex-Nationalists and bring them back into service. The navy commander selected the top recruits with the most important technical skills and knowledge to join his research committee. The committee was fondly nicknamed the "Second Advisory Group" in sly reference to the heavy presence of Soviet advisers. Given the ex-Nationalist officers' familiarity with US and other Western naval affairs, the committee emerged as an important source of information about the US Navy and naval developments in the West. The group provided timely advice about the disposition of the US Navy during the Korean War and translated textbooks and campaign histories in the West, including the curriculum at the US Naval Academy.[33]

The Communist leadership recognized that education was another important source of the navy's intellectual capital. Months before Xiao assumed command of the PLAN, the Central Military Commission began to place the building blocks for educating future generations of naval leaders. In May 1949, the commission established the Andong Naval Academy in Liaoning Province near the mouth of the Yalu River. The mutineers of the *Chongqing* cruiser, numbering 550, were sent to the academy to undergo political reeducation. Ideological indoctrination took priority over naval education and training. The *Chongqing*'s former commanding officer, Deng Zhaoxiang, was appointed the academy's superintendent. The former officers and crew of the *Chongqing* were taught the PLA's fine traditions to prepare them to serve their new Communist masters.[34]

In the summer of 1949 the Central Military Commission dispatched Zhang Xue'en, the deputy superintendent of Andong Naval Academy, to lead a delegation to the Soviet Union. The trip was meant to help the Chinese visitors learn about the Soviet military's professional education system and to recruit Soviet advisers. The group inspected various naval institutions in Moscow and Leningrad to understand the Soviet navy's curriculum, faculty, and academic organization. In early September after concluding agreements with its Soviet naval counterparts, the delegation returned to China.[35] In late November, the Central Military Commission approved the proposal to set up the Dalian Naval Academy and appointed Xiao to serve as superintendent and political commissar, more than two months before he formally assumed his position as navy commander.[36]

The former Nationalists at the Andong Naval Academy, numbering nearly 470, were transferred to Dalian. Among them, about 15 were appointed to serve as instructors. Soviet advisers, 84 of whom arrived in December 1949, also joined the faculty. The former Nationalists drawn from Andong took classes taught by Soviet advisers even as they provided instruction to students at the naval academy.[37] At the same time, Xiao's staff went on a major recruiting drive across the country to attract academic talent. A number of professors from China's topflight schools, including Peking University and Tsinghua University, agreed to serve as instructors. Even recent returnees from overseas graduate programs, including two who had studied at Colorado State University, were hired.[38] With about 100 faculty members and staff in place, the Dalian Naval Academy began its first school year in February 1950, two months before the PLAN headquarters was formally established.

Xiao Jinguang inspected the school in April and spelled out his vision in a speech during his visit to the academy. He identified five areas that would define the school's purpose and mission. The academy must strive to become the center of learning on all naval affairs. It had to strike a balance between political loyalty and technical expertise. While the former enjoyed primacy, the latter was indispensable. The school had to learn from the Soviet navy's experiences, staffed as it was with Soviet experts and consultants. But it also had to infuse the curriculum with the PLA's fine traditions. Finally, the academy had to strictly enforce discipline while fostering a sense of mission about China's quest for sea power.[39] Xiao would go on to establish naval aviation, naval gunnery, and torpedo boat academies in Qingdao and expand the school established by Zhang Aiping's East China Navy in Nanjing.

THE AUGUST 1950 NAVAL CONFERENCE

The Korean War's outbreak on June 25, 1950, raised concerns that the conflict could widen and escalate. The CCP leadership needed to know how the PLAN would play its role in enhancing China's security and in strengthening the nation's coastal defense against possible threats from the sea. On June 30, Premier Zhou Enlai met with Xiao to share the CCP's view of the situation. Zhou conveyed that the leadership would adopt a wait-and-see posture. The plan to attack Taiwan would be delayed, and the services would continue their steady buildups. The premier urged patience. He asserted that several hundred thousand tons of shipping would need to be constructed to transport half a million troops to Taiwan, which would undoubtedly take time.[40] Zhou contended that the navy needed to balance preparations for liberating Taiwan with investments in the service's long-term growth. The two leaders then agreed that the navy would produce a three-year buildup plan.

In mid-July Zhu De, the PLA's commander in chief, wrote a letter to Xiao to communicate his views of the naval buildup. In his missive, Zhu drew attention to infrastructure and shore facilities. He called on Xiao to establish shipyards, aircraft manufacturers, fuel reserves, oil pipelines, and a network of coastal defenses. Echoing Zhou, Zhu advised that the PLAN should not be consumed by plans for a Taiwan invasion and should instead invest in the service's long-term development.[41]

Based on the strategic guidance from Zhou and Zhu, Xiao Jinguang convened a major conference involving twenty-three PLAN leaders to develop the navy's future program.[42] In his capacity as the secretary of the navy's interim party committee, Xiao brought together the stakeholders in the PLAN's future. The attendees included the deputy commander, the deputy political commissar, the chief of staff, leading staff of all navy departments, heads of schools, and representatives from the East China Navy. The landmark gathering, which met for twenty days beginning on August 10, addressed the PLAN's direction as well as the most pressing concerns facing the naval service, including its material conditions and personnel. Notably, members from various units of the East China Navy delivered briefs to the leadership detailing their progress and situation.[43] The attendees clearly sought to learn from Zhang Aiping's experiences over the preceding year to inform their decisions.

Regarding personnel management, the navy leadership emphasized political reliability while acknowledging the importance of technical skills and professionalism. The attendees then agreed to organizational principles that would guide the navy's policies about its officers and sailors. The naval service would not lose sight of the PLA's class and operational origins. The workers and the peasants would remain the "backbone [骨干]" of the organization, while the army would still serve as the institutional foundation.[44] The navy would work to bring in new blood including efforts to absorb revolutionary youths and intellectuals. It would continue the work of the East China Navy to "strive for, unite, educate, and reform" the ex-Nationalists.[45] There was clear recognition that introducing alien elements into the naval service would cause disharmony among the Communist cadre. The navy had to preserve the ideological orthodoxies of the party-army system. Thus, new members would have to strictly adhere to the CCP's "guiding thought [指导思想]." Such a directive undoubtedly reflected Zhang Aiping's own struggles with integrating former KMT officers and men into his ranks.

A contentious issue that emerged at the meeting was the role of Soviet assistance. Mao's declaration in June 1949 to "lean to one side" toward the Soviet Union had largely determined the PLAN's reliance on the Soviet navy as the main source of technical and material support. To Xiao, ideological kinship as well as access to technology and know-how made the Soviet navy a logical politically correct partner. The Soviet navy boasted a fine naval tradition and a longer history in naval construction than China. The Soviets, moreover, had accumulated experience dealing with Western imperial sea powers, a common foe.[46] As Xiao observed in his memoir, "Especially for our navy, which was starting from scratch, it was no good to lean on our own experiences and to grope about by ourselves. Only by learning well and borrowing from other's advanced experiences can we quickly build up a powerful navy that was modern and conventional in character."[47]

Even so, considerable debate divided his subordinates over the extent to which the PLAN should borrow from the Soviets. Former Nationalist naval officers argued that Western navies were far superior to the Soviet navy and were therefore better models for the Chinese navy to emulate. To them, access to Western, particularly British and American, technologies should not be written off. Their proposed motto was "Learn politically from the Soviet Union, learn technologically from Britain and America." Army cadre, including doctrinaire adherents to people's war, contended that they had more to learn from their own civil war experiences than from foreign powers. They bristled at the idea of copying the Soviets, who they felt had provided little assistance during their long revolutionary struggle.

In the end, the conference attendees agreed to guiding principles on the extent to which the Chinese navy should look to itself or to others. The first principle called on the PLAN to insist on "keeping the initiative in our own hands [以我为主]." The Chinese navy would not blindly adopt all things Soviet. It would be selective, rejecting Soviet ways that were unsuited to China's unique local conditions. The PLAN would draw narrow technological and military insights and benefits from the Soviets. But it was imperative for the service to adhere to its own distinctive norms and beliefs surrounding its leadership system, absolute loyalty to the CCP, core organizational tenets, strategic and tactical thought, and fine traditions and operational style. The second principle was one of pragmatism. Even as the PLAN relied on the Soviets, it would still look to Western navies and borrow from their experiences. It would not dogmatically reject useful lessons that China could learn from its ideological and geopolitical foes. The conferees contended that the Chinese navy needed to "study the enemy as well, so as to improve ourselves [也要研究敌人, 改进自己]."[48]

The landmark meeting also produced a lasting influence on the Chinese navy's force structure. The conferees determined that the PLAN would comprise five main combat branches, namely the surface force, the submarine force, the naval air force, the coastal artillery force, and the marine corps. The navy would be employed primarily for coastal operations. It would operate independently or coordinate with the army to conduct landing or counterinvasion operations. Its peacetime and wartime missions included sea-lane defense and counterblockades, protection of fisheries, attacks against enemy harassment at sea and attacks and blockades against enemy ports, mine clearing and minelaying, and defense of naval facilities.[49] Most of these tasks would take place in coastal waters.

The force composition, structure, and missions of the PLAN reflected Xiao's early appreciation for the character of naval warfare and his thinking about how China would wage a war at sea. At the conference, he declared that "modern sea battle is necessarily a kind of three-dimensional war and is a kind of composite war. We must use the aircraft above the waves, the warships on the ocean's surface, the submarines beneath the seas, and artillery along the coast to form a synergy of integrated power. In war, the lack of any one of those capabilities could well spell disaster."[50]

Xiao's earlier metaphor, likening China to a massive aircraft carrier, remained apt. Shore-based assets, such as artillery and aircraft, would project power from the mainland and work in tandem with surface ships and submarines to influence events along the long Chinese coastline.

The conferees further agreed that the nation's dismal economic, industrial, and technological conditions limited the navy's ambitions and options. Moreover, the PLAN clearly could not stand up to the modern navies of the West on equal footing. The immediate Nationalist danger much closer to home also dictated the scope of naval modernization. Xiao thus reiterated his vision outlined at the April opening ceremony of the PLAN's headquarters. China, he argued, needed relatively small and dexterous combatants suited for coastal operations and for the navy's straitened finances. As Xiao argued at the conference, "With an eye toward long-term development and departing from the current situation, we will build light combat power at sea that is modern and offensive in nature. We need to first organize and develop our current capabilities and, on the foundation of those current capabilities, develop torpedo boats, submarines, and naval aviation to gradually build a strong, national navy."[51]

In other words, the PLAN would follow the East China Navy's example, making do with what it had at hand and progressively build a naval force appropriate to China's circumstances. Xiao gave priority to small surface combatants, submarines, and shored-based aircraft, which would serve as the basis for a more ambitious naval buildup should financial and technical circumstances permit. Xiao's directive—later dubbed "*kong* [空], *qian* [潜], *kuai* [快]," Chinese shorthand for "naval aviation, submarines, fast attack craft"—set the course for the PLAN's development over the next two decades.

The decision to acquire shore-based aircraft for maritime defense proved controversial. There was considerable debate about the navy's plan to possess its own aviation arm. Some navy cadre opposed such a program. They argued that the PLA Air Force would be more than adequate for combat missions at sea and that the navy would be duplicating the functions of the independent air service. Still others contended that the Nationalists, which did not possess naval aviation, offered a good model to emulate.[52] The PLAN leadership, however, overruled the objections. Xiao and his team believed that the Chinese navy's surface combatants, which lacked organic air defenses, needed constant cover from the air. Otherwise, the PLAN's warships would be highly vulnerable to enemy airpower. Moreover, the Chinese navy could not count on the air force to provide persistent support, which required close interservice coordination if not integration. Naval aviation thus became a major component of the buildup plan from the start.

In the meantime, the Chinese navy had to cope with severe material shortfalls that continued to plague the service and demanded immediate attention. Given that the construction of an indigenous industrial base would take time, the PLAN had to improvise, just as the East China Navy had to develop ad hoc means to build its fledgling fleet. The attendees of the conference agreed that the navy had to continue the East China Navy's initiatives by repairing damaged ex-Nationalist warships, retrofitting fishing boats and merchant ships with naval weapons, and acquiring foreign vessels via back channels in Hong Kong.

Most importantly, Xiao and his colleagues completed the draft of a three-year buildup plan and, as an element of the program, included their request for obtaining assistance from the Soviet Union. The conferees spent considerable time debating and reviewing the specific capabilities and the expected costs of the naval expansion. The document spelled out the expected numbers of fleets, aviation divisions, and coastal artillery regiments; set forth the numbers of ships, aircraft, and coastal artillery guns to be produced or modified at home and procured abroad; identified the types and numbers of piers, storage facilities, airfields, and prepared sites that would need to be built to support naval bases, coastal garrison divisions, and local patrol and defense commands; and laid out plans for developing various naval academies and training programs for producing the next generation of navy cadre.[53]

To support the buildup, Mao corresponded with Joseph Stalin in October 1950 about acquiring more arms from the Soviet Union. Mao's request included 12 destroyers, 18 frigates, 2 small submarines, 42 submarine hunting ships, 28 submarine hunting patrol boats, 30 minesweepers, 100 torpedo boats, 56 armored boats, 108 torpedo bombers, 10 transport aircraft, and coastal artillery to outfit nine artillery regiments.[54]

After the conference, Xiao delivered the draft proposal to Mao and Zhou for approval.[55] The outbreak of the Korean War and Mao's decision to intervene, however, unraveled the plan. In late October, Zhou Enlai and Nie Rongzhen met with Xiao and his staff about their buildup plan and the equipment orders intended for the Soviet Union. Zhou explained that a crash program to develop airpower would take priority over all other initiatives. The CCP anticipated that Chinese forces in Korea would desperately need air cover, especially since the Soviets had declined to dispatch their air force to help China. Zhou then delivered the bad news. The PLAN had to substantially scale back its plans and expectations. The navy, for example, had to delay the establishment of its naval aviation command and school to free up resources for the air force. Zhou approved a naval aviation department within the navy headquarters and the founding of a torpedo boat training school as a consolation prize.[56]

Finally, Zhou advised Xiao to submit his plan to the Soviet navy for review. To accelerate the consultation process, the premier asked the navy commander to bring the plan with him to Moscow, using it as a basis for further discussions with the Soviet naval leadership.[57] Xiao's reaction to and feelings about the reversal were not documented for the public record. But Zhou's request must have stung. It is easy to imagine the disappointment and the frustration, if not the humiliation, that came with seeking Soviet approval of the Chinese navy's future. As noted above, Mao had written directly to Stalin outlining the ships, aircraft, and supplies that would be needed from the Soviet Union to fulfill the three-year buildup plan. That message too was overtaken by events on the Korean Peninsula.[58] The war in Korea abruptly halted the Communists' nonstop fighting at sea and the hectic and often pell-mell preparations for the PLAN's future since April 1949.

XIAO JINGUANG'S INITIAL CONTRIBUTIONS

Xiao was much more than a loyal apparatchik to the CCP, although his CCP credentials were no doubt a critical qualification to serve as the PLAN's commander. Mao likely set his eyes on Xiao for his political acumen and a deep sense of the PLA's roots and operational style. Xiao did not disappoint. He maneuvered to overcome the institutional preference for subordinating the navy to the army and persuaded Mao to establish the navy as an independent, strategic arm of the CCP. While Xiao accepted Soviet help largely out of necessity, he recognized that the PLA's core beliefs and norms as well as the former Nationalists' expertise and experiences would contribute to the navy's future. He was no narrow-minded ideologue. Like Zhang Aiping, Xiao understood the centrality of human capital to the PLAN's success and stood up the educational and training foundations for the service. He also forged a doctrinal outlook that conformed to China's material, financial, and geographic circumstances and to the PLA's strategic traditions. His decisions would have an enduring influence on the PLAN, some of which are still visible to this day.

NOTES

1. 胡士弘 [Hu Shihong], 张爱萍与新中国海军 [Zhang Aiping and the New Chinese Navy] (Beijing: Renmin, 2015).
2. Hu, 242–43.

3. For details of the minesweeping mission, see 蔡明岑 [Cai Mingling], "突破长江口" [Breaking through the Mouth of the Yangzi River], 舰载武器 [Shipborne Weapons], no. 7 (July 2007): 43–45.

4. 陆其明 [Lu Qiming], 组建第一支人民海军部队的创始人 [The Founder of the People's Navy's First Fleet] (Beijing: Haichao, 2006), 85.

5. 房功利 杨学军 相伟 [Fang Gongli, Yang Xuejun, and Xiang Wei], 解放军史鉴: 中国人民解放军海军史 [History of the Liberation Army: History of the People's Liberation Army Navy] (Qingdao: Qingdao Press, 2014), 110.

6. Fang et al., 110.

7. 王伟 张德彬 主编 [Wang Wei and Zhang Debin, eds.], 渡海登岛: 战例与战法研究 [Cross-Sea Island Landings: Research on Case Studies and Tactics] (Beijing: Military Science Press [military circulation], 2002), 46.

8. Wang and Zhang, 47–48.

9. 中国海军百科全书编审委员会 [Editorial Committee of the Chinese Navy Encyclopedia], 中国海军百科全书 [Chinese Navy Encyclopedia] (Beijing: Haichao, 1999), 1398; and Fang et al., *History of the Liberation Army*, 100–111.

10. Fang et al., *History of the Liberation Army*, 111.

11. Hu, *Zhang Aiping and the New Chinese Navy*, 284.

12. Hu, 293.

13. Hu, 296–97.

14. Mao Tse-tung, *Selected Works of Mao Tse-tung*, Vol. 5 (Beijing: Foreign Language Press, 1966), 15–18.

15. 罗元生 [Luo Yuansheng], 共和国首任海军司令员肖劲光战传 [Biography of First Navy Commander Xiao Jinguang] (Beijing: Great Wall Press, 2013), 156.

16. 吴殿卿 [Wu Dianqing], 三十年海军司令萧劲光 [Thirty-Year Navy Commander Xiao Jinguang] (Taiyuan, Shanxi: Shanxi People's Press, 2013), 165.

17. 吴殿卿 [Wu Dianqing], 蓝色档案—新中国海军大事纪实 [Blue Files—A Documentary of the Main Events of New China's Navy] (Taiyuan: Shanxi People's Press, 2015), 87.

18. 萧劲光 吴宏博 [Xiao Jinguang and Wu Hongbo], "组建新中国海军领导机关" [The Founding of the New Chinese Navy's Leading Institutions], 军事历史研究 [Military History Research], no. 6 (November 2016): 119. This article is Xiao's oral history edited by the Political Department's editorial division of the PLAN. Wu Hongbo is an editorial staff member of the Political Department and edited the oral history.

19. Wu, *Thirty-Year Navy Commander Xiao Jinguang*, 167.

20. 邓礼峰 [Deng Lifeng, ed.], 中华人民共和国军事史要 [Military History of the People's Republic of China] (Beijing: Military Science Press, 2005), 188. Members of the Military History Research Center of the Academy of Military Science compiled the study. See also 当代中国丛书编辑部 [Editorial Department of the Contemporary China Book Series], 中国人民解放军 (下) [People's Liberation Army (Vol. 2)] (Beijing: Contemporary China Publisher, 1994), 27.

21. Xiao and Wu, "The Founding of the New Chinese Navy's Leading Institutions," 121.

22. Xiao and Wu, 121.

23. Xiao and Wu, 121.

24. Wu, *Thirty-Year Navy Commander Xiao Jinguang*, 180–83.

25. 海军史编委 [Editorial Committee of History of the Navy], 海军史 [History of the Navy] (Beijing: Liberation Army Press, 1989), 20–21. The head of the editorial

committee was Adm. Zhang Lianzhong, the former commander of the PLAN from 1988 to 1996.

26. Xiao and Wu, "The Founding of the New Chinese Navy's Leading Institutions," 120.

27. Wu, *Blue Files*, 90.

28. 房功利 杨学军 相伟 [Fang Gongli, Yang Xuejun, and Xiang Wei], 中国人民解放军海军60年 [60 Years of the Chinese People's Liberation Navy] (Qingdao: Qingdao Press, 2009), 80. The volume was published to commemorate the sixtieth anniversary of the PLAN's founding in April 1949.

29. Xiao and Wu, "The Founding of the New Chinese Navy's Leading Institutions," 119.

30. Fang et al., *60 Years of the Chinese People's Liberation Navy*, 80.

31. Fang et al., *History of the Liberation Army*, 80–88.

32. Wu, *Thirty-Year Navy Commander Xiao Jinguang*, 171.

33. Wu, 173.

34. 杨国宇 主编 [Yang Guoyu, ed.], 当代中国海军 [Contemporary Chinese Navy] (Beijing: China Social Science Press, 1987), 105. Consultants to the book's editorial committee included Xiao Jinguang and Liu Daosheng, the former deputy commander of the PLAN from 1973 to 1982.

35. Yang, *Contemporary Chinese Navy*, 105.

36. Wu, *Thirty-Year Navy Commander Xiao Jinguang*, 77–78.

37. 刘华清 [Liu Huaqing], 刘华清回忆录 [Memoirs of Liu Huaqing] (Beijing: Liberation Army Press, 2004), 254. Liu Huaqing, who would later serve as the PLAN's commander in the 1980s, was appointed deputy superintendent of the Dalian Naval Academy in March 1953. Liu managed day-to-day affairs at the academy and supervised political work on the campus.

38. Wu, *Thirty-Year Navy Commander Xiao Jinguang*, 80–81.

39. Wu, 183–87.

40. 吴殿卿 [Wu Dianqing], "海军第一个五年建设计划制订经过" [The Process of Developing the Navy's First Five-Year Buildup Plan], 党史博览 [General Review of the Communist Party of China], no. 2 (2011): 38.

41. Wu, "The Process of Developing the Navy's First Five-Year Buildup Plan," 38.

42. See also Martin Murphy and Toshi Yoshihara, "Fighting the Naval Hegemon: Evolution in French, Soviet, and Chinese Naval Thought," *Naval War College Review* 68, no. 3 (Summer 2015): 27–29.

43. 曲令泉 郭放 [Qu Lingquan and Guo Fang], 卫海强军—新军事革命与中国海军 [Maritime Defense and Strong Military—The New Military Revolution and the Chinese Navy] (Beijing: Haichao, 2004), 110.

44. Editorial Committee of History of the Navy, *History of the Navy*, 32.

45. Deng, *The Outline of the Military History of the People's Republic of China*, 187. For a speech Zhang Aiping delivered to outline the CCP's policies on former Nationalists, see 汪世喜 [Wang Shixi], "张爱萍将军与华东海军" [General Zhang Aiping and the East China Navy], 党史文汇 [Corpus of Party History], no. 12 (2008): 36–37. Wang was a former Nationalist sailor who had mutinied and joined the Communist cause.

46. Wu, *Thirty-Year Navy Commander Xiao Jinguang*, 192.

47. 萧劲光 [Xiao Jinguang], 萧劲光回忆录 [Memoirs of Xiao Jinguang] (Beijing: Contemporary China Press, 2013), 231.

48. Fang et al., *History of the Liberation Army*, 63.

49. Yang, *Contemporary Chinese Navy*, 42.

50. Xiao, *Memoirs of Xiao Jinguang*, 227.

51. Xiao, 227. See also Deng Lifeng, *The Outline of the Military History of the People's Republic of China*, 187; and 师小芹 [Shi Xiaoqin], "小型舰艇的历史定位与中国式均衡海军" [The Historical Place of Small Combatants and a Balanced Navy with Chinese Characteristics], 军事历史 [Military History], no. 1 (2011): 38.

52. 刘道生 [Liu Daosheng], "毛泽东, 人民海军的缔造者" [Mao Zedong, the Architect of the People's Navy], 湖南党史月刊 [Hunan Party History Monthly], no. 13 (1993): 6. From 1950 to 1953, Liu Daosheng was the PLAN's deputy political commissar and the director of the navy's Political Department.

53. Fang et al., *History of the Liberation Army*, 57.

54. 中国人民解放军军史编写组 [Editorial Team of the Chinese People's Liberation Army's Military History], 中国人民解放军军史 第四卷 [Military History of the Chinese People's Liberation Army, Vol. 4.] (Beijing: Academy of Military Science, 2011), 51.

55. Wu, *Blue Files*, 108.

56. Wu, "The Process of Developing the Navy's First Five-Year Buildup Plan," 39.

57. Wu, *Blue Files*, 108.

58. 吴殿卿 [Wu Dianqing], "毛泽东与萧劲光大将" [Mao Zedong and Xiao Jinguang], in 毛泽东与海军将领 [Mao Zedong and His Navy Generals], 主编 吴殿卿 袁永安 赵小平 [Wu Dianqing, Yuan Yongan, and Zhao Xiaoping, eds.] (Beijing: People's Press, 2013), 33.

The Xiamen, Jinmen, and Zhoushan Campaigns

The Third Field Army's offshore campaigns began in earnest over the summer of 1949. The 10th Army, under Ye Fei, was the first to attempt a major island-seizing operation and would go on to take islands off the Zhejiang and Fujian coasts. The army's early experiences would inform the strategies and planning of the Fourth Field Army documented in chapter 6. The Third Field Army's encounter with the seas resulted in successes and failures. Notably, the fiasco at Jinmen had an outsize influence on PLA strategy and on the course of Cold War history, including the permanent division of China. The Jinmen campaign thus possesses both operational and strategic meaning that reverberates to this day. Given that the amphibious landings took place in similar geographic settings within a single theater of operations, the battles provide a laboratory to assess the causes behind the triumphs and the reversals. In short, the campaigns offer an opportunity to evaluate the field army's generalship and strategy.

PRELUDE TO THE XIAMEN AND JINMEN CAMPAIGNS

The PLA's successful campaign to cross the Yangzi River and the subsequent fall of Nanjing and Shanghai opened the door to southern China. As 120,000 Nationalist forces fled south to Fujian Province and another 60,000 fell back eastward to Zhoushan Island at the mouth of Hangzhou Bay, the Third Field Army embarked on an aggressive pursuit of the remaining KMT troops. The 10th Army began its drive south in early July and attacked Fuzhou on August 6. The Communists seized the city in about two weeks, wiping out 40,000 enemy troops.

During the final phase of the Fuzhou campaign, the 10th Army ordered the 28th Corps to Pingtan Island, the largest offshore island of Fujian Province. The Communist troops hailed from Shandong Province and were strangers to combat at sea. Ye thought that the island-seizing operation would earn the unit much-needed experience for the trials ahead.[1] The 28th Corps faced ten thousand Nationalist defenders, the remnant force that had fled Fuzhou. The attackers spent about half a month searching for and conscripting civilian fishing vessels for the water crossing.[2]

The Communists adopted a mini island-hopping approach from the north, seizing adjacent islands as they crept south toward Pingtan Island. On the night of September 12 the 28th Corps launched its attack against its first objective, Xiaolian Island. PLA forces seized the small feature with little difficulty the following morning. On September 14, the corps directed its troops on Xiaolian to land on the adjacent Dalian Island. After the first wave landed on Dalian, the staging base for the main assault on Pingtan, a storm hit the area, preventing the transports from bringing follow-on troops ashore. Those who reached Dalian had to fend for themselves for about a day before reinforcements arrived to overwhelm the defenders.[3] The Communists then pulled off the final push against Pingtan, killing or capturing about 6,000 men. Notably, local insurgents on Pingtan aided the 28th Corps' landings and advance on the island.[4] The surviving Nationalists fled by sea. The successful battle provided much-needed experience for the amphibious operations ahead. But it also hinted at the logistical and meteorological challenges that would later confound the Communists.

The series of rapid successes, including the defeat of the Nationalists at Zhangzhou on September 25, 1949, brought the Communist forces in control of the main coastline facing Taiwan. More importantly, they were positioned to seize key offshore terrain, Xiamen and Jinmen, the key Nationalist holdouts and a gateway to Taiwan. On September 26, 1949, Ye Fei convened a strategy session in Quanzhou to discuss plans for taking Xiamen and Jinmen. Initially, his subordinate commanders agreed to seize Xiamen and Jinmen simultaneously. Encounters in the preceding months, during which the Communists repeatedly steamrolled the Nationalists, suggested that the dispirited and weakened defenders would shatter on contact. PLA commanders also worried that a sequential attack against each target in turn would permit defenders from one island to escape to the other. They thus sought to sweep up the enemy in one step.[5]

However, this ambitious scheme quickly fell apart. The lack of shipping became a severe constraining factor. The 10th Army ordered the 31st Corps camped in Zhangzhou and the 28th Corps and the 29th Corps bivouacked in Quanzhou to collect local boats for the operation. In Quanzhou, the local party leadership formed a "supply committee [供应委员会]" to help the PLA recruit boatmen and gather serviceable vessels.[6] The three corps struggled to meet their requirements. The retreating Nationalists had seized or destroyed most of the seaworthy local fishing boats before the Communists arrived. The 10th Army also had trouble enlisting the help of locals. Most of the PLA's officers and soldiers hailed from other parts of China. As a result, cultural and linguistic barriers hampered the newly arrived outsiders' interactions with the southern fishermen.[7] The locals were also likely suspicious of the Communists and understandably feared the expropriation of their boats, the main sources of their livelihoods. They were, after all, new subjects of an occupying force.

To make matters worse, the 28th Corps had already lost many boats to bad weather during the Pingtan campaign. Since they were recruiting from the same area, the 28th and 29th Corps found themselves competing over scarce resources in a zero-sum game that led to unnecessary infighting and delays.[8] After an extensive survey of their situation, the Communists found that they were unable to press into service adequate numbers of local fishing boats to carry troops to Xiamen and Jinmen at the same time. During the first half of October, the 10th Army managed to enlist 630 wooden boats of varying sizes and performance and about 1,600 boatmen. Problematically, most of the vessels were flat-bottom riverboats unsuited for even short-distance sea crossings. The 29th and 31st Corps assigned to take Xiamen could only muster a fleet capable of transporting three regiments, while the 28th Corps destined for Jinmen could collect enough ships for just one regiment.[9] Left with no other choice, the 10th Army decided that it would first take Xiamen and turn to Jinmen next.

XIAMEN CAMPAIGN (OCTOBER 9–17, 1949)

The strategically located Xiamen Island is a doorway to the seas along China's southeast coast. Xiamen (previously known as Amoy in the West) occupies an important place in China's historiography. Zheng Chenggong, commonly known as Koxinga in the West, used the area around Xiamen as a base from which to end Dutch rule on Taiwan in 1662. Xiamen was the site of a Sino-British battle during the First Opium War and became an open port under the "unequal" treaty system. Japan's invasion of southeastern China in 1938 began at Xiamen and Jinmen. The island metropolis, long a major commercial hub, has a land area of about 140 square kilometers. The mainland surrounds Xiamen on three sides, and about one nautical mile separates the island's coast closest to the mainland.

The plan to take Xiamen involved three parts. A reinforced regiment from the 31st Corps would attack Gulang Islet just off the southwest coast of Xiamen. This was meant as a diversionary assault to draw Nationalist defenders away from the main line of attack to the north. The 28th Corps and elements of the 29th Corps were tasked to conduct another deceptive attack against Dadeng Island and Xiaodeng Island located just north of Jinmen. The goal was to sow more enemy confusion by misdirecting the defenders' attention to Jinmen. It was hoped that the Nationalists might be deceived into believing that both Xiamen and Jinmen were under threat. The 29th and 31st Corps would form the main assault force to sneak up on Xiamen's northern coast while the

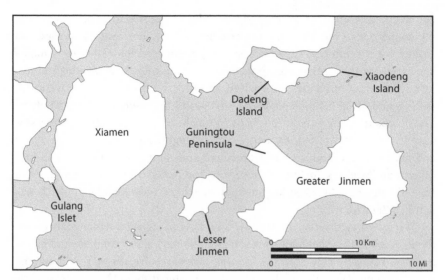

MAP 5.1. Xiamen and Jinmen campaigns, October 1949

© Toshi Yoshihara

Nationalists scrambled to defend Gulang Islet to the southwest and the Dadeng and Xiaodeng Islands north of Jinmen.[10]

On the night of October 9, the 10th Army commenced the first moves to seize Dadeng and Xiaodeng Islands. The Communists favored nighttime operations to avoid detection and harassment by Nationalist airpower, which was largely employed during daytime, and to maximize surprise against island garrisons. The main objective, Dadeng, is a narrow strip of island that stretches west to east just less than one nautical mile off the mainland shores. The sea separating the island from the mainland is very shallow. At low tide, which occurs for short periods twice a day, the watery terrain is passable by foot. The local commanders gambled that their forces could cross without boats, which had been consumed entirely by the main operation against Xiamen. It was a risky if not reckless decision. The 251st Regiment of the 28th Corps and the 259th Regiment of the 29th Corps spearheaded the attack. The three battalions of the 259th Regiment waited until the waters receded to its lowest point in the early evening and waded across waist-high water to reach the eastern portion of Dadeng. Each battalion then advanced independently against the island defenders.

Alerted to the assault, the Nationalists dispatched reinforcements by sea from Jinmen, about four nautical miles to Dadeng's south. The incoming KMT defenders quickly threatened to upend the tactical balance. To make matters worse, the tide had reversed, and the follow-on troops on the mainland were cut off by the sea from their trapped comrades on the island. To compound the regiment's dangerous situation, the crossing over shallow water and mudflats soaked the ammunition supplies, rendering them unusable. The Communists had carried with them only one light artillery piece with three working rounds. The regiment commander improvised and ordered his troops to advance in small groups deep behind enemy lines to disrupt the Nationalists' momentum. The troops then fired the three shells in quick succession, feigning a massive assault. The trick worked. Expecting an onslaught, the Nationalists panicked and fled. The Communists surged forward and captured about one thousand officers and soldiers, including those who had just arrived from Jinmen.[11] On the following day the 251st Regiment attacked and took Xiaodeng, which was lightly defended.

While the tactical encounter was a success, it signaled dangers ahead for the PLA. Had it not been for the local commander's quick thinking and clever stratagem as well as the Nationalists' utter lack of resolve, the tidal shift and the poor handling of supplies might have led to disaster. It should have been an early warning to the 10th Army's high command that its forces needed to account for the demands of nature and logistics. Rather than take heed, the 10th Army neglected to closely study the battle for lessons and chose to press ahead.[12]

When Xiaodeng fell, the Communists had not only achieved their initial objectives but had also successfully tricked the Nationalists into thinking that Jinmen was next, forcing the defenders to reinforce the island. On October 15, the Communists launched another diversionary attack. The 271st Regiment and the 277th Regiment under the 31st Corps were to land separately on the southwest coast of Gulang Islet, while the 273rd Regiment would conduct a follow-on amphibious assault. It was thought that the 31st Corps' contribution to the cross-river campaign along the Yangzi had prepared it well for the cross-sea landing. The commanders had conflated riverine conditions with ocean currents. Moreover, during the Yangzi campaign, the corps was part of the second wave and had landed on the river's south bank unopposed. It had never experienced exposure to hostile fire while in transit at sea. To make matters worse, the troops hailed from the plains of northern China and were unfamiliar with nautical affairs.

At four o'clock in the afternoon, the Communists unleashed salvos of artillery fire to destroy enemy coastal defenses. However, the commanders had ordered the artillery units to avoid hitting structures built by Western imperial powers when Gulang was a treaty port. The high command had hoped to keep the historic buildings intact. As a result of such tactical constraints, the shells either landed harmlessly or inflicted superficial damage. The barrage also alerted the island defenders to the impending attack, eliminating the element of surprise. Then the fine weather suddenly darkened. Strong gusts delayed the departure of the Communist flotilla for hours, which in turn bought time for the Nationalists to shore up their defenses.

But more trouble awaited the attackers after they finally set sail. As the transports neared the island, a sudden shift in wind direction combined with high seas broke the flotilla's formation, scattering them in different directions. Some boats were damaged, and others sank. Some were even blown back to where the troops had originally embarked. The boats that were able to stay on course came under heavy enemy fire from an enemy warship and shore-based artillery as they approached Gulang's beaches. More vessels were damaged or sunk. More than half of the hand-selected civilian sailors pressed into service were wounded or killed.[13]

The surviving troops who managed to land were spread too widely across the beach, unable to provide mutual support. Worse still, they had come ashore into kill zones where the defenders had set up overlapping fires on the landing sites. Despite heroic efforts, most were cut down before they could advance beyond the beach. Only seven companies of the 271st Regiment were able to move farther inland. The regiment commander and the deputy regiment commander were killed in action. The second wave of reinforcements, comprising three battalions of the 273rd Regiment, could not make the crossing owing to persistent bad weather. Those stranded on Gulang, including entire companies, were wiped out, many running out of ammunition and supplies. The heavy losses forced the 31st Corps to call off the attack and redirect resources to the main assault against Xiamen. The foundering battle produced the intended effect by convincing the defenders on Xiamen to divert forces to the southwest. But it came at a high price: 464 killed, 426 wounded, and 411 missing in action.[14]

The main assault against Xiamen's northern shores took place concurrently with the attack on Gulang. The Communists employed five regiments: the 274th Regiment and the 275th Regiment were responsible for the western sector of the coast, the 254th Regiment and the 255th Regiment attacked the central sector, and the 256th Regiment was tasked to take the eastern sector. On the night of October 15, the troops embarked on 250 boats of varying sizes and took three separate routes to reach their designated landing zones.[15] On the western front, the operation almost failed from the start. The transports that had quietly neared the coast under the cover of darkness belatedly discovered that shallow waters and mudflats beneath them, stretching about one thousand meters from the coastline, surrounded the approaches to the island. The ill-timed landings coincided with the receding tides, trapping the boats and the men. When the troops sought to wade ashore, they were mired in knee-deep muck.[16] The Nationalists discovered the botched landings and began to direct withering fire on the exposed, slow-moving soldiers. After hours of heavy fighting, including multiple Nationalist counterattacks that the

Communists somehow fended off, the landing forces secured a beachhead and broke through the first line of defenses.

The forces on the central front successfully landed in secret and surprised the Nationalist units. The Communists directed accurate gunfire against enemy defenses, which quickly collapsed by the morning of October 16. One company of the 254th Regiment defied the odds and seized the airport, a key operational objective. Despite repeated Nationalist counterattacks, using numerically superior forces, the Communists held on.[17] The troops on the eastern sector landed at the geographic seam of two KMT coastal surveillance units, an area that each side considered the responsibility of the other. As a result, the defenders mistook the amphibious troops as friendly forces, compounding the surprise.[18] The 256th Regiment then secured a beachhead and pushed inland. By noon on October 16, all five regiments shattered the Nationalist defenses along a ten-kilometer front, allowing reinforcements to flow uninterrupted onto the beachheads and opening the way for an aggressive advance. By the afternoon of October 16, the Communists reached the waist of Xiamen. At the end of that day the defenses collapsed, compelling the Nationalists to flee south to be rescued by sea.

As it became clear that the Nationalist position was untenable, the 273rd Regiment, the follow-on force that could not reach Gulang Islet owing to bad weather, dispatched a battalion to take Gulang in the wee hours of October 17.[19] Unlike the clashes on October 15 when the Nationalists wiped out the attackers, the Communists landed successfully and quickly seized key terrain. The battalion then captured about one thousand enemy troops who failed to escape by sea in time. That day, the rest of Xiamen fell to the Communists. Out of the forty-five thousand defenders, two thousand were killed or wounded and about twenty-five thousand were captured. The campaign against Xiamen Island proper took only two days to complete. The diversionary attacks, one of which was sacrificed almost entirely to the Nationalists, had worked. The battle appeared to be a rout, one in a succession of quick wins. But the success disguised the challenges that would plague the 10th Army in its plans against Jinmen. Shipping, a vital commodity in amphibious operations, was already scarce and made scarcer still by attrition in battle. The campaign also revealed that the Communists had much to learn about the unforgiving and unpredictable weather conditions at sea as well as the currents, the tides, and coastal terrain. These shortfalls and general inexperience with offshore combat would prove disastrous in the next campaign.[20]

THE JINMEN CAMPAIGN (OCTOBER 24–28, 1949)

The Nationalist-held Jinmen comprises a cluster of islands, with the largest feature, Greater Jinmen, located about five nautical miles east of Xiamen and about five nautical miles from the mainland. Positioned astride maritime communications around Xiamen, the island redoubt was a strategic prize for both sides. The Communists perceived Nationalist control of Jinmen as a major obstacle to a prospective cross-strait campaign. The CCP leadership also saw Jinmen, Xiamen, and the surrounding areas as a natural launch pad for invading Taiwan. Possession of Jinmen, then, determined whether Mao Zedong could vanquish Chiang and decisively conclude the civil war. Geographic advantage also beckoned: the mainland coast surrounded Jinmen on three sides, while only the southern coast faced the open waters of the Taiwan Strait. The defeats and retreats of the preceding months, including the fall of Xiamen, had further exhausted and demoralized the Nationalist defenders. The PLA command, buoyed by its recent successes, sensed an opportunity to deliver a decisive blow.

However, as noted earlier, the Xiamen campaign and its aftermath had direct bearing on the conduct of the Jinmen operation. In their quest to take Xiamen, the Communists suffered significant losses in shipping during the various battles. After experiencing the terrors of taking Xiamen, many conscripted boatmen, who were expected to contribute again to the Jinmen effort, refused to serve or fled with their vessels.[21] The Nationalists also continued their raids to destroy seagoing craft along the mainland coast. The availability of transports thus became the determining factor in how the Jinmen campaign would be waged.

Initially, the 10th Army ordered the 28th Corps to organize and lead the campaign against Greater Jinmen and tasked the 31st Corps to seize Lesser Jinmen, located just west of the main island. But after the 28th Corps discovered that there were only enough boats to carry one battalion, the 10th Army scrapped the 31st Corps' mission. The Communists realized that they lacked the shipping to conduct both operations and decided instead to focus their efforts on Greater Jinmen. After several more delays to the start of the campaign, the Communists were able to conscript about 350 boatmen and 320 boats.[22] The 28th Corps acquired enough shipping to transport just three regiments, numbering some 9,000 troops. The scarcity of local manpower and resources was severe: the army had to draft almost all the boatmen from Quanzhou some fifty kilometers to the north and from as far as Fuzhou about two hundred kilometers up the coast. This too would have an impact on the course of the campaign.

Military intelligence estimated that the Nationalist garrison on Jinmen numbered about twenty thousand. It was determined that an equal number of Communist troops would be enough to defeat the enemy. But even if this optimistic forecast was accurate, the 10th Army clearly did not possess enough ships to throw the same ratio of attackers against the defenders in a single transit. To bring the requisite number of troops ashore to even the tactical balance, PLA planners determined that the transports would have to land the first wave on Jinmen and then make a return trip to fetch the second tranche waiting on the opposite shore. The initial assault would have to hold firm on the beachheads or overcome enemy defenses on their own until the follow-on forces arrived. The planners apparently believed that the troops could be brought ashore in two successive waves in one night. However, according to a retrospective study, even under fair weather conditions and with no opposing forces to contest such passage, it would have taken the boats four to five hours to make a single roundtrip, covering about five nautical miles each way.[23] Such was the confidence, if not the hubris, of the Communists.

Intelligence, though shaky, also indicated that the Nationalists were preparing troops and transports to reinforce Jinmen. The Communists did not know at the time that in the weeks leading up to the campaign, Generalissimo Chiang Kai-shek had ordered a continuous buildup of the garrison. One People's Republic of China study claims that island defenders had already swelled to at least forty thousand by October 24, double the initial estimates upon which the campaign was based.[24] One ROC article states that the Nationalists had stationed up to thirty thousand troops on Jinmen by the time of the campaign.[25] In short, the Communists had significantly undercounted their adversary's presence on the island, a defending force that was at least three times larger than the attackers.[26] Faulty intelligence led Ye Fei to conclude that his army could still act before the local military balance tilted too far, foreclosing the opportunity to strike. There was thus a great sense of urgency to finish off the Nationalists, despite the lack of boats and the risks that a two-wave assault entailed.

The operational plan was to form six regiments for the campaign. The 28th Corps, the leading organization, would contribute four regiments to the fight and draw two more from the 29th Corps. Each of the two waves would comprise two regiments from the 28th Corps and one regiment from the 29th Corps. The 82nd Division of the 28th Corps would have overall command of the forces. The 28th Corps had to leave behind a division in Fuzhou for garrison duty and thus had to settle for a clunky division of labor in which one corps oversaw units of another corps.[27] The first wave would hit the beaches on the western sector of the island, and the second wave would attack the eastern portion. For the first wave, the flotilla would attempt a three-pronged assault on a landing area in the northwest corner of Jinmen. The 244th Regiment, the 251st Regiment, and the 253rd Regiment were responsible for seizing the eastern, central, and western sectors of the beach, respectively. According to the plan, the 244th Regiment was to drive south along the narrow waist and midsection of Jinmen to cut off east-west communications. The other two regiments were to take the main county township.[28] Pulling together regiments from two different corps for the crucial first landing complicated the command and control of forces, compounding the risks of an operation that was already quite complex with many moving parts.[29]

On the evening of October 24, the troops assembled at Lianhe, Dadeng Island, and Wotou just north of Jinmen and boarded the ships. Attesting to the disorganization that plagued the campaign, regiment commanders found to their dismay that there were still not enough ships to transport the entire first landing group. Several platoons and even an entire company had to be left behind and were ordered to join the subsequent wave of attack.[30] At around midnight, the nonmotorized fishing vessels set sail for Jinmen. The flotilla, composed of sailing boats of uneven size and speed, struggled to maintain its formation. The boatmen from Quanzhou and Fuzhou were strangers to local sea conditions, while poor ship-to-shore communications severely hampered coordination. The boats operated independently of each other. A sudden change in the current and wind direction further scattered the fleet. Elements of the left and central tines went well off course and ended up with the right wing.

To make matters worse, the 244th Regiment lost the element of surprise as it neared its landing zone.[31] A Nationalist patrol accidentally set off a mine at the beach close to the regiment's area of disembarkation. Hearing the explosion, defenders along the shoreline turned on their search lights and, to their shock, discovered that an enemy flotilla was attempting to sneak troops ashore. They immediately began to direct their fire at the approaching boats and alerted the entire command to the impending invasion. This early detection and initial contact contributed in part to the subsequent Communist casualties and the breakdown in operations. A mishap helped to mitigate, if not foil, the surprise attack on the eastern sector.

Under the cover of darkness, the other two regiments were able to spring tactical surprises on the KMT defenders and secure footholds. However, as troops waded ashore, spread out along a ten-kilometer stretch of beach, chaos reigned. The units scattered on the beach lacked unified command and were unable to restore any degree of organizational cohesion. In some cases, a battalion commander had communications with no more than one company.[32] Without an overall command structure to guide their actions, each unit operated on its own and proceeded according to the plan, as if it were a script, without regard to radically changed circumstances on the ground. The various uncoordinated parts of the force sought to advance to their original operational objectives without pause and without a tactical reassessment.

In the meantime, frontline units defending the beaches put up ferocious resistance, inflicting significant casualties on the assault forces. Nationalist naval vessels, including a minesweeper, a gunboat, and a tank landing ship, arrived on the scene to interdict shipping, suppress enemy artillery on the mainland,

and bombard troops who landed on Jinmen.[33] Within hours, the Communist offensive began to stall. After blunting the initial assault, Nationalist infantry units, backed by M5A1 Stuart tanks and artillery, launched a three-pronged counteroffensive before daybreak.[34] The tanks would earn the nickname "the bears of Jinmen" for their devastating effectiveness against troops who lacked adequate numbers of antiarmor weaponry. Two prongs pushed west from Jinmen's waist, the central segment of the island, while one prong advanced north from the southwest. In the morning, the Nationalists launched air sorties to suppress Communist artillery positions opposite Jinmen and bombard enemy units on the island.[35] The counterattack rolled back the adversary's territorial gains and progressively pushed Communist units into the Guningtou peninsula, a pocket on Jinmen's northwest tip.

On the beaches, the high tide that brought the transports close to shore receded drastically, miring the entire flotilla in the exposed mudflat.[36] The stranded ships came under unrelenting artillery fire and naval gunfire from nearby positions. When day broke, the Nationalist aircraft bombarded the trapped vessels. The combined firepower of land, air, and sea forces destroyed every single boat and killed or maimed fishermen pressed into service by the Communists. The second-wave troops waiting on Dadeng Island for the returning wooden sailing boats watched helplessly in horror at the fiery wreckage on the opposite shore.[37] Not only did the capacity to reinforce, a centerpiece of the operation, vanish, but the ability of the three regiments to escape also disappeared.

By noon, the 244th regiment ran out of ammunition and was virtually wiped out. The 251st regiment, which was pinned down on the beach by Nationalist shore-based artillery, had already lost a third of its troops. The regiment lost another one thousand troops in fierce fighting before breaking out of an encirclement on the afternoon of October 25. One embattled element of the regiment was down to two squads after resisting multiple Nationalist counterattacks over nine hours.[38] The remnants of the 251st and the 253rd Regiments joined up and limped to the beachhead along the Guningtou peninsula.

As the day wore on, the 251st and 253rd Regiments defended a shrinking and tenuous perimeter on Guningtou peninsula. Unwilling to admit defeat, the 10th Army ordered the 246th and 259th Regiments to send in reinforcements. The decision was reckless at best. The Communists were able to scrounge enough ships to carry only four companies. Owing to high winds parts of the fleet were blown off course, while the rest were only able to land ten platoons on Guningtou on the night of the October 25, making a negligible impact on the local military balance.[39] The remaining troops resisted in the hope that more boats would arrive to retrieve them.

By October 27th, headquarters lost communications with those trapped on Jinmen. Outgunned, outsized, out of ammunition and food, and out of options, the Communist remnants were crushed on the afternoon of October 28. The commander of the 246th Regiment, sent to rescue his comrades, committed suicide in a final desperate act. After days of intense clashes, an eerie silence descended over the island. The operation was a fiasco. The 10th Army lost all three regiments, nearly 5,000 dead and 4,000 captured, and over 300 boatmen pressed into service. The Nationalists suffered over 6,000 casualties, including nearly 2,500 killed in action and some 3,700 wounded.[40] For the Communists, the string of easy victories throughout 1949 came to an abrupt halt.

In the aftermath of the catastrophe, Mao conceded that the PLA had suffered its greatest loss in Jinmen during the entire Chinese Civil War. Coming less than a month after the founding of the People's Republic of China on October 1, the defeat must have stung. Mao urged his subordinates to reflect on the lessons of the abortive campaign. Sobered by the failure, his subsequent communications with commanders in charge of seizing Taiwan demonstrated a newfound respect for the complexities of an amphibious campaign. Upward estimates about how much would be needed to take Taiwan reflected the high command's recognition that a cross-strait operation would demand careful planning, thorough preparation, and substantial if not overwhelming forces to succeed.

The lopsided victories by the Third Field Army after crossing the Yangzi, including the quick collapse of Xiamen's defenses, clearly influenced the haphazard planning and execution of the Jinmen campaign. One study attributes the failure of the campaign to underestimation of the enemy, impatience, failure to assess the enemy's situation, lack of preparedness for an amphibious operation, and flawed organization of combat forces.[41] Another calls attention to the absence of naval and air support, inadequate troop transports, unfamiliarity with the meteorological conditions, and poor intelligence of the opponent's disposition.[42] The official history of the Third Field Army notes that the 10th Army had prematurely shifted its focus to the expected administration of liberated territories while delegating the planning and command responsibilities to its subordinate command, the 28th Corps. The poor decision underscored the "blind optimism" that had characterized the 10th Army's assessments.[43]

In one of the best anatomies of the disaster, Miles Yu identifies more reasons for the failure. Local hostilities toward the Communists, especially among the fisherman, deprived the 10th Army adequate shipping to bring the troops ashore. Poor strategic and operational intelligence pitted the Communists against a stronger willed and more powerful enemy than anticipated. Major delays to the flotilla's departure truncated the nighttime operation, a crucial period when the forces could fight without fear of Nationalist airpower, restricted as it was to daylight missions. Uncoordinated command and control of forces led to chaos and confusion when the assault forces landed on the island.[44]

One ROC study finds tactical shortfalls that hampered Communist operations. The absence of proper communication equipment aboard the ships contributed to the chaotic landings at the beaches. Shore-based artillery units on the mainland suffered from short ranges and limited ammunition, precluding them from providing adequate support to the landings on Jinmen. Improper use of the few antiarmor weapons exposed the troops to the withering firepower of Nationalist tanks.[45] Another ROC article points out that the Communists had not properly secured the beachheads after landing their troops. Among the three regiments, only the 253rd Regiment left one battalion to protect its lodgment. The rest of the forces charged inland without regard to their tenuous footholds on the beach. This neglect allowed the Nationalists to seal the various breakthrough points along the shoreline as soon as the day broke on October 25. Had the Communists secured the beachheads with an adequate reserve force, they might have been better positioned to support their comrades attacking inland; monitor, delay, constrain, or prevent Nationalist movements; and counterattack when circumstances warranted.[46]

In his memoir, Ye Fei concedes many of the mistakes cited above. He acknowledges that he was consumed by the job of administering the newly conquered Xiamen, a major economic hub. For him, it was essential to maintain social stability in this vital urban area. The battles along the Fujian coast had proved highly disruptive to the local economy. Retreating Nationalists had forcibly seized resources across the region. By the time the Communists took Xiamen, fuel and food shortages were emerging as major problems. The war's disruption to shipping, so essential to transporting goods to the island, only worsened scarcity.[47] Thus, the caring and feeding of Xiamen's population, numbering some two hundred thousand, competed for Ye's attention.

Ye further admits that the 28th Corps did not possess enough boats. He confirms that the campaign against Xiamen led to serious losses in transports that could not be replaced. Yet, the afterglow of the Xiamen victory led Ye and his subordinates to paper over the difficulties and dangers of cross-sea invasions. He also identifies a major operational error: the failure of the landing force to secure the beachhead. After getting to shore, the three regiments rushed headlong toward their objectives without regard to the logistical foundation of the campaign. They left only one battalion to defend the boats and the lodgments. Ye further finds fault with the command arrangement. Not a single divisional commander accompanied the first wave of attackers to provide overall unified direction. This only compounded the lack of coordination between the hodgepodge of regiments when the troops came ashore. Finally, Ye observes that the operation violated a basic principle of modern warfare. The PLA did not possess the wherewithal to contest the air and the seas, much less command them. The complete absence of airpower and naval power put the entire force at grave risk.[48] These lessons learned would inform the Fourth Field Army's campaign against Hainan Island (detailed in chapter 6).

ZHOUSHAN ISLANDS CAMPAIGN (AUGUST 18–NOVEMBER 5, 1949)

The Zhoushan archipelago is located just east of Ningbo on the southern mouth of Hangzhou Bay. More than four hundred islands and islets comprise this offshore cluster, covering an area of about 1,200 square kilometers. Zhoushan Island, the largest feature, is about 500 square kilometers in size. The islands sit astride north-south communications along the mainland coast and could serve as either a protective screen for or a launch pad against such major cities as Shanghai, Hangzhou, and Ningbo. When Nationalist defenses collapsed around Shanghai and Ningbo, the forces retreated to Zhoushan, a stronghold blocking the Communist path to the seas. In July 1949, the KMT established a new command on Zhoushan overseeing about sixty thousand defenders. Nationalist naval and air assets based on the island provided naval gunfire support and close air support to the ground troops.

The Third Field Army began planning for seizing the islands as soon as Shanghai fell in May and ordered the 7th Army to take charge of the operation. The 7th Army commanded about four divisions numbering forty thousand troops, mostly infantry with some limited artillery support. In late July, commanders and planners began to examine their options. It was decided that the 22nd Corps would have overall responsibilities for carrying out the mission. The 22nd Corps would also command the 61st Division of the 21st Corps. Given the qualitative and quantitative inferiority of forces, the shortage of shipping, and the complete lack of experience with amphibious operations, the 7th Army adopted a conservative approach to the campaign.[49]

First, the 7th Army trained and prepared. Most of the soldiers came from China's interior and were utterly unfamiliar with maritime affairs. They had to learn to cope with waves, maneuver around obstacles on the beach laid by the enemy, and advance across beaches.[50] Second, the 7th Army planned to conquer the islands piecemeal. It would first take on strongpoints along Zhoushan's periphery, particularly the smaller islands closest to the mainland. Localized operations would allow the Communists to amass forces against numerically inferior defenders at those specific locales in decisive engagements. The goal was in part to fight battles of annihilation that would deliver a psychological shock against the enemy and progressively chip away the adversary's overall strength. The battles would also help the troops test their newfound skills and accumulate much-needed experience in amphibious operations.

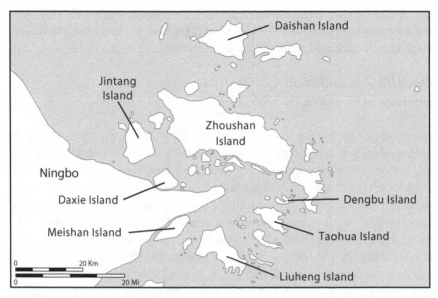

MAP 5.2. Zhoushan Islands campaign, August–November 1949

© Toshi Yoshihara

By mid-August, it was decided that the 7th Army would target Daxie Island, an atoll about a third of a nautical mile offshore and a gateway to the main Zhoushan Island. About one thousand defenders were garrisoned on Daxie. The 22nd Corps formed three infantry regiments and an artillery regiment to overwhelm the opposing force. Four battalions would comprise the first wave of the assault, while three battalions would deliver the follow-on units. The artillery regiment would be deployed to provide fire support. Another regiment would seize two nearby islets to guard against a counterattack by a garrison stationed on Meishan Island to the south. All preparations for the assault took place in utmost secrecy. On August 17, some two hundred boats were hidden or camouflaged along the bay stretching several kilometers. Artillery pieces were also surreptitiously pulled into prepared firing positions. These quiet movements and concealed sites avoided detection by Nationalist reconnaissance forces.[51]

On August 18 the 22nd Corps launched a night attack, using the cover of darkness to maximize surprise. After a barrage of artillery fire, boatmen rowed furiously to bring the four regiments across the water. Gunners aboard the boats provided suppressing fire against enemy positions as they approached Daxie. It took only fifteen minutes for the vessels to reach the opposite shore. The deception measures and the lightning strike surprised the defenders. The attackers took three separate routes and quickly surrounded the Nationalist command post on the island. The garrison fell on the 19th at dawn. The following day, the Nationalists attempted a counter amphibious assault with the support of five naval vessels and five combat aircraft, but the attack was repulsed. Upon hearing the news of Daxie's collapse, the Nationalist unit based on Meishan Island abandoned its post. This first operational success boosted the confidence of the 7th Army and offered important lessons for amphibious operations to come.

The 7th Army then turned to grab Jintang Island, a larger feature than Daxie located just west of Zhoushan. The occupation of Jintang and Daxie would position the Communists to close in on Zhoushan, the main prize, in a pincer movement. After the disaster at Daxie, the Nationalists were no longer confident in the stopping power of water. Recognizing that Jintang could be the next target, they began to construct bunkers at key defensive locations on Jintang.

In early September, the 22nd Corps decided that four regiments would conduct the main assault while one regiment would serve as a reserve unit. Another smaller force would feint toward Liuheng Island, the southernmost feature of the archipelago. The goal was to tie down the defenders there to prevent the flow of reinforcements to the besieged garrison on Jintang. Three artillery regiments would provide fire support, including long-range gunfire to bombard and suppress nearby naval ports and airbases. This coordinated campaign would isolate the battlefield on Jintang and would overwhelm the defenders with superior numbers in men and firepower.

However, bad weather intervened throughout the second half of September. A series of storms hit the area, severely damaging roads, bridges, and pier-side facilities. The damage to logistical infrastructure severely disrupted preparations for the campaign. It was not until early October, after heroic efforts to restore critical services, that the command decided the time was right to attack. But the weather would not cooperate. The 22nd Corps delayed again. Careful study of local terrain and meteorological conditions had taught the Communists that Jintang was a hard target. Mudflats surrounded the island, and the tides receded dramatically. Tidal conditions suitable for an amphibious assault were available for only six days a month, and high tide for each of those six days lasted for just four hours.[52] The window, already narrow, was closing on the Communists.

On October 3, the day before the high tides would recede, the 22nd Corps ordered the attack despite continuing rains and high winds. That afternoon when the weather lifted for a brief moment, forty-nine artillery pieces opened fire on Jintang, and some three hundred boats rushed toward the island.[53] It took the vessels about seventy-five minutes to cross nearly two nautical miles of water. Heavy rains resumed as the forces landed on the beaches, complicating the planned advance. But the weather also grounded Nationalist airpower based at Dinghai airbase on Zhoushan. The Communists pushed north, cutting off east-west communications and severing access to harbors on either side of the island. When they reached the northern end of the island, some elements of the force crossed over to an adjacent islet on the northwestern coast, completing the conquest. The operation ended at dawn on October 5.

Jintang's collapse, which brought the Communists significantly closer to Zhoushan, compelled the Nationalists to withdraw forces from outposts on the exposed southern edge of the defensive perimeter, including Liuheng Island and Xiashi Island. The 61st Division of the 21st Corps, responsible for taking offensive operations from the south of Zhoushan, immediately seized those islands in the wake of the Nationalist retreat. Fresh from another success, the Communist high command decided to ride the momentum of victory and ordered the 61st Division to attack Taohua Island, sandwiched between Xiashi to the south and Zhoushan to the north. According to PLA historiography, the locals at Xiashi purportedly pleaded with their liberators to free their neighbors on Taohua.[54] In a show of their putative enthusiasm, they dug up boats that they had buried on the beaches or brought up vessels that they had scuttled and readied seventy boats in three days.

On the afternoon of October 18, artillery shells rained down on Taohua. Following an hour of preparatory bombardment, four battalions set sail for the island. Once on the beach, the troops scaled cliffs, while suppressing fires kept enemy forces fixed at their defensive positions. The Nationalists were again unable to stop the advance beyond the beach. The main attacking force, after reassembling, drove deep into the island and, after a night of fierce fighting, reached the two main harbors to the north, cutting off the escape routes by sea. The island fell in just twenty hours.

The series of defeats forced the Nationalists to reorganize their defenses. They established a new command structure, appointed new commanders, redeployed additional naval assets to Zhoushan and neighboring Changtu Island, accelerated work on an airfield at Daishan Island to accommodate bombers, and reinforced Zhoushan with additional troops, increasing the garrison to ninety thousand men.

To complete the encirclement of Zhoushan Island along its southern flank, the 61st Division prepared to seize Dengbu Island. Located on the southeast corner of Zhoushan, Dengbu is just one and a half nautical miles to the northeast of Taohua Island. The target was the remaining physical barrier standing between the Nationalists on Zhoushan and the Communists. The 61st Division assigned the 182nd Regiment and one battalion of the 183rd Regiment to serve as the first landing wave and one battalion and one company of the 183rd Regiment to act as the reserve force. Twelve pieces of mountain guns emplaced on

Taohua would provide fire support. The division assembled a flotilla that could carry two regiments.[55] There were concerns that the amphibious force did not possess enough lift. The operation to capture Taohua cost the Communists some forty boats, and losses continued to mount as the Nationalists conducted their air raids against vessels. But the high command insisted that the operation proceed as scheduled.[56]

On the afternoon of November 3, artillery units on Taohua delivered suppressive fire against Nationalist positions. While bad weather grounded the ROC Air Force, Nationalist army units on Dengbu and naval vessels answered with counterbattery fire.[57] That night the first echelon, carried by about one hundred boats, surged toward Dengbu. But high winds and a rapid shift in tidal currents prevented large elements of the flotilla from reaching their intended destinations. Initially, only seven and a half infantry companies and two gunnery companies, numbering about one thousand men, made it to shore. This small contingent was able to secure beachheads and break through thinly defended positions along the coastline, allowing follow-on forces to arrive and gradually strengthen the attackers. Over a night of heavy fighting, the Communists held about three-quarters of the island and pushed back the defenders to Dengbu's northern corner. It appeared that victory was at hand.

However, the Nationalists were not ready to give up. The Zhoushan Defense Command dispatched reinforcements in the wee hours of November 4. Naval transports brought four regiments to shore up the besieged defenders behind a shrinking perimeter.[58] The tactical balance of power instantly flipped against the Communists. With naval gunfire support and close air support, the Nationalists counterattacked with two advancing columns and broke out to the southeast and southwest.[59] During the counteroffensive, the ROC Air Force employed three B-25 bombers, seven Mosquito fighter-bombers, and seven P-51 fighters to harass and interdict the enemy.[60] The Communists, who thought they were on the verge of success, were suddenly greatly outnumbered and knocked back into a full retreat. They then took their stand at separate locations in the middle of the island. The unceasing firepower that the Nationalists unleashed from land, air, and sea proved devastatingly lethal. Cut off from resupply, the encircled troops eventually ran out of ammunition and food. Some units resorted to desperate hand-to-hand combat, resulting in grievous losses. In one instance, the 1st Battalion of the 183rd Regiment was whittled down to one political officer and some forty men.

That night, the 61st Division dispatched reinforcements totaling eleven companies, including those that had failed to reach the island in the first wave. These forces successfully landed and joined up with the embattled remnant defenders. While they inflicted substantial casualties on the attacking Nationalists and clawed back some key positions, the enemy had absolute tactical superiority and was growing stronger as more troops flowed onto the island. And the 61st Division had depleted its reserves of manpower. On November 5, fine weather enabled the Nationalists to maximize their air and naval superiority to pummel the Communists, while ground forces pushed farther south, occupying key terrain.[61] The situation was becoming untenable. According to the PLA's official history, the surviving units withdrew on the night of November 5. One ROC source claims that most of the Communist units on Dengbu were wiped out and that only a few managed to escape by boat to Taohua.[62] Coming on the heels of the Jinmen disaster, this defeat further underscored the lesson that amphibious operations were inherently complex and risky especially in the face of a resolute and resourceful foe.

The Third Field Army's scathing after-action report laid out the factors that had contributed to the failure at Dengbu. Materially, the Communists lacked naval and air support, which would have otherwise furnished them the means to contest the Nationalists' use of the air and the seas. Inadequate shipping deprived the 61st Division of the capacity to bring enough troops to deliver a decisive blow with overwhelming force. The 7th Army and its subordinate 22nd Corps, which had overall command of forces, had failed to pay close attention to weather and hydrological conditions. The assault forces under the 61st Division were poorly trained and ill-prepared for the task at hand. The commanders had further neglected to anticipate setbacks and, when the first echelon foundered, were unable to reinforce those trapped on Dengbu quickly enough and thereby shift the tactical balance back in their favor.[63]

Another study contends that Communist forces were already overextended by the time Taohua Island had fallen. Measured by distance, Communist forces had stretched about twenty-five nautical miles in the seaward direction from the mainland through Meishan, Liuheng, Xiashi, and Taohua Islands. As the attacker captured each island it had to leave behind a garrison, progressively siphoning off forces available to conduct offensive operations.[64] In Clausewitzian terms, the Communists had reached or gone beyond the culminating point of attack by the time planning for Dengbu began. Still another retrospective argues that poor intelligence and overconfidence contributed to the failure. The Communists believed that only four enemy battalions were on Dengbu and that those defenders would go largely unsupported. Frontline commanders were unaware that Nationalist forces had poured onto Zhoushan at the end of October and failed to consider the possibility of reinforcements reaching Dengbu from the main island. The attackers thus received provisions for a short campaign, expecting the island to fall quickly like the others before it.[65]

In a counterfactual analysis, one ROC source contends that had the Communists been able to land four battalions in the first assault wave as originally planned, they might have achieved a quick win.[66] The initial breakthroughs on the night of November 3 had sowed chaos and confusion among the Nationalist defenders. But with only two battalions and an overstrength company ashore, the attackers were unable to exploit their tactical successes. Their inability to ride the circumstances to victory gave the Nationalists time to send in reinforcements, thereby closing the window of opportunity for a rapid, decisive conquest. As the troops lost their operational momentum, they were forced to fight a series of bloody attritional engagements. Moreover, the KMT's air and naval forces accelerated the losses on the ground. Like the predicament at Jinmen, the Communists lacked adequate numbers of long-range artillery to support the offensive ashore and disrupt Nationalist naval sorties. Together, these factors contributed to the reversal of fortunes.

The setback bought the Nationalists time to substantially boost the size of the garrison on Zhoushan Island, ballooning to around 120,000 troops during November. By the end of 1949, the KMT command decided to use Zhoushan as a base for offensive operations against the mainland, including a blockade of the Yangzi River delta; maritime interdiction against coastal traffic and Communist-held offshore islands; air bombardment of shore facilities, coastal cities, and rail transportation; and small hit-and-run raids against coastal targets by special forces.

To eliminate the threat from Zhoushan, the Communists began a buildup of its own to oust their dug-in opponent. By April 1950 they had amassed some 375,000 troops, 44 surface combatants, 38 amphibious assault craft, and bombers and tactical aircraft, including the Soviet-supplied MiG-15.[67] They deployed air force units to Shanghai, Hangzhou, and Xuzhou from February to March 1950 and were able to contest the Nationalist command of the air by April. On April 25, Commanders of the Third Field Army convened a joint planning conference for a combined land-air-sea campaign against Zhoushan. It was decided that the 7th and 9th Armies would command a force of six corps to conquer the island stronghold.[68] But the plan was soon overtaken by events. The fall of Hainan Island on May 1 (detailed in chapter 6) sent shockwaves across the Nationalist high command. At the same time, it was clear to the KMT leadership that the military balance around Zhoushan had shifted in the Communists' favor. On May 10, Chiang Kai-shek ordered the evacuation of forces from Zhoushan Island to Taiwan.[69] In mid-May, the Nationalists quietly withdrew some 125,000 troops by sea without any losses over the course of three days.[70] The operation, involving tight coordination among the army, navy, and air force, preserved a major component of Chiang's fighting forces. The retreat left Zhoushan open to the Communists.

A MIXED RECORD

The Third Field Army's performance at sea was spotty at best. The destruction of a diversionary force marred Xiamen's seizure. The Jinmen disaster overturned key assumptions about the PLA's prospects for conquering Taiwan. The Zhoushan campaign stalled after the Nationalists repulsed the Communist advance on Dengbu Island. The Nationalists were then able to withdraw all of their forces from Zhoushan unscathed. Terrible consequences followed whenever the Third Field Army violated basic principles of warfare. The 10th Army and the 7th Army appeared to have succumbed to victory disease as they pressed on their offensives in the expectation of further easy wins. But at Jinmen and Dengbu Islands they had clearly gone beyond the Clausewitzian culminating point of attack. At the same time, the campaigns demonstrated the centrality of interaction between two living forces in war. Once Chiang decided to reinforce his strongpoints at Jinmen and Zhoushan, the Communist amphibious operations stopped in their tracks. The Fourth Field Army to the south would learn much from the Third Field Army's experiences and adapted its strategy accordingly to avoid the costly mistakes of its comrades on the Fujian and Zhejiang coasts.

NOTES

1. 叶飞 [Ye Fei], 叶飞回忆录 [Memoirs of Ye Fei] (Beijing: Liberation Army Press, 2007), 414.
2. 南京军区编辑室 [Editorial Office of the Nanjing Military Region], 中国人民解放军第三野战军战史 [War History of the Third Field Army of the People's Liberation Army] (Beijing: Liberation Army Press, 2008), 379. The study was originally published in 1996.
3. Editorial Office of the Nanjang Military Region, 379.
4. Ye, *Memoirs of Ye Fei*, 414.
5. 郭德宏 主编 [Guo Dehong, ed.], 解放军史鉴: 解放军史 (1945–1949) [The Annals of the Liberation Army: History of the Liberation Army (1945–1949)] (Qingdao: Qingdao Press, 2014), 894.
6. 汪庆广 主编 [Wang Qingguang, ed.], 岛屿登陆战斗 [Island Landing Operations] (Beijing: Military Science Press [military circulation], 2001), 26.
7. 卓爱平 [Zhuo Aiping], "'漳夏金战役'金门失利原因探究" [An Investigation of the "Zhangzhou-Xiamen-Jinmen Campaigns" and the Cause of the Jinmen Defeat], 军事历史研究 [Military History Research], no. 1 (2003): 38.
8. Ye, *Memoirs of Ye Fei*, 415.
9. Editorial Office of the Nanjing Military Region, *War History of the Third Field Army*, 382–83.
10. Editorial Office of the Nanjing Military Region, 383–84.
11. Guo, *The Annals of the Liberation Army*, 896.
12. Guo, 897.
13. Guo, 898.
14. For a blow-by-blow account of the abortive Gulang assault, see 陈广相 [Chen Guangxiang], "渡海解放鼓浪屿之战" [The Cross-Sea Battle to Liberate Gulang Islet], 党史纵览 [Overview of Party History], no. 6 (2016): 51–53. The author is a senior colonel at the Editorial Board of the Political Department of the Nanjing Military Region, a military historian, and an author of a history of the 10th Army's 29th Corps.

15. Guo, *The Annals of the Liberation Army*, 899.

16. Editorial Office of the Nanjing Military Region, *War History of the Third Field Army*, 385.

17. Guo, *The Annals of the Liberation Army*, 899.

18. Guo, 900.

19. Guo, 900.

20. For an excellent summary of how the Xiamen campaign had a knock-on effect on the Jinmen campaign, see Zhuo, "An Investigation of the 'Zhangzhou-Xiamen-Jinmen Campaigns' and the Cause of the Jinmen Defeat," 37–41.

21. 张茂勋 丛乐天 邢志远 [Zhang Maoxun, Cong Letian, and Xing Zhiyuan], "金门失利原因何在?" [What Were the Reasons for the Jinmen Failure?], 百年潮 [Hundred Year Tide], no. 1 (2003): 34. All three authors were staff members of the assault force destined for Jinmen and were eyewitnesses to key events surrounding the disaster.

22. 王洪光 [Wang Hongguang], "对金门战役'三不打'的考证" [Research on the "Three No Strikes" Instruction regarding the Jinmen Campaign], 军事历史 [Military History], no. 4 (2012): 22.

23. Zhang et al., "What Were the Reasons for the Jinmen Failure?," 35.

24. Zang et al., 31.

25. 林福隆 [Lin Fulong], "金門古寧頭之戰: 從戡亂到保臺" [The Battle of Jinmen-Guningtou: From Suppression to Securing Taiwan], 軍事史評論 [Military History Review], no. 26 (June 2019): 30. This periodical is published by the Administration Office of the ROC Ministry of National Defense. The June 2019 issue commemorates the 70th anniversary of the Jinmen and Dengbu island campaigns.

26. 陈新民 徐国成 罗峰 主编 [Chen Xinmin, Xu Guocheng, and Luo Feng, eds.], 岛屿作战研究 [Research on Island Operations] (Beijing, Military Science Press [military circulation], 2002), 13. The study estimates that the ratio between the attacker and the defenders was one to four.

27. Ye, *Memoirs of Ye Fei*, 415.

28. 邢志远 [Xing Zhiyuan], "金门失利原因何在?" [What Were the Reasons behind the Jinmen Defeat?], 百年潮 [Hundred Year Tide], no. 1 (2003): 37. The author was a staff member of the 244th Regiment.

29. Chen, Xu, and Luo, *Research on Island Operations*, 14.

30. 丛乐天 [Cong Letian], "金门之战始末" [The Beginning to End of the Battle for Jinmen], 北京档案 [Beijing Files], no. 6 (2000): 52. The author, a staff member of 244th Regiment, was among those left behind on Dadeng Island owing to the lack of shipping. The author was an eyewitness to the destruction of the stranded boats on Jinmen.

31. 萧鸿鸣 萧南溪 萧江 [Xiao Hongming, Xiao Nanxi, and Xiao Jiang], 金门战役: 记事本末 [The Jinmen Campaign: A Record of Events] (Beijing: China Youth Press, 2016), 243–50.

32. Editorial Office of the Nanjing Military Region, *War History of the Third Field Army*, 388.

33. 陳偉寬 [Chen Weikuan], "古寧頭戰役: 海,空軍作戰研究" [The Guningtou Campaign: Research on Naval and Air Operations], 海軍學術雙月刊 [Navy Professional Journal] 53, no. 6 (December 2019): 13. This bimonthly periodical is published by the ROCN Headquarters. The author is a retired ROC Air Force colonel and a lecturer at the ROC National Defense University.

34. 王明瑞 [Wang Mingrui, ed.], 古寧頭戰役70周年紀念冊 [The Guningtou Campaign: 70th Anniversary Memorial Book] (Taipei: ROC Ministry of National

Defense Administration Office, 2019), 53–58. This volume provides an overview of the Jinmen battle from the Nationalist perspective.

35. Chen, "The Guningtou Campaign," 14.

36. 刘统 [Liu Tong], 跨海之战: 金门 海南 一江山 [Cross-Sea Battles: Jinmen, Hainan, and Yijiangshan] (Beijing: SDX Joint Publishing, 2010), 100–102.

37. Cong, "The Beginning to End of the Battle for Jinmen," 52.

38. Editorial Office of the Nanjing Military Region, *War History of the Third Field Army*, 389.

39. Editorial Office of the Nanjing Military Region, 389.

40. 陳偉忠 [Chen Weizhong], "金門保衛戰之研析" [Analysis of Defense of Jinmen], 軍事史評論 [Military History Review], no. 26 (June 2019): 77.

41. 杨贵华 主编 [Yang Guihua, ed.], 中国人民解放军战史教程 [Course Materials on the Chinese People's Liberation Army's War History] (Beijing: Military Science Press, 2013), 156.

42. He Di, "The Last Campaign to Unify China: The CCP's Unrealized Plan to Liberate Taiwan, 1949–1950," in *Chinese Warfighting*, ed. Ryan et al., 78.

43. Editorial Office of the Nanjing Military Region, *War History of the Third Field Army*, 390.

44. Yu, "The Battle of Quemoy," 91–107.

45. Chen, "Analysis of Defense of Jinmen," 90–91.

46. 陳明仁 [Chen Mingren], "古寧頭戰役對我遂行島嶼登陸作戰之啟示" [The Guningtou Campaign and Its Lessons for Carrying Out Island Landing Operations], 海軍學術雙月刊 [Navy Professional Journal] 54, no. 6 (December 2020): 134. The author is a colonel of the ROC Marine Corps and a faculty member of the ROC National Defense University.

47. Ye, *Memoirs of Ye Fei*, 413.

48. Ye, 419–20.

49. Editorial Office of the Nanjing Military Region, *War History of the Third Field Army*, 400–401.

50. Editorial Office of the Nanjing Military Region, 401.

51. Editorial Office of the Nanjing Military Region, 402.

52. Editorial Office of the Nanjing Military Region, 403.

53. Editorial Office of the Nanjing Military Region, 404.

54. Editorial Office of the Nanjing Military Region, 404.

55. 户辉 郑怀盛 [Hu Hui and Zheng Huaisheng], "登步岛渡海登陆作战经过与思考" [The Conduct of the Cross-Sea Landing Operation against Dengbu Island and Some Thoughts], 军事历史 [Military History], no. 3 (2007): 22. Hu Hui was the chief of staff for operations of the 21st Corps at the time of Dengbu Island campaign.

56. 毕建忠 [Bi Jianzhong], "登步岛战斗受挫的原因与启示" [The Causes and Implications of the Setback during the Dengbu Island Combat], 军事历史 [Military History], no. 1 (2000): 7. The author is a historian at the Academy of Military Science.

57. 況正吉 [Kuang Zhengji], "登步島戰鬥之研究" [Research on Dengbu Island Combat], 軍事史評論 [Military History Review], no. 26 (June 2019): 104–5.

58. The official war history of the Third Field Army asserts that the Nationalists dispatched four regiments, while Bi Jianzhong states that the Nationalists sent three regiments. See Editorial Office of the Nanjing Military Region, *War History of the Third Field Army*, 406; and Bi, "The Causes and Implications of the Setback during the Dengbu Island Combat," 8.

59. Hu and Zheng, "The Conduct of the Cross-Sea Landing Operation against Dengbu Island," 23.

60. 孫祥恩 主編 [Sun Xiangen, ed.], 登步島戰役70周年參戰官兵訪問記錄 [The 70th Anniversary of the Dengbu Island Campaign: A Record of Interviews with Veteran Officers and Troops] (Taipei: Administration Office of the ROC Ministry of National Defense, 2019), 20.

61. 王懷慶 [Wang Huaiqing], "析論1949年金門及登步兩島作戰對國共雙方的影響 與啓示" [An Analysis of the 1949 Jinmen and Dengbu Island Operations and Their Influence and Lessons for the Nationalists and the Communists], 陸軍學術雙月刊 [Army Bimonthly] 55, no. 567 (October 2019): 16. This periodical is published by the ROC Army Headquarters. The author is a colonel of the ROC Army and an instructor at the ROC National Defense University.

62. Wang, "An Analysis of the 1949 Jinmen and Dengbu Island Operations," 16.

63. Editorial Office of the Nanjing Military Region, *War History of the Third Field Army*, 406.

64. Bi, "The Causes and Implications of the Setback during the Dengbu Island Combat," 9–10.

65. Hu and Zheng, "The Conduct of the Cross-Sea Landing Operation against Dengbu Island," 25.

66. Kuang, "Research on Dengbu Island Combat," 123–26.

67. 鄭維中 王懷慶 [Zheng Weizhong and Wang Huaiqing], "1950年國軍舟山轉進作 戰情報作爲與得失啓示" [The 1950 Nationalist Information Operations during the Zhoushan Withdrawal and the Lessons from the Gains and Losses], 陸軍學術 雙月刊 [Army Bimonthly] 56, no. 574 (December 2020), 84.

68. Editorial Office of the Nanjing Military Region, *War History of the Third Field Army*, 408.

69. Zheng and Wang, "The 1950 Nationalist Information Operations during the Zhoushan Transition," 91.

70. It is notable that ROC studies treat the withdrawal from Zhoushan as a major Nationalist operational success, akin to Britain's famous Dunkirk evacuation. 晏楊清 [Yan Yangqing], "國軍撤守舟山轉進臺灣之研究" [Research on Nationalist Withdrawal from Zhoushan and Transition to Taiwan], 軍事史評論 [Military History Review], no. 27 (June 2020): 142–43.

SIX

The Hainan and Wanshan Campaigns

The Fourth Field Army under the legendary commander Lin Biao carried out an amphibious operation against Hainan Island that remains the largest in the PLA's history. Hainan, comparable in size to Taiwan, was viewed as strategic terrain only second in significance to Taiwan. The island was an operational prize that dwarfed Xiaman, Jinmen, and Zhoushan in scale and complexity. Contrasting sharply with the Third Field Army, the preparations for the campaign, including strategy formulation, logistics, and training, were meticulous and methodical. During his visit to Moscow in early 1950, Mao Zedong paid personal attention to the operation and delivered instructions to Lin attesting to the importance Mao attached to conquering Hainan. The multistage campaign, which involved close coordination with indigenous insurgents on the island, showed how the Communists learned from their previous failures and adapted their strategies based on a sound appraisal of themselves and of their adversary.[1] In short, the campaign's success reflected good strategy. The subsequent Wanshan campaign saw the PLA engage in its first joint army-navy operation far from shore support. Both campaigns are remembered today as major milestones in the PLA's combat history.

PREPARATIONS (DECEMBER 18, 1949–MARCH 4, 1950)

On October 2, 1949, the Communists launched the Guangdong campaign. Within two weeks, the 15th Army captured Guangzhou. The surviving Nationalist forces fled southwest. The 4th Army pursued and caught up with the enemy, destroying 40,000 troops near Yangjiang and Yangchun during the Liangyang campaign. The Fourth Field Army drove west into Guangxi Province beginning on November 6. By mid-December, the Communists annihilated 170,000 enemy forces in Guangxi. The remaining survivors, numbering about 20,000, staggered into Vietnam. Only Hainan Island remained out of the CCP's hands in southern China.

Hainan, covering nearly 34,000 square kilometers of territory, is roughly the size of Maryland and at the time of the campaign was home to three

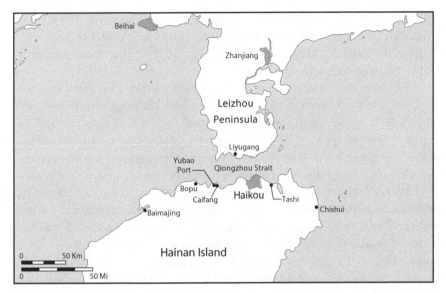

MAP 6.1. Hainan Island campaign, March–May 1950

© Toshi Yoshihara

million people. Qiongzhou Strait separates Hainan from Leizhou Peninsula, an appendage of Guangdong Province. The strait is 11 nautical miles at its narrowest and is 27 nautical miles at its widest, about 10 nautical miles wider than the Strait of Dover. Smooth winds and currents would allow a sailing boat to make the crossing in five to seven hours.[2] To some Chinese strategists, only Taiwan rivaled the geostrategic importance of Hainan in the seaward direction. The Communists feared that the tropical island's size, proximity to the mainland, resource base, and access to the sea would enable the Nationalists to stage a major counteroffensive against the newly established regime on the mainland. Possession of Hainan in turn would give the CCP a commanding position over the maritime approaches to southern China while extending Chinese territory southward into the South China Sea by more than two hundred kilometers.

In December 1949, Generalissimo Chiang Kai-shek appointed Gen. Xue Yue to lead the Hainan Defense Command. Xue divided the island's defense into the northern, eastern, western, and southern sectors and coordinated the land, air, and sea forces to keep the Communists at bay. A force about one hundred thousand strong defended this last bastion in the south.[3] Xue commanded five armies of nineteen divisions, fifty warships from the ROCN's Third Squadron, a marine corps regiment, and four air groups of fighters, bombers, and transports numbering forty-five aircraft.[4] The KMT possessed command of the air and local sea control. In addition to the watery barrier that was at least twice as wide as the channel that separated Jinmen from the mainland, Xue enjoyed strategic depth and room for operational maneuver on Hainan. Coming on the heels of the Jinmen disaster, the bristling defenses on Hainan seemed a formidable challenge to the Communists.

Unlike the rushed operations of the Third Field Army, a key feature of PLA planning for the Hainan campaign was the close consultations between the Fourth Field Army's high command, the local theater commanders, and the political leadership, including Mao and the Central Military Commission. From December 1949, when the discussions of the operation began, to February 1950, Mao telegraphed Lin no fewer than four times. Attesting to the value that Mao attached to the campaign, the correspondence took place during his high-stakes visit to Moscow when he negotiated with Joseph Stalin the future of Sino-Soviet relations. Mao instructed his subordinates to consider a wide range of issues, from the timing of the operation to the size of the invasion force, command arrangements, and shipping equipment.[5] Mao's attention to detail down to the tactical level for the planned Hainan assault contrasted sharply with his apparent silence during the Jinmen campaign.[6]

The Jinmen debacle weighed heavily on Mao. Referring to the Jinmen campaign in his December 18 message to Lin, Mao warned, "You must study this lesson . . . [,] avoid underestimating the enemy . . . [, and] prevent repeating the same mistakes made at Jinmen." Mao instructed Lin to learn directly from Su Yu, the Third Field Army's commander, about the "entire experience" of Jinmen.[7] In the same message, Mao pointed out that "a cross-sea operation is completely different from all of our army's past combat experiences. We must pay attention to tides and wind direction. We must concentrate all forces to transport at least one army (40,000 to 50,000 troops) in a single transit, possess more than 3 days of food, land on the enemy's forward area and establish a firm beachhead, and immediately conduct an independent attack without relying on reinforcements."[8] Mao was clear that half measures and piecemeal improvised efforts that characterized the Jinmen campaign would not be repeated at Hainan.

Determined to employ the best units for the campaign, the Fourth Field Army assigned the 15th Army's 40th Corps and 43rd Corps, numbering about one hundred thousand troops, to spearhead the assault. The two elite corps distinguished themselves in the Liao-Shen and Ping-Jin campaigns that decisively turned the tide of the civil war on the mainland. Each corps would be supported by an artillery regiment, an air defense artillery regiment, and a combat engineering unit. Yet, the Communists still lacked an air force and a navy to protect the amphibious forces. And the landing sites across the strait were well beyond the range of shore-based artillery.

But the Communists had a resident advantage in Hainan. A Communist-led armed group, known as the Qiongya Column (琼崖纵队), had been operating actively on Hainan since the mid-1920s. The insurgents survived for decades in the inaccessible mountainous interior, harassing Japanese occupiers and Nationalist troops alike. By the time of the Japanese surrender in 1945, the guerrilla force had grown to fifteen thousand men and controlled a base area inhabited by half of Hainan's population.[9] By January 1950 Feng Baiju, the column's leader, commanded ten regiments, numbering about twenty-five thousand troops, and controlled up to two-thirds of the territory and two-thirds of the population.[10] To compensate for its inability to project power, the 15th Army coordinated with the Qiongya Column, which boasted superior knowledge of local conditions, to facilitate the amphibious landings. The Communists also hoped that diversionary attacks and sabotage by the irregular forces on Hainan would threaten the KMT's rear areas, drawing some of its attention away from the seaward direction.

From mid-December through January, commanders and planners of the 15th Army debated their options for seizing Hainan. They gathered as much information as they could about the local conditions surrounding the island and examined the various amphibious operations in the European and Pacific theaters of operations during World War II. The commanders and planners also studied the Third Field Army's failures at Jinmen in October 1949.[11] They met repeatedly to hash out the operational details and engaged in frank discussions about the risks and benefits of their evolving strategy and then briefed the Fourth Field Army leadership in Wuhan and the Central Military Commission in Beijing about their findings and recommendations. These consultations helped the 15th Army obtain support from the top leadership about its proposed plan of attack.

In early February, the 15th Army convened a commanders' conference in Guangzhou to reach consensus on the overall direction of the upcoming campaign. The participants first engaged in a net assessment of the military balance.[12] On the one hand, certain conditions favored the Communists. The Nationalists on Hainan were mostly troops defeated on the mainland. The best units had already been wiped out in earlier phases of the civil war. They were outsiders on the island, had few intrinsic stakes in defending territory that was not their hometown, were unfamiliar with local circumstances, and suffered from low morale. The Communists, by contrast, boasted high morale following the conquest of the Chinese heartland and possessed superior warfighting skills. They also enjoyed the support of the Qiongya Column and large elements of the local population. This indigenous grassroots movement could help to tilt the balance. On the other hand, the Nationalists had control of the air and the sea and possessed qualitatively superior weaponry, while the Communists had no naval power or sea power to speak of. And significantly, the PLA lacked experience in large-scale amphibious operations.

After debating the strengths and weaknesses of each side, the conferees considered ways to exploit Nationalist weaknesses and minimize Communist weaknesses while playing on PLA strengths. The participants homed in on basic geography. Unlike the small island of Jinmen, Hainan is big. The coast directly facing the Leizhou Peninsula alone is more than seventy kilometers wide. Despite the seemingly impressive numbers on the island, the Nationalists simply did not have the manpower and the naval assets to monitor and defend the entire coastline. Hainan's shores were therefore far more porous than they appeared. Yet, it was unlikely that the Communists could conscript and build enough shipping to transport troops across the strait in a single transit by the spring or early summer of 1950, the anticipated time frame for the campaign. Even if they could somehow produce such a fleet, a large and concentrated amphibious force would have been vulnerable to Nationalist air and naval interdiction in the absence of a strong Communist navy and air force to cover the sea crossing.

The commanders and planners thus arrived at a novel solution to the operational problem. They would rely on secrecy, deception, and surprise to exploit the permeable character of the Nationalist defense perimeter while minimizing their exposure to the KMT's superiority in technology and firepower. And they would fall back on a core tenet of their warfighting strategy: people's war. They agreed on the guideline of "actively smuggle across, make small transits in batches, and combine forces during the final landing [积极偷渡, 分批小渡 与最后登陆相结合]," which the Central Military Commission subsequently approved.[13] It was an innovative and audacious plan. According to the directive, the 40th and 43rd Corps would initially slip units across the Qiongzhou Strait to test and probe enemy defenses. After landing on Hainan, these advance teams would join up with the Qiongya Column and, in cooperation with the guerrilla forces, harass, distract, and tie down Nationalist forces on the island. By drawing KMT defenders away from defensive strongpoints along the coast, the Communists hoped to create more favorable conditions for the main assault on the island.[14]

To ensure success, the Communists engaged in meticulous planning and painstaking preparations. First, they acclimated the officers and troops to the entirely new operational environment. Many from the hinterlands did not know how to swim, much less cope with undertow, waves, and surf. Many were complete strangers to the ocean, and the sight of the seas frightened them. They worried incessantly about the boats overturning and being drowned. In the eyes of the local commanders, they were also excessively fearful of Nationalist airpower and naval power. To restore confidence in these elite units, the Communists turned to their playbook of political indoctrination to reeducate their forces.[15]

Second, the 15th Army intensified intelligence work. The 40th and 43rd Corps established coastal surveillance stations to monitor Nationalist traffic at sea and in the air to discern patterns in behavior. They stood up meteorological survey teams to better understand and predict the hydrology around the Qiong-zhou Strait. Frogmen disguised as fishermen infiltrated deep behind enemy lines to gather local intelligence about the disposition of Nationalist defenders.[16] The Communists linked up with the Qiongya Column and instructed the guerrillas to gather as much information about the enemy as possible.

Third, the 15th Army scrambled to assemble a fleet capable of transporting at least fifty thousand troops under the command of the two corps. Like the predicament of the Third Field Army, the Fourth Field Army faced an acute shortage of boats. During their retreat from the mainland to Taiwan, Nation-alist forces had denuded the area of vessels to deprive their adversary of the means to transit by sea. During the KMT's evacuation of southern China, its forces brought many seagoing ships to Taiwan and destroyed those that they could not send to its main island stronghold. Many local fishermen opposed to Communist rule buried, hid, or scuttled their boats to preclude their use.

Initially unit commanders, under pressure to act quickly, dispatched troops to forcibly conscript operable boats in the area. The effort apparently back-fired owing to strong resistance among the local population. The two corps then resorted to renting boats from the residents, producing about six hun-dred vessels in a month. They also requisitioned boats from recently conquered territory such as Weizhou Island, west of the Leizhou Peninsula in the Gulf of Tonkin. It appears that the 15th Army had to fall back on coercion to seize boats from the surrounding communities to meet its needs. Over the course of three months, the Communists mobilized some four thousand boatmen and about two thousand vessels for the operation.[17] Attesting to the anticipated scale of the operation, this amphibious force dwarfed the flotilla assembled for the Jinmen and Zhoushan campaigns under the Third Field Army. In the meantime, the Communists sought to motorize as many of the wooden sailing boats as they could.

Fourth, the two corps engaged in intensive training to ready the force for the rigors of at-sea operations. The troops took crash courses to obtain basic sail-ing and navigational skills. Many had to learn how to swim. The Communists had to raise a new cohort of sailors to handle the boats. Given that the boats came in various sizes and conditions, the trainees practiced techniques to stay in formation against changing winds and tides. The assault troops repeatedly rehearsed ways to assemble at prepared sites and embark on ships in an orderly and efficient fashion. They developed ploys to camouflage vessels along the coasts, tactics against air and naval interdiction, and various communications methods while in transit. As the force improved, the units conducted exercises to sharpen such skills as small-scale landings, major amphibious assaults, and combat at sea.[18] The vigorous and rigorous training heightened morale and confidence among the troops, many of whom had initially recoiled from the prospects of fighting at sea.

Fifth, the Communists emplaced long-range coastal artillery and air defense units along the shores of the Leizhou Peninsula to protect their ships and troops training in the area from the Nationalist navy and air force. The 28th Artillery Regiment positioned an artillery battalion on the southeastern, south-central, and southwestern sectors of the peninsula. Each battalion fielded heavy guns that boasted maximum ranges of thirteen to fourteen kilometers covering the northern portions of the Qiongzhou Strait.[19] The 1st Air Defense Regiment protected the airspace over ports, ships, troops training at sea, and the artillery positions on the Leizhou coast. These deployments effectively ended Nationalist air and naval raids against the assembling Communist forces.[20]

Sixth, the 15th Army mobilized the local industries and communities to provide rear-area support. Nationalized factories lent their facilities, engineers, technicians, and workers to modify and repair boats and parts. Spare fuel of all kinds and essentials at sea, such as life jackets, were requisitioned. The local government in Guangzhou formed committees to register and keep track of conscripted vessels. In three months, the Communists had mobilized almost a million civilians to engage in infrastructure work; repaired or restored over 3,000 kilometers of roads, 96 bridges, and 6 ferry crossing points; expropriated 37.5 million kilograms of food; and acquired some 45,000 ox-drawn carts to transport supplies and ammunition.[21]

Finally, the 15th Army directed the Qiongya Column to prepare for the landings. The guerrillas began to fight back more aggressively against the Nationalists' counterinsurgency campaign intended to wipe out the column and its supporters on Hainan and also began to accelerate hit-and-run attacks to tie down frontline KMT units. In addition, the guerrillas engaged in sabotage warfare to disrupt Nationalist operations and to destroy various defensive works and positions along the coast. They also mobilized local populations to facilitate the expected arrival of Communist forces. An underground network drawn from various communities geared up to provide logistical support, ambulatory and medical assistance, local guides for arriving units from the mainland, and resupply of food and ammunition and to stand watch against enemy movements and supply on-the-ground intelligence.[22] Such attention to detail on issues big and small stood in sharp contrast to the rushed and precarious approach of the Third Field Army.

PRELUDE TO THE MAIN OFFENSIVE (MARCH 5–APRIL 1, 1950)

In early March 1950, the Communists were ready to commence the campaign. The 15th Army assigned the 40th Corps and the 43rd Corps each to sneak a reinforced battalion across the strait on March 5. The two battalions, one drawn from the 352nd Regiment of the 40th Corps and the other from the 383rd Regiment of the 43rd Corps, would make the first passage. The battalions would avoid frontal assaults against the coast opposite Leizhou Peninsula, which was closest to the mainland but also the most heavily fortified part of the island's defense perimeter. Instead, they would sail farther down the coast to land forces behind the enemy on the eastern and western sides of Hainan in a pincer-like movement. This stowaway operation would serve as proof of concept developed in February.

One reason for the assault was the need to reinforce the Qiongya Column on Hainan. Beginning in the summer of 1949, the Nationalists launched a series of counterinsurgency operations to clear and suppress the irregular armed group. But these initial campaigns proved ineffective. After assuming command of the island's defenses in December 1949, Gen. Xue Yue developed a comprehensive plan to roll back the Qiongya's positions. The Nationalist commander understood that he faced a two-front war. He had to balk the growing amphibious threat on the Leizhou Peninsula and squeeze the insurgent movement within Hainan. To disrupt Qiongya's ability to link up with the Communists from the mainland, Xue's forces conducted a series of sweeps deep into Hainan's interior in February 1950. According to one ROC campaign history, the offensives proved quite effective. The Nationalists defeated and forced the retreat of the insurgents in multiple engagements in early March.[23] The initial Communist effort to transport forces to the island was designed in part to relieve the growing military pressure on Qiongya.[24]

On the night of the assault on March 5, there was no wind where the 43rd Corps had embarked its troops. It was decided that the 40th Corps would proceed as planned and that the 43rd Corps would launch its assault whenever the wind picked up again. It was thought that the staggered arrival of units might confuse the enemy. About eight hundred troops of the 352nd Regiment set sail aboard thirteen boats on their own that evening. The wind ceased at midnight after the crew had been at sea for more than four hours, so they had to row. When the transports encountered ten Nationalist motorized patrol craft and four aircraft overhead, they disguised themselves as fishing boats and avoided detection.

It was not until early afternoon the following day that the small flotilla transited over forty nautical miles to arrive off Hainan's northwest coast near Baimajing. As the boats approached the shoreline, two KMT naval vessels and four fighters discovered their presence and opened fire on them. Nationalist forces ashore also trained their guns on the vessels. The battalion pressed on, landed, seized the beachhead, and advanced immediately inland, defeating two coastal defense units along the way. On May 7, the battalion linked up with two regiments of the Qiongya Column. The successful experiment validated a key element of the Communist strategy and buoyed confidence among those preparing to cross the seas.[25]

On March 10, a reinforced battalion from the 43rd Corps' 383rd Regiment and an infantry artillery company, numbering about one thousand troops, finally found the right wind conditions to set sail. The twenty-one wooden sailing boats were to transit over fifty nautical miles to land on the northeast coast of Hainan near Chishui Port. Light rain and low visibility meant that the flotilla would be safe from Nationalist airpower. But the vessels ran into a night squall: six boats lost their masts, and two boats overturned, with one hundred aboard lost to the seas. After battling the storm for ten hours, the flotilla finally disembarked its troops at the designated area. The forces defeated a Nationalist coastal defense garrison and linked up with an independent regiment of the Qiongya Column. Two KMT battalions then gave chase. The Communists managed to escape the pursuers, destroying an enemy battalion in the process. The infiltrators, assisted by the irregulars, reached their haven in Hainan's interior under Qiongya's control.[26]

With these successes, the Communists gambled on a more direct line of attack for their second attempt. The 15th Army directed the 40th Corps and the 43rd Corps each to put ashore a reinforced regiment on the east and west sides of Haikou, the largest city on Hainan, located directly across from the Leizhou Peninsula. The proximity of the targets and the shallow beaches of the landing zones favored the attackers. Friendly guerrilla forces also maintained a strong presence in the area. However, Haikou was home to the headquarters of the Nationalist military command and was the most heavily defended city on the island. Better road infrastructure would also allow the defenders to bring in reinforcements much more rapidly. The Communist commanders decided that it was still worth a gamble.

On March 26, the 40th Corps embarked two battalions of the 352nd Regiment and a battalion of the 353rd Regiment, totaling 2,900 men, aboard eighty-one boats. The flotilla was to conduct an overnight transit sixteen nautical miles to landing areas just west of Haikou around Lingao Point. About an hour after the boats set sail, the winds and currents changed direction and forced the crew to row, substantially slowing progress. To make matters worse, poor visibility precluded communications via light signals. Relying only on radios, the boats were unable to determine each other's relative positions and courses. The forces afloat lost unified command and struggled to maintain formation.[27] When the scattered flotilla neared the coast, the tactical commanders discovered that the boats had gone well off course to the east of the landing zone. The boats reassembled off Yubao Port at daybreak on March 27. Many boats had to rely on visual contact with the shoreline to navigate toward the rallying point.

The commanders calculated that it would take two to three more hours to reach Lingao Point to the west. But the forces risked being discovered by Nationalist naval and air patrols in daylight hours. It was thus decided that they would land wherever they could to avoid interdiction. The flotilla haphazardly disembarked its troops along a twenty-kilometer front with little to no coordinated command. The units fought their way past coastal defenders and pushed their way inland. In the meantime, a fierce battle raged near the rendezvous point where the incoming Communists troops were supposed to be met by friendly insurgents operating behind enemy lines. The Qiongya Column and the 352nd Regiment's battalion that had landed in early March were to link up with the newcomers. Instead, they ran into stiff Nationalist resistance near Lingao Point. They eventually disengaged, joined up with new arrivals on March 29 at Meihou Village nearly fifty kilometers inland, and proceeded to Qiongya's base area. The flotilla lost one boat to a Nationalist warship, and several boats were lost at sea in transit.[28]

The 43rd Corps assigned the 379th Regiment and a battalion from the 381st Regiment, numbering over 3,700 troops, to transit about twenty-two nautical miles and conduct their assault on a sector near Tashi, more than twenty kilometers east of Haikou. On March 31, the troops boarded eighty-eight fishing boats and set sail at about eleven o'clock in the evening. The flotilla was composed of two escort groups that flanked each side of the amphibious force.

Before midnight, Nationalist patrol boats began to approach the fleet. Following a brief exchange of fire, the KMT vessels retreated. Then the wind changed direction, slowing the boats to a crawl. It was at this moment of vulnerability that the Nationalists dispatched a much larger naval force from Haikou. Five boats on escort duty belonging to the 5th Company of the 379th Regiment peeled away from the main body and charged at the closest oncoming KMT warship. Each seven-meter-long wooden vessel carried a reinforced squad armed with mortars, rocket launchers, grenade launchers, and satchel charges that the Communists had seized from surrendered Nationalists troops.[29] The crews had no choice but to close the distance to get within range. As they drew near under heavy enemy bombardment, the troops held their fire, maintaining impressive discipline. At about one hundred meters from the target, they unleashed their first salvo and launched another at about seventy meters.[30] The damaged Nationalist vessel turned and fled. Forty-five troops aboard three ships were killed in the exchange.[31]

Similar scenes of melee continued for about two more hours before it was decided that the amphibious force would advance to the landing zone, leaving behind the escorts. It was hoped that the escorts would tie down the Nationalist warships, allowing the transports to escape and disgorge the troops ashore. The wind picked up, and the transports were finally able to approach the shores of Tashi at five o'clock in the morning on April 1. The ships then ran into a hail of artillery shells from KMT positions along the coast. Under intense bombardment, the troops charged ashore to suppress enemy fire. As they fought through the first line of defense, the 383rd Regiment that had landed twenty days earlier and an element of the Qiongya Column attacked the enemy's rear. Threatened on two fronts, Nationalist resistance collapsed. The Communists then joined up and fought their way to a base area in the interior.[32]

The cross-sea assault proved costly for some. Four of the escorts, which attempted to fend off the Nationalist warships in an earlier encounter, went off course and landed two companies near Haikou, the enemy stronghold. The Nationalists pounced on these exposed forces. Surrounded and under heavy fire from land, sea, and air, the units fought desperately for two days. They exhausted their ammunition and food and were eventually overrun.[33] Only eighteen troops survived the ordeal.[34] These and other experiences over the course of the two crossings demonstrated the potential high costs of landing forces when a determined opponent contests both the waters and the shores. Despite the difficulties of each voyage, the 40th Corps and the 43rd Corps had managed to slip across two reinforced battalions, one battalion, and two regiments totaling about eight thousand men. By early April the 15th Army had an advance force, nearly the size of a full division, on Hainan that was well positioned to prepare the way for the main assault.

However, it is likely that the PLA writings have downplayed the extent of Communist losses during this stage of the campaign. One ROC study notes that the Nationalists inflicted about 500 casualties against the 383rd Regiment and elements of the Qiongya Column on March 17.[35] During the fighting against the 352nd and 353rd Regiments near Yubao Port on March 27, the Nationalists reportedly killed some 950 troops, wounded more than 120 others, and captured some 171.[36] According to the KMT's account, the two companies that had mistakenly landed near Haikou on April 1 fought tenaciously against the island defenders. But the threat of annihilation and adept Nationalist psychological warfare convinced many Communists to surrender.[37] In this version of events, the two companies did not resist as heroically as the PLA literature has portrayed them in the battle. From mid-February to the eve of the main cross-sea assault on April 15, the Nationalists purportedly sank 197 boats, killed or captured some 8,000 Communist troops, and failed to keep out about 1,900 infiltrators.[38]

CIA reporting at the time, likely based on Nationalist intelligence, shows that the Communists probably suffered more losses than depicted in the official PLA histories. In late January, Nationalist naval raids damaged Communist vessels near Beihai, Guangxi, and Anpu, Guangdong, while one patrol intercepted a boat on Hainan's east coast. In early February, a Nationalist warship sank over 60 vessels near Beihai.[39] Between early January and late February, according to one CIA report, the ROCN destroyed 122 boats, seized 10 boats, and captured 75 PLA officers and men.[40] Still another noted that the first amphibious assault launched on March 5 was only "partially successful." Of the 2,000 troops who landed on Hainan, only 300–400 linked up with the Qiongya Column and escaped into the interior. The rest were killed, wounded, or captured.[41] CIA reports issued in late March recorded that the ROC Army, Navy, and Air Force continued to intercept and sink junks carrying troops and supplies to Hainan.[42] In one case, defenders on Hainan's west coast repulsed a night landing by ten junks carrying 1,000 enemy troops.[43] Just before the main Communist invasion in mid-April, the Nationalists captured 1,000 men, including a regimental political commissar, following the defection of an entire flotilla.[44]

THE DECISIVE SEA CROSSING (APRIL 16–MAY 1, 1950)

On April 10, the Communists convened a commanders' conference for the final cross-sea offensive. The participants developed an overall plan for the frontal assault. The 40th and 43rd Corps would concentrate all their manpower in the effort. The 40th Corps would call on the entire 119th Division, the 118th Division's 354th Regiment, two battalions from the 353rd Regiment, and the 358th Regiment of the 120th Division. The 43rd Corps would employ the 128th Division's 382nd and 383rd Regiments and one battalion from the 384th Regiment. Totaling twenty-five thousand men, these forces would constitute the first wave of the amphibious landings. The units under the 40th Corps would be responsible for the western sector of the landing zone, while the 43rd Corps would oversee the advance on the eastern sector. Maniao harbor, about forty-five kilometers west of Haikou, would serve as the rough dividing line between the western and eastern sectors.[45] The Communists had clearly learned from past failures such as those during the Jinmen and Zhoushan campaigns, when one corps was given command responsibilities over units of a different corps.[46]

Echelon forces, under the command of the 43rd Corps, would follow the first wave. The reinforcements would be composed of the 380th Regiment, two battalions from the 381st Regiment, two battalions from the 384th Regiment, the 385th Regiment, and the 386th Regiment, numbering nearly twenty thousand troops. The Qiongya Column and the advance forces from the 40th Corps would push toward Lingao to support and link up with the arriving units of the 40th Corps in the western sector. Another Qiongya group and the advance team from the 43rd Corps would similarly drive north to assist with the landings on the eastern sector. Other irregular units would cut roads and blow up bridges to immobilize the Nationalists, while others would conduct diversionary attacks to draw the enemy's attention away from the main offensive and tie down resources.

In each sector, the Communists would seek to punch through the frontline defenses; cut across the main bodies of the enemy's army, slicing them into separate segments; and encircle each segment. Part of the goal was to lure Nationalist reinforcements toward the isolated pockets in which their besieged comrades would be trapped. As the rescuers neared those pockets, the Communists would mass forces against them in battles of annihilation to progressively wear down the Nationalists. This operational concept replicated that employed during the major civil war campaigns on the mainland.

On April 16, the Communists launched the main assault. The troops, assembled in areas east and west of Liyugang on the south coast of Leizou, embarked on some 380 wooden sailing boats and a small number of motorized vessels.[47] The flotillas of the 40th Corps and the 43rd Corps departed their ports simultaneously at around 7:30 p.m. Given the scale of the operation, Communist preparations for the launch were visible to the Nationalists. The defenders were thus ready. The moment the transports sailed halfway across the strait, KMT warships and aircraft began to interdict the amphibious force. Troops aboard the boats directed small-arms fire against the aircraft, while "escort firepower boats [护航火力船]" steered toward the Nationalist combatants. The crews on the Communist vessels employed their night fighting skills and close combat to negate the technological superiority of their adversary.[48] They maneuvered into the blind spots of the larger warships and concentrated their fire on vital targets, such as the ship's bridge. After three hours of engagement, the wooden boats managed to heavily damage the KMT's *Taikang* frigate, the flagship of the Third Squadron.[49]

In the early hours of April 17, the flotilla broke through the blockade and neared Hainan's shores.[50] Between 2:00 and 4:00 a.m., the 43rd Corps successfully seized a beachhead between Yubao harbor and Caifang harbor. Following closely behind, the 40th Corps landed along the beaches near Bopu harbor between 3:30 and 6:00 a.m. on its designated western sector. Events unfolded quickly after the Communists waded ashore. The 40th Corps defeated two Nationalist battalions, overran a series of fortifications, and seized the strategic high ground at Gaoshan Ridge. Another element of the corps surrounded Lingao township, while the main force dashed southward. By April 19, the 40th Corps had advanced about thirty kilometers inland in a series of encirclement and annihilation battles. In the meantime, the 43rd Corps took Caifang Ridge and pushed south, surrounding Huachang Village.

To prevent the Communists from severing Haikou's communications to the west, the Nationalists rushed forces to defend Fushan. The combined forces of the newly arrived PLA units and the advance team that landed in March defeated the approaching reinforcements while another overstrength battalion occupied Fushan, about fifteen kilometers from the coast.[51] The decision to smuggle troops across the strait in March proved prudent: the resulting shift in the tactical balance allowed the Communists to overpower or preempt the Nationalists.

The KMT command rushed five divisions to Meitin and Chengmai to stop the eastward advance of the 43rd Corps from Fushan toward Haikou. Sensing an opportunity to engage in a decisive battle, the Communists ordered the 40th Corps to swing its forces toward Chengmai and ordered the 43rd Corps to head toward Bailian and Meitin to cut off and annihilate Nationalist reinforcements destined for Chengmai. Three regiments and a battalion of the 43rd Corps reached and held their positions at Huangzhu and Meitin located along the route to Chengmai. Another element of the corps occupied high ground in the same area. On the morning of April 20, Nationalist ground forces with the aid of airpower collided into these two components of the 43rd Corps and encircled them, leading to intense attacks and counterattacks.

The 40th Corps first reached Chengmai on the morning of April 21 and then redirected its main units toward Meitin to relieve the surrounded 43rd Corps. The 40th Corps' forces split into two prongs and attacked the Nationalist flanks from the east and west in a counterencirclement. The KMT offensive stalled and then began to crumble. Realizing that they had been outmaneuvered, the Nationalists retreated headlong back to Haikou. One KMT regiment, unable to break the Communist siege, was completely wiped out. The 40th Corps and the 43rd Corps joined forces and gave chase. Nationalist resistance quickly collapsed thereafter. On April 23, the Communists entered Haikou's outskirts and then captured the city that morning. The previous day, Nationalist general Xue Yue issued an order to abandon northern Hainan, including Haikou, and to withdraw forces to more defensible positions along southern sectors of the island.[52] Xue also requested the dispatch of naval vessels to Yulin on Hainan's southernmost tip to prepare for the evacuation of his troops.

On the evening of April 23 the Communists launched the second wave of troops, directing it against Haikou. The troops landed in succession between 1:00 and 4:00 a.m. on April 24 along the coast of Tianwei harbor west of Haikou. With the entire force assembled ashore, the balance of power shifted dramatically in the Communists' favor. Sensing collapse in Nationalist morale and strength, the 15th Army embarked on a full-court press to pursue, search, and destroy the remaining enemy forces. Leaving behind two regiments to hold Haikou, the rest of the army shifted to an all-out offensive. They raced south to major ports to cut off the Nationalist retreat by sea. A combined force of the 40th Corps and the 43rd Corps along with elements of the Qiongya Column pushed down the east coast to reach Yulin. Another component of the 43rd

Corps cut through the middle of the island and headed toward Beili and Basuo located on the southwest coast, while a reinforced battalion of the 40th Corps went by sea along the west coast to reach Beili and Basuo.[53]

On their three-pronged drive south, the Communists rapidly smashed through feeble Nationalist defenses or caught up to those seeking to escape the island. One unit sped south toward Yulin in 40 vehicles captured from surrendered enemy forces. By May 1, the Communists obtained control over the entire island of Hainan. Over the course of nearly two months, they destroyed five divisions numbering about 33,000 men, including the capture of nearly 25,000 troops. The ROCN evacuated about 50,000 personnel from Hainan to Taiwan.[54] Nationalist equipment, including 481 artillery pieces, 4 aircraft, 7 tanks and armored personnel carriers, and 140 vehicles, fell into Communist hands. During the campaign, the Communists shot down 2 aircraft, sank 1 warship, and damaged 5 other vessels.[55] About 4,500 troops under the 15th Army were killed or missing in action.[56]

The Fourth Field Army's official history attributes the operational success to four factors. First, the 15th Army coordinated and consulted closely with the Central Military Commission and the Fourth Field Army leadership on such key issues as timing, scale, transportation methods, and tactics of the enormous amphibious undertaking. Second, the local commanders prepared meticulously for the assault. They dedicated significant time and resources to conscript shipping and seamen, indoctrinate the troops, and train the forces for the sea crossings. Third, PLA planners carefully assessed all the relevant factors that had bearing on the campaign, including the weather, the tides, the geographical and meteorological conditions, the landing zones, the strengths and weaknesses of the Nationalists, the local population on Hainan, and so forth. At the same time, they closely studied themselves to maximize the command and control of forces, ensure the unity of command, and strengthen the independent ability of seagoing forces to operate and land troops. Finally, they relied on the locals to obtain critical resources, including ships, skilled sailors, supplies, and food. Above all, the Qiongya Column on Hainan proved indispensable to shifting the military balance. Indeed, the indigenous insurgents tied up nearly half of the Nationalists' manpower.[57]

According to one ROC account, the victory may have had as much to do with fatal Nationalist weakness as with superior Communist strategy. On paper, the Hainan Defense Command boasted as many as 160,000 troops, including navy and air force personnel. But the five armies and three divisions under Gen. Xue Yue's command were severely undermanned. Field inspections later revealed that Xue may have only had 70,000 to 80,000 active troops, about half of the official figures. The Nationalist defenders were armed with aging equipment. They lacked adequate ammunition, spare parts, medical supplies, and heavy weaponry. American aid had ceased, adding to the material woes. The KMT's main forces were also stretched thin, divided as they were between Taiwan, Zhoushan, and Hainan. Reinforcements and reallocation of resources were simply not forthcoming.[58] Under the circumstances, it was perhaps inevitable that the Nationalist resistance collapsed so quickly and so completely once the main Communist assault took place.

THE WANSHAN CAMPAIGN (MAY 25–AUGUST 4, 1950)

The Wanshan Islands are located about ten nautical miles south of Hong Kong's Lantau Island and due southeast of Zhuhai. The archipelago, comprising forty-eight islands and rocks, lies astride critical sea lines of communications near the Pearl River estuary, the epicenter of maritime commerce in southern China. The islands also enclose the main entrance to Guangzhou, a major economic hub. They could serve as a gateway or barrier to Communist China's seaborne trade.

Some elements of the Nationalist forces defeated on the mainland retreated to Wanshan in December 1949. The KMT's high command decided to use the islands as a base for counteroffensive operations against nearby Communist forces and targets along the coast. The Nationalists established a command center on Lajiwei Island that oversaw a marine battalion, an armed fishing flotilla, and naval combatants drawn from the Third Squadron. The navy there performed blockade duty against seaborne traffic around the Pearl River delta and safeguarded the sea-lanes connecting Taiwan and Hainan. The navy also engaged in harassment operations along the Guangdong coast.[59]

After Hainan Island fell in May 1950, the KMT reinforced the garrison on Wanshan by dispatching additional marines, an army battalion, four companies that had evacuated Hainan, and local militia totaling some three thousand men. The Nationalist flotilla consisted of frigates, minesweepers, and landing craft numbering about thirty combatants.[60] Units based on the islands were well positioned to blockade nearby waters, disrupt local fishing and seaborne trade, and conduct harassing attacks on the mainland.

Recognizing the potential threat that the Nationalists posed to the security and economic recovery of the region, Mao decided it was time to "concentrate power to clean up our doorstep."[61] The Central Military Commission and the Fourth Field Army directed the 15th Army's Guangdong Military Region Riverine Defense Command to oversee the campaign. The operation would be undertaken by forces drawn from different services, regions, and commands.

The 15th Army assigned the battle-hardened 392nd Regiment and the 393rd Regiment of the 44th Corps to spearhead the assault. In addition, the joint and combined force included naval units under the riverine command,

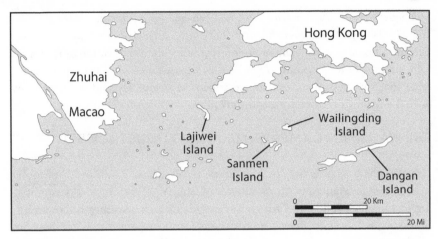

MAP 6.2. Wanshan Islands campaign, May–August 1950

© Toshi Yoshihara

numbering twenty-nine combatants; an artillery regiment from the Pearl River military subregion; an artillery battalion from the 139th Division; an artillery company from the South Central Military Region; an artillery company drawn from the 50th Corps; and an artillery company of the 130th Division totaling some ten thousand men.[62]

The joint army-navy team decided to concentrate forces with utmost speed, actively prepare for landing operations, strike early, and hit fast. The main tasks for the navy were to attack enemy warships, transport and put ashore army units, and defend the sea-lanes.[63] Specifically, the naval flotilla would spearhead the offensive by transiting at night, conducting surprise attacks against enemy units in their home ports, engaging in close-in night combat, and screening the amphibious assault forces.[64] Through these sudden raids the Communists hoped to progressively seize islands, using captured islands as the basis for taking the next set of islands.

While the operational orders were clear, the Communists' capacity to implement the plans was not straightforward. The riverine command's navy, such as it was, possessed only a handful of seaworthy vessels. It had just two ships that could be counted as surface combatants: a World War II–era American-built infantry landing ship displacing 358 tons, armed with two guns, and an unarmed British-made landing craft dating from World War I. In addition to these ships, five gunboats and nine small landing craft would form the task force for the mission.[65] Most of the officers and men were drawn from the army, while former Nationalist naval personnel constituted a portion of the manpower. Many of the ground pounders had never seen the ocean before.

Beginning on May 8, 1950, the various elements of the assault force assembled at Zhongshan, located north of Zhuhai on the western shores of the Pearl River estuary. Over the course of two weeks they planned, prepared, and trained for the operation.[66]

In the wee hours of May 25, sixteen combatants and eight civilian transports left Tangjia Bay located just north of Zhuhai and headed toward Lajiwei Island, home to the KMT's main garrison. The riverine command divided the amphibious assault force into a "firepower fleet [火力船队]" that would attack enemy ships at anchor and a transport flotilla that would put troops ashore.[67] The firepower fleet would split into two spears to tie down KMT ships anchored off Lajiwei, while the transports would be afforded the chance to land troops on Qingzhou and Sanjiao Islands, located less than six nautical miles west of Lajiwei. These two islands would then serve as launch pads for an eastward offensive.

The expedition started off badly. Owing to the lack of experience in navigation and poor communications equipment, the two groups lost contact with each other despite a short transit distance of just twenty nautical miles. Each group was on its own without the benefit of mutual support. To make matters worse, the lead escort, the *Jiefang*, reached Mawan harbor at Lajiwei well ahead of its own group before dawn. Finding itself alone among some thirty much larger warships at anchor, the landing craft nevertheless crept into the port undetected. The 28-ton boat closed to about one hundred meters of the 1,240-ton KMT flagship *Taihe* and opened fire. The Nationalists were completely caught off guard. In the ensuing clash, the outgunned *Jiefang* suffered grievous losses, with thirteen casualties out of a crew of nineteen. After losing its guns to enemy fire, the boat retreated to the open sea.[68]

Another Communist landing craft, the *Guishan*, caught up to the *Jiefang* and entered Mawan harbor as the fighting broke out. The ship's captain decided to reposition the vessel to intercept Nationalist ships fleeing the port. However, as soon as day broke it became clear to the KMT defenders that they faced only two small vessels. They thus poured their fire into the *Jiefang* and the *Guishan*.[69] While the *Jiefang* was able to escape, the *Guishan* was not so lucky. After taking multiple hits to the hull and deck, the ship caught fire and started to take on water. With the commanding officer dead and with over half the crew killed or maimed, the ship diverted and beached itself at Lajiwei's Diaoting Bay. The surviving troops aboard had no choice but to storm the island. They engaged in a bloody, hopeless assault and were cut down to the last man.[70]

Meanwhile, in waters just east of Lajiwei, the gunboats *Xianfeng* and *Fendou* encountered two enemy patrol boats and immediately closed in on the combatants. At nearly point-blank range, the *Xianfeng*'s crew threw grenades aboard the KMT vessel and then stormed it with bayoneted rifles to engage in hand-to-hand combat.[71] The Nationalists quickly surrendered. The other boat tried to flee the scene, but the *Fendou* caught up to the boat and sank it.

The initial sneak attack against Mawan harbor and the subsequent engagements took a surprisingly outsize toll on the Nationalists. Major combatants including the *Taihe*, an amphibious assault vessel, and a minesweeper took serious hits. One gunboat was sunk, while virtually all other ships suffered some damage. In the confusion of the battle the Nationalist ships withdrew from Lajiwei, retiring to Taiwan for repairs. However, the tactical outcome may not have been as lopsided as the PLA writings suggest. According to a CIA report, the Nationalists captured two hundred enemy troops, seized one steamer, and sank nine gunboats during this initial encounter.[72]

With the seas largely uncontested around the western and central segments of the archipelago, the Communists began to seize and occupy various island features. On the opening day of the campaign, amphibious assault ships successfully landed troops on Qingzhou and Sanjiao Islands, rendering the rest of the Nationalist positions untenable. Indeed, Lajiwei, Dazhizhou and Xiaozhizhou Islands, Datouzhou Island, and Hetan Island fell in quick succession from May 26 to 28.

As the Communists progressively ate away at Nationalist holdings, they were able to parry enemy counterattacks. On May 29 after running into a KMT picket ship, a Communist landing craft, No. 509, trained a mountain artillery piece on the enemy combatant, forcing it to retreat. The following day, four Nationalist warships approached Sanjiao Island from the west and began shelling Communist positions there. The defenders waited until the vessels were two nautical miles from shore before unleashing a fusillade of gunfire that damaged three combatants. On May 31, the Communists put ashore a reinforced platoon that captured Dongao Island. Five days later, Dawanshan and Xiaowanshan Islands, Baili Island, Zhuzhou Island, and Hengzhou Island fell to amphibious assaults. On June 10, two platoons waded ashore and captured Aizhou Island.

These Communist advances compelled the Nationalists to fall back to Wailingding Island, ten nautical miles east of Lajiwei, and to Dangan Island, the last line of defense. The Nationalists also deployed the First Squadron in place of the battered Third Squadron. The KMT committed a sizable force comprising some ten surface combatants, including a destroyer, two frigates, two landing craft, four minesweepers, and multiple gunboats. These vessels sought to lure the Communists into an open sea engagement without much success. They also shelled enemy positions on the islands and interdicted transports on their way to resupply and reinforce the garrisons across the archipelago.

During the first half of June the Communists took an operational pause to regroup and draw lessons from the previous fighting, including the difficulties with unity of command during the attack on Lajiwei Island. To ensure improved coordination for the next phase of the campaign, the leadership formed an interim joint organization that could assert unified command over the infantry, artillery, and naval units.[73] During this lull, local commanders set up observation posts on Aizhou and Zhizhou Islands to discern patterns in KMT patrols. To answer the Nationalist harassment, the riverine command formed a new flotilla comprising three amphibious assault ships, a landing craft, a barge, and a tugboat. The command retrofitted all the vessels with the army's guns, turning them into mobile artillery platforms at sea. Most unorthodox, the tugboat was assigned to pull the barge bristling with cannon pieces.

The Communists were now ready for the next move. On the night of June 27, the flotilla quietly cruised from Aizhou Island to the unoccupied Sanmen Island, less than four nautical miles to the east and just over three nautical miles south of Wailingding. The ships put ashore infantry and artillery units on Sanmen under the cover of night and then positioned themselves for battle. The ground forces worked through the night to set up their firing positions. The KMT forces were unaware of these surreptitious movements and the trap that awaited them.

The following morning as a Nationalist minesweeper headed for Sanmen on a regular patrol, the Communists struck first. The artillery on Sanmen fired a salvo at the approaching warship, damaging it. At the same time, the landing ships and the barge concentrated their gunfire on the ships that lay at anchor off Wailingding. The barrage sank one gunboat and damaged two others. The Nationalists immediately dispatched the rest of the flotilla to assist the minesweeper. The Communists waited until the enemy task force came within range of their firepower at sea and ashore and then opened fire simultaneously. The guns on the island and aboard the barge completely surprised the KMT forces. Under the cover of shore-based artillery, the Communists' makeshift fighting ships maneuvered and engaged in a five-hour sea battle, sinking one Nationalist gunboat and inflicting damage on a minesweeper and other gunboats. Even the destroyer, the capital ship of the flotilla, took hits that resulted in casualties.[74]

The Nationalists finally gave up contesting the waters around the Wanshan Islands and retreated to Taiwan. Wailingding fell on July 1. A month later the Communists captured Dangan Island and Jiapeng Island, the eastern perimeter of the archipelago. On August 4, the ground forces moved farther south and landed on Zhiwan, Beijian, and Miaowan Islands. Three days later the Communists seized the last feature, Wenweizhou Island, thus concluding the Wanshan Island campaign.

The struggle, which lasted seventy-five days, was the PLA's first exposure to sea combat and first joint maritime campaign. The Communists sank four warships, damaged eleven ships, captured eleven vessels and nearly two hundred men, and inflicted more than seven hundred casualties. The campaign eliminated a Nationalist foothold in the South China Sea. Moreover, for a military that had never operated so far offshore, the campaign was a significant achievement. The distance from the first island captured in the west to the last islands to fall in the east was about thirty-four nautical miles. The Communists not only had to cross the seas to attack and seize enemy garrisons, but they also had to hold the islands and resupply the occupying forces. They conducted an island-hopping campaign in a theater where the seas were contested by a materially and technologically superior foe.

AN IMPRESSIVE RECORD

Lin Biao's Fourth Field Army acquitted itself well, especially when compared with the Third Field Army's indifferent performance. Several key factors contributed to the field army's success. Following the disaster at Jinmen, Mao Zedong was personally invested in the Hainan campaign's success. The stakes were high, and the field army was under intense pressure to succeed. Lin and his subordinate commanders methodically debated and prepared for the operation. They developed a campaign plan based on a sober assessment of their own forces and of the Nationalist opponent, carefully weighing each side's strengths and weaknesses. The scheme to smuggle advance units to the island and link up those units with the Qiongya insurgents proved essential to the main assault's success. The Communists spent time and resources to train and equip the landing troops and to ensure that the size of the transport fleet was more than adequate for the task ahead. They spared no effort to develop and strengthen the logistical infrastructure and the supply chain to support what would become a massive undertaking. The shock of Jinmen and the lessons from that disaster undoubtedly influenced the design and execution of the campaign. Even so, some of the tactical actions were close-run things and could well have ended in catastrophe if not for the fifth column forces on the island. Despite initial setbacks during the Wanshan campaign, the Communist forces, organized as a joint army-navy team, were able to steadily advance. They took an operational pause to reassess the situation and adapt to new circumstances on the newly occupied island positions, suggesting an improved capacity to resupply and sustain operations while relatively far from their home base on the mainland. The evident learning and adaptation that took place for these campaigns to succeed would pay more dividends in future encounters with the Nationalists.

NOTES

1. For an early comprehensive account of the Hainan campaign, see Reed Richards Probst, "The Communist Conquest of Hainan Island," PhD diss., George Washington University, 1982.

2. 第四野战军战史编写组 [Editorial Team of the Fourth Field Army's War History], 第四野战军战史 [War History of the Fourth Field Army of the People's Liberation Army] (Beijing: Liberation Army Press, 2008), 585. The official history was originally published in 1998.

3. According to a January 16 CIA information report, Xue Yue claimed that he commanded five armies and other independent units as well as air and naval forces that numbered 150,000 men. CIA Information Report, "Nationalist Military Information, Hainan," January 16, 1950, CREST, CIA-RDP82-00457R004200040010-4.

4. Editorial Team of the Fourth Field Army's War History, *War History of the Fourth Field Army*, 586.

5. Editorial Team of the Fourth Field Army's War History, 589–95.

6. As Xiaobing Li notes, "No existing Chinese record reveals serious discussions at the high command on the Jinmen Operation before October 28, 1949," the day the Communist regiments were wiped out on Jinmen. Xiaobing Li, *A History of the Modern Chinese Army* (Lexington: University of Kentucky Press, 2007), 131.

7. Editorial Team of the Fourth Field Army's War History, *War History of the Fourth Field Army*, 590–91.

8. 魏碧海 [Wei Bihai], "海南岛战役渡海登陆作战的历史经验与思考" [The Historical Experience of and Thoughts on the Cross-Sea Landing Operations of the Hainan Island Campaign], 军事历史 [Military History], no. 1 (2001): 8.

9. For an in-depth history of the Qiongya Column and the decades-long insurgency on Hainan, see 陈泽华 [Chen Zehua], 解放战争海南敌后游击战纪实 [A Documentary of Guerrilla Warfare behind Enemy Lines on Hainan during the War of Liberation] (Beijing: Liberation Army Press, 2011). Col. Chen Zehua is director of the editorial office of Guangzhou Military Region's Political Department.

10. Editorial Team of the Fourth Field Army's War History, *War History of the Fourth Field Army*, 586. According to the CIA, the Qiongya Column fielded five divisions numbering about 17,500 men. CIA Information Report, "Communist Order of Battle, Hainan," April 11, 1950, CREST, CIA-RDP82-00457R004600580012-9.

11. 杨迪 [Yang Di], 创造渡海作战的奇迹—解放海南岛战役决策指挥的真实记叙 [Creating the Miraculous Cross-Sea Operations—The True Story behind the Campaign Command Decisions in Liberating Hainan Island] (Beijing: Liberation Army Press, 2008), 41. The author was the chief of the operations section of the 15th Army during the Hainan campaign. As a member of the frontline command, he was intimately involved in the planning and major decisions of the operation.

12. Editorial Team of the Fourth Field Army's War History, *War History of the Fourth Field Army*, 593–94.

13. Yang, *Course Materials on the Chinese People's Liberation Army's War History*, 158.

14. For an excellent account of the Guangzhou conference, see Yang, *Creating the Miraculous Cross-Sea Operations*, 67–78.

15. Editorial Team of the Fourth Field Army's War History, *War History of the Fourth Field Army*, 596–97.

16. Editorial Team of the Fourth Field Army's War History, 597–98.

17. Editorial Team of the Fourth Field Army's War History, 599. According to the CIA, by early March the Communists had conscripted up to 1,400 boats along the mainland's southern coast, stretching from Yangjiang in Guangdong to Qinzhou in Guangxi. See CIA Information Report, "Chinese Communist Military Activities, South Kwangtung," March 10, 1950, CREST, CIA-RDP82-00457R004500110002-2.

18. Editorial Team of the Fourth Field Army's War History, *War History of the Fourth Field Army*, 599–601.
19. The artillery pieces included American-built 75mm field guns that the Communists had captured from the Nationalists. See CIA Information Report, "Communist Order of Battle, Hainan and Kwangtung," February 20, 1950, CREST, CIA-RDP82-00457R004400010008-0.
20. Yang, *Creating the Miraculous Cross-Sea Operations*, 111–12.
21. Editorial Team of the Fourth Field Army's War History, *War History of the Fourth Field Army*, 602.
22. Editorial Team of the Fourth Field Army's War History, 602–3.
23. For an excellent summary of the Nationalist counterinsurgency campaign, see 陳偉忠 [Chen Weizhong], "戡亂海南島戰役之研究" [Research on the Suppression Efforts in the Hainan Island Campaign], 軍事評論史 [Military History Review], no. 27 (June 2020): 75–78.
24. 王伟 张德彬 主编 [Wang Wei and Zhang Debin, eds.], 渡海登岛: 战例与战法研究 [Cross-Sea Island Landings: Research on Case Studies and Tactics] (Beijing: Military Science Press [military circulation], 2002), 37; and Yang, *Creating the Miraculous Cross-Sea Operations*, 199.
25. Editorial Team of the Fourth Field Army's War History, *War History of the Fourth Field Army*, 604–5.
26. Editorial Team of the Fourth Field Army's War History, *War History of the Fourth Field Army*, 605–6.
27. Wang and Zhang, *Cross-Sea Island Landings*, 38.
28. Editorial Team of the Fourth Field Army's War History, *War History of the Fourth Field Army*, 607–8.
29. Wang, *Island Landing Combat*, 25.
30. For a blow-by-blow account of the engagement, see 王文清 梁玉师 郁汉冲 [Wang Wenqing, Liang Yushi, and Yu Hanchong], 中外岛战 [Chinese and Foreign Island Wars] (Beijing: Liberation Army Press, 2009), 207–8.
31. Editorial Team of the Fourth Field Army's War History, *War History of the Fourth Field Army*, 608.
32. For a vivid account of this operation, see 宋维枝 [Song Weizhen], "'叶挺独立团'跨海征琼崖—忆海南岛战役中的第127师" ["Yeting Independent Group" Cross-Sea Mission to Qiongya—In Remembrance of the 127th Division in the Hainan Campaign], 军事历史 [Military History], no. 4 (2001): 67–71. Brig. Gen. Song Weizhen was formerly the deputy political commissar of the Fuzhou Military Region. During the Hainan campaign he was the political commissar of the 127th Division and took part in the assault.
33. Yang, *Creating the Miraculous Cross-Sea Operations*, 165.
34. Editorial Team of the Fourth Field Army's War History, *War History of the Fourth Field Army*, 609.
35. Chen, "Research on the Suppression Efforts in the Hainan Island Campaign," 89.
36. Chen, 91.
37. Chen, 91.
38. Chen, 95. The author concedes that the figures likely overstate Communist losses and understate the number of successful infiltrations.
39. CIA Information Report, "Communist Preparations for Hainan Invasion: Nationalist Naval Patrols, Hainan," February 23, 1950, CREST, CIA-RDP82-00457R004400300009-8.

40. CIA Information Report, "Nationalist Naval Forces, Hainan," March 14, 1950, CREST, CIA-RDP82-00457R004500110003-1.
41. CIA Information Report, "Situation, Hainan; Supply of Nationalist Guerillas, China Mainland," March 17, 1950, CREST, CIA-RDP82-00457R004500400003-9.
42. CIA Information Report, "Nationalist Operations against Communist Landings and Guerillas, Hainan," March 27, 1950, CREST, CIA-RDP82-00457R004600100007-7.
43. CIA Information Report, "Nationalist Military Operations, Hainan," March 28, 1950, CREST, CIA-RDP82-00457R004600160004-4.
44. CIA Information Report, "Communist Landings, Hainan," April 17, 1950, CREST, CIA-RDP82-00457R004700420004-7.
45. Editorial Team of the Fourth Field Army's War History, *War History of the Fourth Field Army*, 611.
46. See chapter 3. During the Jinmen campaign, the 82nd Division of the 28th Corps had overall command of all forces to include the regiments of the 29th Corps. For the Zhoushan campaign, the 22nd Corps had overall responsibilities for carrying out the operation and was also given command of the 61st Division of the 21st Corps. These mixed command relationships led to serious problems in coordination, communications, and command and control.
47. Editorial Team of the Fourth Field Army's War History, *War History of the Fourth Field Army*, 611–12.
48. Wang et al., *Chinese and Foreign Island Wars*, 212–13.
49. Editorial Team of the Fourth Field Army's War History, *War History of the Fourth Field Army*, 612.
50. The PLA's official history does not reveal the extent of Communist losses at sea.
51. Editorial Team of the Fourth Field Army's War History, *War History of the Fourth Field Army*, 613.
52. Chen, "Research on the Suppression Efforts in the Hainan Island Campaign," 101.
53. Editorial Team of the Fourth Field Army's War History, *War History of the Fourth Field Army*, 617.
54. Chen Weizhong, "Research on the Suppression Efforts in the Hainan Island Campaign," 107.
55. 朱冬生 主编 [Zhu Dongsheng, ed.], 江河海岛作战卷 [Volume on Riverine and Island Combat] (Beijing: Liberation Army Press, 2010), 393.
56. Editorial Team of the Fourth Field Army's War History, *War History of the Fourth Field Army*, 619.
57. Editorial Team of the Fourth Field Army's War History, *War History of the Fourth Field Army*, 623–28.
58. Chen, "Research on the Suppression Efforts in the Hainan Island Campaign," 108–11.
59. Editorial Team of the Fourth Field Army's War History, *War History of the Fourth Field Army*, 620.
60. Editorial Team of the Fourth Field Army's War History, *War History of the Fourth Field Army*, 621.
61. 陆儒德 [Lu Rude], 中国海军之路 [The Path of the Chinese Navy] (Dalian: Dalian Press, 2007), 238.
62. Editorial Team of the Fourth Field Army's War History, *War History of the Fourth Field Army*, 621.
63. 梁芳 主编 [Liang Fang, ed.], 海战史与未来海战研究 [The History of Sea Battles and Research on Future Sea Battles] (Beijing: Haiyang, 2007), 195. Senior Colonel

Liang Fang is a professor in the strategy department at the PLA National Defense University.

64. Zhu, *Volume on Riverine and Island Combat*, 408.

65. According to the CIA, the Communists possessed four former Nationalist gunboats, two landing craft, two hundred motorized boats, and one hundred junks prior to the invasion in late June. CIA Information Report, "Chinese Communist Strength, Chungshan," June 28, 1950, CREST, CIA-RDP82-00457R005100710004-7.

66. In the months preceding the operation, the Communists employed five hundred fishing boats carrying PLA observers to scout the Wanshan Islands and track the patterns and timing of Nationalist naval patrols. CIA Information Report, "Communist Plans for Wanshan Assault," March 29, 1950, CREST, CIA-RDP82-00457R00 4600260012-4.

67. Zhu, *Volume on Riverine and Island Combat*, 409.

68. Zhu, 410–11.

69. Zhu, 410–11. There is some discrepancy over how the *Guishan* came under attack. In another telling, the *Guishan* was on its way to disgorge troops on Qingzhou and Sanjiao Islands. But a Nationalist ship, fleeing the chaos at Mawan harbor, intercepted and engaged the *Guishan*. For this version of events, see Liang, *The History of Sea Battles and Research on Future Sea Battles*, 196.

70. Zhu, *Volume on Riverine and Island Combat*, 411.

71. Zhu, 411.

72. CIA Information Report, "Communist Military Losses in Wanshan (Ladrone) Islands," June 7, 1950, CREST, CIA-RDP82-00457R005000490005-2.

73. Zhu, *Volume on Riverine and Island Combat*, 415.

74. Zhu, 413.

SEVEN

An Assessment of the PLA's Seaward Turn

Over the course of eighteen months, Mao Zedong and his subordinates stood up an independent strategic naval service while the PLA fought a series of offshore operations. Institutionally, the Communist leadership confronted mind-boggling material, personnel, and intellectual challenges as they sought to establish a new navy. The PLAN's founders, including Zhang Aiping and Xiao Jinguang, developed novel workarounds and solutions to overcome the staggering obstacles. Notably, the efforts to integrate former Nationalist foes into the navy's ranks reflected the desperate needs of the Communists at a critical moment in China's postrevolution history.

Operationally, the PLA conducted island-seizing campaigns that were diverse in scale, intensity, and complexity. Some of the contested landings, such as those on Hainan, were spectacular successes, while others, such as those on Jinmen, were disastrous failures. The quality of strategy, planning, preparations, and operational art was often the arbiter that decided those outcomes. The play of chance, ever present in any war, also contributed to the PLA's performance on the battlefield. Today, Chinese analysts continue to draw lessons from these early amphibious assaults and apply those lessons to possible real-world contingencies over Taiwan. The following synthesizes the major themes and findings from the preceding chapters.

INSTITUTIONAL ASSESSMENT

Several themes emerge from the history of the Chinese navy's founding. The navy was not an afterthought. From the start, it was a strategic project that was designed to vanquish the remaining Nationalists on Taiwan and offshore islands and conclusively end the Chinese Civil War. The highest levels of authority made crucial choices about sea power. The timing of those decisions turned on the CCP's assessment of the civil war. As it became evident that the Nationalist's seaward retreat would change the conflict's character into a maritime contest, acquiring sea power and airpower became an urgent priority. At critical junctures Mao Zedong played an important role in signaling the CCP's intent, and his public declarations served as a stimulus to the naval buildup. Mao's meeting with the former Nationalists in August 1949 was a gesture of reconciliation that made further collaboration possible. It is worth pondering the course of the naval buildup had the outbreak of the Korean War not interrupted the planned cross-strait campaign.

The Communists benefited from the defeated Nationalists, who in the wake of their defeat passed on hardware and software to the civil war's victors. Defections and mutinies not only accelerated the collapse of KMT resistance but also made available to the winning side vessels, officers, and sailors. After the cross-river campaign, shore facilities and personnel along the Yangzi and around Shanghai, the epicenter of maritime industry and activity, fell wholesale to the Communists. Surface combatants of the Second Squadron and a variety of Nationalist assets formed the nucleus of the PLAN. The CCP had no choice but to live with—and build on—a hand-me-down navy.

But it was in the area of software, including education, experience, technical expertise, institutional memory, and naval culture, where the Nationalist influence seemed most pronounced. Nationalist officers assumed key positions in the fleet and headquarters of the East China Navy and later the PLAN. They made important decisions about education, force structure, and modernization and were the first to command the PLAN's warships. Indeed, in a sweeping lateral move, the CCP reassigned former commanding officers, executive officers, and department heads of the ROCN to the same positions and duties aboard ships of the new navy. As many as a third of the officers and sailors were ex-Nationalists.[1] Many would go on to lead the PLAN with distinction. Despite their small numbers within the new navy, the Nationalists wielded an outsize influence during this formative period. One study estimates that by the end of 1955, former KMT personnel constituted only 2.1 percent, or about 4,000 people, of the 188,000-strong navy.[2]

The defeated Nationalists' intellectual contributions were notable. Both Zhang Aiping and Xiao Jinguang welcomed the expertise of high-ranking Nationalist officers, despite nagging doubts about the ex-KMT officers' loyalty and their Western educations. Zhang repeatedly turned to the most knowledgeable and experienced Nationalist officers, many trained in the United Kingdom, the United States, and Japan, for advice and promoted them to key positions in research, education, and ship construction. Xiao followed Zhang's example and formed his own research committee, drawing members from Zhang's team in the East China Navy. This "second advisory group," a sly reference to the primacy of Soviet advisers, furnished insights about Western navies and passed on critical intelligence about the US Navy.

Material and intellectual poverty forced the naval commanders to strike a balance between pragmatism and the CCP's ideological imperatives. While the

CCP's political primacy over all naval affairs was firmly established from the start, Zhang and Xiao took steps to ensure that professional expertise played a role alongside party loyalty. Despite the massive cultural, intellectual, and ideological chasms that divided the Communist cadre and the ex-Nationalists, they pressed ahead with integrating the two former enemies. Choosing reconciliation over retribution was not easy. Like an immune system that produces antibodies to attack harmful foreign viruses, some of the cadre assailed the Nationalists out of fear that ideological impurities might contaminate the CCP and the army. Zhang found himself scrambling to mollify such reactions to sustain unity of effort.

Scarcity also compelled improvisation. The surviving Nationalist navy had already withdrawn its best assets to Taiwan. The Communists were left with an assortment of combatants of uneven quality and questionable seaworthiness. Desperate for ships, they pooled together existing resources, including from the civilian sector, to serve as a stopgap measure. The East China Navy retrofitted amphibious assault ships and even merchant and fishing vessels, equipping them with army guns. This ad hoc approach would continue under the PLAN and would later be codified by the August 1950 navy conference. To bring officers and crew to full strength, the Communists took drastic shortcuts in education and training that horrified their Soviet advisers.

Lingering questions, however, remain about the current historiography of the PLAN. While the writings suggest that the Communists sought to reconcile with the Nationalists, it is possible that efforts to move past the civil war were far more contentious than the narratives let on. To what extent the Nationalists were coerced into cooperating is not clear. For example, the climactic meeting between Liu Bocheng and Rear Adm. Lin Zun over the fate of the Second Squadron could well have been less than cordial. It is likely that these magnanimous gestures were merely instrumental, a Machiavellian expedient to win over Nationalist cooperation that the Communists would sustain only as long as they needed it. This would be consistent with the united front strategy that the Communists had employed for decades.

Indeed, it is noteworthy that Zhang's tenure from April 1949 to February 1951 preceded the crescendo of ideological warfare that Mao would unleash on his people, including against the former Nationalists.[3] The Korean War further heightened suspicions of KMT loyalty and fear of subversive forces sponsored by the Nationalists on Taiwan. Successive waves of counterrevolutionary campaigns that culminated in the Cultural Revolution likely fell hard on the ex-Nationalists. It is unclear to what extent the hard-won experiences, lessons, and expertise that Zhang and Xiao worked to cultivate and pass on from the ex-KMT officers and sailors to the cadre survived the subsequent years of tumult.

The literature also seems to deliberately underplay the significant Soviet role in aiding the PLAN while lending far more prominence to the ex-Nationalists' contributions. Many writings surveyed in this study make passing or grudging references to the Soviet advisers' presence. The emphasis on the Chinese origins of the PLAN may be a product of shifting national attitudes. Over the past two decades, the PLAN has put to sea a balanced fleet constructed by China's own shipyards. The era of heavy dependence on Soviet and, later, Russian technology and assistance is long past. Growing domestic confidence that China can chart an independent course on sea power without foreign help may explain the attempts to downplay Soviet assistance.

The writings about integration of the former Nationalists into Communist ranks may have reflected the more complex and interdependent relationship with Taiwan in recent years. ROC president Ma Ying-Jeou's tenure from 2008 to 2016 led to a temporary thaw in cross-strait relations. This period produced national feelings on the mainland that were less reflexively hostile to the Nationalists. Softening public attitudes toward Taiwan, for a time, may have made it possible to retell the reconciliation efforts with the KMT. In other words, the PLA literature may have as much to do with Beijing's current worldview and policy agenda as with an accurate reconstruction of events.

Despite the potential analytical distortions, these histories nevertheless challenge long-standing conventional wisdom about Chinese sea power. The preceding narrative counters widely held Western assumptions that the Communists were inattentive to maritime affairs during the early years. The PLA leadership issued directives to build a navy ten months before the establishment of the People's Republic. Mao understood that sea power was essential to ending the civil war and defending China's long coastline and inland rivers against the predations of hostile powers. Mao was personally involved in making personnel decisions, handpicking both Zhang and Xiao, and was instrumental in overruling the Central Military Commission and the General Staff Department about the navy's fate while siding with Xiao's position that the navy had to be conceived as an independent, strategic service.

Contrary to earlier Western judgments, the Soviets did not monopolize the influence on Chinese naval thought. Nor were the Communists intellectual automatons who unthinkingly adopted and borrowed from Soviet doctrine and hardware. Both Zhang and Xiao adapted the navy to China's peculiar conditions. They insisted on a Chinese way on doctrine, force structure, education, and training. Xiao repeatedly underscored the primacy of the PLA's strategic and operational traditions in determining the PLAN's purpose and design. Following Zhang's cue, Xiao appointed former Nationalists to positions of authority within the fleet and headquarters that conferred to them a direct institutional role in shaping the PLAN. In sum, a hybrid of intellectual influences, both foreign and indigenous, shaped the PLAN's first years.

The Communist-Nationalist collaboration, in turn, enabled imaginative workarounds to make the most of the ramshackle navy. Notably, the conscription of the merchant and fishing fleets suggests that the civil-military integration of maritime power dates back to the earliest days of the PLAN. In light of this history, perhaps it is not surprising that China has been so adept at seamlessly employing a combined fleet of naval combatants and civilian maritime law enforcement vessels in recent years.

OPERATIONAL ASSESSMENT

The PLA conducted a remarkably diverse set of offshore campaigns. The scale of the landings and the physical terrain varied significantly. The operational objectives ranged from tiny islets to Hainan, China's major offshore island second in size only to Taiwan. The force sizes differed accordingly. A battalion numbering several hundred infantry personnel took Tanxushan Island, while forty-five thousand troops took part in the final Hainan landings in addition to the eight thousand–strong advance force that snuck across the Qiongzhou Strait in earlier assaults.

The methods and tactics also varied. During the Xiamen campaign, the 10th Army employed diversionary attacks against Gulang Islet and areas north of Jinmen to draw Nationalist attention and forces away from the main line of attack on the northern shores. The Jinmen campaign was a blunt head-on assault on the beaches. The abandoned plan against Dachen Island would have been a direct attack as well. The Zhoushan campaign followed a sequential path that seized secondary objectives closer to the mainland on its way to the main prize. Similarly, the island landings off Shanghai's south shore were designed to take bite-size chunks out of Nationalist defenses. The Pishan and the Wanshan campaigns were notable for their jointness, involving as they did army-navy coordination.

The outcomes were quite diverse. Jinmen and Dengbu were clearly defeats. The former had an outsize strategic impact because it altered the high command's calculus about the invasion of Taiwan. The latter halted further attempts to take Zhoushan. Nationalist reinforcements and the KMT's demonstrated determination to hold its positions stopped the Communists in their tracks. Even the apparent victories disguised deadly problems that the PLA faced at sea. The attack against Pingtan, the 10th Army's first foray in cross-sea landings, almost foundered. The diversionary assault against Gulang during the Xiamen campaign was devastatingly costly. The experiences at Pingtan and Gulang were early warnings of the calamity to come at Jinmen.

Many of the success stories were close-run things. It was the foiled plot to spring a surprise on the defenders at Dachen that led to the attack against an alternate site, Pishan. Coordination of forces, often complicated by the weather and currents, was a perennial difficulty. In an early attempt to smuggle forces onto Hainan, the scattered fleet barely made it to shore. The Pingtan campaign might have come to grief had the stranded troops been driven off the beaches at Dalian, the staging area for the attack on Pingtan. In short, many operations that turned on luck or Communist resolve could have easily ended like Jinmen or Dengbu.

The operations shared important characteristics. These commonalities stemmed from the PLA's warfighting traditions and, relatedly, the Communists' material inferiority. Throughout the period covered in this study, the Nationalists enjoyed superior weaponry and deployed naval and air forces that could interdict transiting Communist vessels. The PLA, by contrast, possessed few tools to contest the enemy's use of the air and the seas. To address this power asymmetry, PLA leaders brought to bear tactical superiority at the scene of action while fighting from an overall position of strategic inferiority. They first attacked weakly defended garrisons or isolated island outposts with overwhelming force. The mismatch in the local military balance allowed the PLA to smash enemy forces, gain experience, buoy confidence, and chip away at the adversary's power. Chinese military commanders were clearly taking a page from Mao's playbook in the earlier phases of the civil war when the Communists were strategically inferior to the Nationalists.

For the East China Navy's initial forays at sea, Zhang Aiping deployed a numerically superior force against small island garrisons close to the mainland to secure quick victories before he ordered more ambitious operations farther offshore. Similarly, the Third Field Army's Zhoushan campaign first involved attacks against Daxie and Jintang, satellite islands that were within easy reach, using greater numbers to overpower defenders. The Fourth Field Army's initial smuggling operations were directed at landing sites well behind the enemy's front lines where the beaches were lightly defended. Such an indirect approach increased the chances of success, while the insertion of the advance troops helped tip the military balance in the Communists' favor.

Driven by necessity, the Communists developed plans that minimized, if not negated, their adversary's aerial and maritime dominance. The Communists used camouflage, dispersal, and deception to deny the adversary intelligence about where the troops would embark and when the transports would set sail. All the vessels sailed by night to avoid detection and maximize surprise against the defenders. On one occasion, bad weather worked in the Communists' favor as it grounded the ROC Air Force based on Zhoushan. As noted above, the PLA conducted tactical feints to draw the adversary's attention away from the main attack against Xiamen. Or, in the case of Hainan, the boats sailed to weakly garrisoned areas behind enemy strongpoints to unload troops. But nighttime transits frequently came at the expense of ship-to-ship communications and navigation, complicating the command and control of forces.

In combat, the local commanders sought to turn their weaknesses into strengths. Their boats were invariably much smaller than those of their Nationalist counterparts, and few had organic firepower. To compensate for the lack of weight and offensive punch, they leveraged the agility of their boats to close in on enemy combatants to deliver small-arms fire. Such a tactic put the vessels in the adversary's blind spots, in areas well inside the effective firing ranges of the enemy's naval guns, rendering them unusable. The Communist troops aboard the ships then poured gunfire and grenades onto vital targets, such as the bridge and the senior officers aboard, to knock out the combatant. In one instance, the Communists almost pulled off a sneak attack against anchored Nationalist vessels at Lajiwei Island during the Wanshan campaign. While the tactical encounter was a failure, the psychological shock of the surprise attack forced the Nationalists to withdraw, opening the way for further PLA advances. The combat is remembered favorably in Chinese naval historiography.

The Communists clearly understood the relationship between battle and fighting spirit. Zhang's plan to first take a modest objective in a progressive, island-hopping campaign and the 7th Army's seizure of Daxie Island, the first assault in the larger Zhoushan operation, were not merely initial attempts to test the troops' skills in amphibious landings. The leaders believed, correctly, that successes in these early experiments would boost confidence among the officers and the men for the more difficult actions ahead. Similarly, the smuggling operations to insert forces behind enemy lines at Hainan were not only designed to tilt the local military balance in the Communists' favor but they also served as trial balloons that, if successful, would bolster morale. This judgment proved correct. Zhang insisted that his naval flotilla had to seize Pishan, when Dachen became an impregnable garrison, to maintain operational momentum and morale. On a related point, the PLA pitted its much weaker naval units against the Nationalist navy in the belief that the moral factor would overcome the material asymmetries in power. Some of the frontal assaults against better-equipped KMT ships verged on suicidal, as the high costs in men killed and boats sunk amply attested. But in the case of the Wanshan campaign, the psychological edge conferred initiative and delivered a shock to the Nationalists that proved salutary to the conflict's outcome.

The PLA brought into play elements of people's war doctrine in all its offshore campaigns. Each operation required the Communists to obtain the cooperation of local communities to achieve success. They had to enlist local support to acquire junks and boatmen to sail them. For Hainan, the scale of the people's assistance was enormous: some two thousand boats and six thousand boatmen took part in the final assault. Equally important, the resident communities provided insights and knowledge about the unique terrain, weather conditions, and ocean currents of their regions. Such information allowed the

22nd Corps to gamble on the timing of its attack on Jintang despite bad weather and enabled the East China Navy to press ahead against Pishan. The Communists learned, as they did repeatedly in the past, that winning local hearts and minds was not easy. Attempts to forcibly conscript vessels quickly produced a backlash. Some frightened fishermen fled with their boats when faced with the prospect of danger. Others destroyed or buried their craft. When the PLA had no choice but to recruit outsiders unfamiliar with local conditions for the Jinmen campaign, the resulting confusion and mistakes during the nighttime transit proved lethal.

The Hainan campaign perhaps best exemplified the role and effects of people's war. The Qiongya Column, an indigenous insurgent force akin to the Viet Cong in South Vietnam, proved invaluable to the operation's success. The local armed group provided intelligence about the disposition of the Nationalist defenders on the island. The group's superior knowledge of local circumstances and terrain no doubt aided the Communist cause. The column's leaders coordinated closely with their comrades on the mainland to join up with the smuggled-in troops and guided the newcomers through hostile terrain to reach the Qiongyas' base areas. Their safe havens located in Hainan's inaccessible mountain interior ensured the survival of the newly arrived PLA units. That the armed group was able to sustain, feed, arm, and supply an outside force numbering eight thousand troops demonstrated the significant resources they enjoyed, including the support of local communities. They then combined forces with the advance PLA troops to conduct harassment attacks and feints to tie down the Nationalists during the main cross-strait assault against Hainan. These actions almost certainly tipped the balance in the Communists' favor.

The PLA was very adept at pragmatic workarounds. The transports were almost entirely civilian in character. During the Hainan campaign, the 15th Army scrambled to motorize as many of the junks as possible. The PLA improvised to enhance the firepower of its fledgling fleet. The East China Navy converted civilian vessels for military use by retrofitting army artillery aboard the ships. The Wanshan campaign featured boats armed with army weaponry that provided gunfire support to forces ashore and engaged in combat at sea. In one instance, a tugboat pulled a barge armed to the teeth with artillery pieces. Throughout this period PLA planners displayed a high degree of comfort—in part out of necessity and in part owing to their tradition of people's war—with merging civilian platforms with military capabilities.

During the offshore campaigns, the PLA exhibited key characteristics that remain central to the Chinese military's institutional identity and operational style. Local commanders emphasized resourcefulness and improvisation in the face of a materially and technologically superior foe. Fighting from a position of relative weakness meant that superior organization and operational art were crucial to success. The commanders acted in the belief that fighting spirit could overcome some of their material shortfalls. They employed deception, surprise, close combat, and night operations to compensate for their technical and physical inferiority while maximizing the effects of their tactics. They not only relied on the civilian population for resources and expertise but also demonstrated a high degree of comfort with fashioning military power out of civilian capabilities, merging seamlessly the irregular elements of warfare with conventional combat.

ASSESSING CHINESE APPRAISALS

Chinese analysts have sought to apply the historical lessons from this period of intense fighting to modern-day circumstances. By examining those lessons, outside observers can evaluate how Chinese strategists think about the relevance of their past to modern amphibious operations and how they plan to fight. Below is a sample of writings that links explicitly the past to the present and future.

A Chinese National Defense University study draws four broad lessons from the amphibious operations. In future wars, according to the report, the PLA must accurately appraise the enemy's situation; engage in thorough operational planning; provide ample material support to the landing forces, especially shipping; and conduct intensive training in cross-sea combat. The study also draws attention to the vital importance of keeping the sea-lanes secure, balking enemy blockades and interdiction, and rapidly seizing and holding a large beachhead to enable a decisive breakthrough. Intriguingly, the study finds value in conquering secondary targets before turning to the main operational objective. The study also notes that the seizure of satellite islands near Pingtan and Jinmen were important preconditions to the final assaults.[4]

Zhao Huanming, a researcher at the Academy of Military Science, provides an informed comparative assessment of the Jintang, Dengbu, and Jinmen campaigns.[5] In justifying his case selection, he notes that the three operations took place within weeks of each other and shared similar meteorological and hydrological conditions. Yet, they produced vastly different outcomes: Jintang was a clear win, while Dengbu and Jinmen were serious setbacks. Given that the environmental factors were roughly similar, Zhao attributes the losses at Dengbu and Jinmen to poor strategy.

Zhao believes that material readiness, preparedness, and a proper assessment of the adversary were crucial to explaining variation in the outcomes. The 22nd Corps, responsible for the Jintang operation, was methodical in its planning and execution. It spent two months searching for vessels and boatmen across cities along Hangzhou Bay's south bank, from Ningbo all the way to Shaoxing, some eighty-five kilometers to the west. During that time, the corps conscripted about 500 boats and repaired over 350 junks. It was determined to have adequate shipping to transport a reinforced division, comprising four regiments, in a single overnight transit. The corps did not count on the second wave of reinforcements, which it judged too risky, for success. The leadership then ordered battalion and company commanders to organize the flotilla; refine and tighten the command and control of forces; study the weather, the tide, and the terrain; participate in training; experiment with the troops; and develop doctrine. The tactical leaders, in turn, insisted on intensive and repeated training and exercises to master combat techniques at sea. Newly minted sailors and troops tested out tactical concepts, including nighttime transits over open water, landings, and maneuver at beaches, until they were confident of their skills.

The 10th Army at Jinmen, by contrast, underestimated the enemy, lacked shipping, and failed to understand the maritime environment. The PLA planners hastily concluded that a one-to-one ratio between Communist attackers and Nationalist defenders would still lead to success, violating a basic precept that defense is the stronger form of war especially when the offense is launched from the sea. The 10th Army assumed that the seas would be uncontested and believed that a single flotilla could bring two waves of assaults on Jinmen in a single night. The army recruited boatmen who were unfamiliar with the local conditions. Its command structure, in which the 28th Corps oversaw the regiments of the 29th Corps, caused confusion and undermined unity of effort. The 10th Army's planning and preparations were haphazard, focused as they were on administering the recently conquered Xiamen. And the army did little to study the battlefield, the weather, and the seas. In sum, the 10th Army's leadership exhibited hubris and an alarming disregard for the harsh realities of amphibious operations.

Similarly, the 61st Division was unprepared for the assault on Dengbu. Like the 10th Army at Jinmen, it too thought that the Nationalist defenders were weak and would shatter on contact. The local commanders originally intended to land four battalions on the islands but possessed shipping for transporting only two battalions and one company. Yet, the division still proceeded with the attack. While the seven and a half companies that reached and stormed the beaches initially made impressive advances to drive off the Nationalists, they became overextended and were overwhelmed by enemy reinforcements from the sea. Worse, the division lacked the boats to dispatch a second wave of troops to restore the tactical balance of power. The division might not have needed follow-on forces had it sent forth a large contingent in the first attempt. Neither the 10th Army nor the 61st Division seriously considered the worst-case scenario and largely discounted the possibility that the Nationalists would substantially buttress their garrisons.

For Zhao, these contrasts between one success and two failures illustrate the requirements for waging modern amphibious warfare. To prevail in future ship-to-shore operations, Zhao contends that the PLA must acquire a deep understanding of the adversary and of itself and obtain a firm grasp of the operational terrain. It must thoroughly plan, prepare, and organize its forces and must always consider the worst-case scenario while avoiding wishful thinking. Notably, Zhao argues that the failures at Jinmen and Dengbu had as much to do with "intellectual paralysis [思想麻痹]" as with material shortfalls.[6] In short, sharp intellect and a proper mindset about the challenges at hand might have changed the course of those battles. Finally, Zhao advocates for delivering overwhelming power in amphibious operations. The landing force must be large enough to secure the beachhead, stand its ground, break through enemy defenses, and conduct deep follow-on attacks independent of reinforcements. Ample and accurate firepower are a precondition for suppressing enemy fire and for supporting the amphibious troops.

In an extensive study on the role of logistics in amphibious operations, two senior colonels assess the Hainan campaign and its implications for future landing campaigns.[7] While they acknowledge that the PLA's material backwardness at the time renders comparisons to contemporary amphibious operations difficult, they see value in understanding how the Communists succeeded despite their inferiority in equipment. In other words, the two colonels anticipate that the PLA in the twenty-first century would still be required to fight against technologically superior adversaries. To them, four logistical factors proved decisive at Hainan.

First, the 15th Army's work on gathering the transports, numbering some two thousand, was especially crucial to success. The crash program to motorize the larger wooden sailing boats was also important to the transit. Second, the 15th Army's various logistical units played a critical role prior to and after combat operations on Hainan. Many deployed to the front to serve as clearinghouses for the provision of goods and services. After the main assault secured the beachheads and took Haikou, these units swiftly crossed the strait to sustain the flow of supplies and help with administering Haikou.

Third, the logistics arm enabled the 15th Army to adjust to local conditions. The staging area around the Leizhou Peninsula was poor and lacked resources. Moreover, the tropical environment in the deep south and the many associated diseases proved especially debilitating to the northerners who comprised the main force. Logistics was essential to feeding and caring for a forward-deployed force of over one hundred thousand troops in what amounted to an alien land. Fourth, the Communists drew from local communities in Guangzhou, Hainan, and other provinces to logistically support the campaign. For example, the PLA recruited some seven hundred boatmen in Wuhan, more than 1,200 kilometers to the north, to fill the ranks of the transport flotilla.[8] As noted above, the Qiongya Column and its base areas were reportedly amply supplied to sustain eight thousand outsiders.

Liu Xing, Liu Chang, and Li Yuanxing, three scholars from the Military Transportation University, assess the Jinmen campaign to consider the importance of civilian transports in modern amphibious operations. They recount the woefully inadequate shipping that contributed to the disaster at Jinmen. The authors contend that civilian vessels should remain a major component of the PLA's future landings on hostile shores. They depict the nonmilitary logistical component of the PLA's power projection as a "foundational strength [基础力量]." The analysts draw attention to five areas to which military planners should pay attention.

The PLA, they believe, should actively promote modifications to new civilian ships (ranging in displacement from 5,000 to 10,000 tons) that incorporate capabilities for wartime contingencies. The military should compile a digital database and registry that would enable the rapid mobilization of civilian ships. Civilian crews should engage in regular peacetime training and coordination with the military. Liu, Liu, and Li are especially concerned with wartime command and control of forces, which was a major complicating factor during the transit to Jinmen. Finally, the scholars call on mid- to large-scale maritime transport industries to contribute to the formation of "a powerful civilian logistics fleet."[9]

In another insightful analysis, Dou Chao sees four lessons from the Jinmen fiasco that would be relevant to a future conflict with Taiwan.[10] First, as documented repeatedly in this study, the 10th Army lacked the material wherewithal to effectively prosecute the campaign. From shipping to ammunition, the PLA was inadequately equipped for the operation. Second, the Communist planners clearly underestimated the island defenders. Third, the author sees the nighttime transit as a symptom of a deeper problem: the absence of airpower and naval power to keep the seas free from enemy interdiction. The flotilla's utter destruction on the beaches of Jinmen was also the result of the PLA's inability to contest Nationalist use of the air and the seas. Fourth, the ground operations on Jinmen were not supported by a secure beachhead, were hampered by uncoordinated action between the three regiments, and were unprotected by shore-based artillery, naval gunfire, and airpower. While Communist field artillery on the mainland could have reached Jinmen, poor communications prevented accurate and timely gunfire support while substantially increasing the risk of fratricide. The troops could only count on the weapons and ammunition they brought ashore.

To Dou, the PLA must avoid or minimize the four problems that led to the Jinmen catastrophe if it is to succeed in a cross-strait invasion. The amphibious force must possess more than enough shipping to carry the first wave of landings on Taiwan's beaches. Given that civilian transports lack survivability, military warships must constitute the bulk if not the entirety of the first wave. Civilian vessels must be relegated to the subsequent phases of attack after the PLA has crushed enemy resistance. The first wave of troops and equipment must be supplied amply with ammunition, fuel, and food to conduct independent operations without the expectation of reinforcements. The PLA must also resist the temptation to take lightly the ROC armed forces. Many on the mainland have become dismissive of Taiwan's military, convinced that it is equipped with outdated and inferior weaponry, suffers from low morale, and lacks fighting spirit. Dou warns against such condescension, arguing that similar wishful thinking led to disaster at Jinmen.

The PLA must contend with enemy interdiction that would be far more lethal and effective than in 1949. It faces all-weather, day-and-night precision firepower from ROC and possibly American forces. Without command of the commons, China's transports, no matter how numerous or well defended, would not survive the transit across the strait. As such, Dou argues, China's air, naval, and rocket forces must possess "absolute superiority [绝对优势]" in firepower over their island defenders. And they must have ample firepower to deter and, failing that, punish third parties seeking to intervene on Taiwan's behalf. Dou pays special attention to preparatory fires designed to suppress and soften up enemy defenses, which in his view are essential to keeping the sea-lanes open and secure. According to Dou, the PLA forces "must concentrate their power to the maximum extent possible to conduct strikes that would seek to paralyze most, if not all, of the enemy's counter landing combat systems. The key targets of the attack should be the enemy's command and control systems, the communications systems, naval and air bases, air defense systems, and so forth.[11]

Dou further notes that the PLA must possess a substantial follow-on force to keep the strait clear of enemy forces and to prevent the adversary from cutting off the units that had already landed on Taiwan's coast. This reserve force would keep the frontline invading forces well supplied and prevent them from being stranded on the island. Dou explicitly harkens back to the Jinmen disaster to underscore the importance of preserving the link between forces ashore and the logistical chain that would stretch across the Taiwan Strait to the mainland.

Intriguingly, Dou advocates for shipborne army artillery units to complement the firepower delivered from air and naval assets. He notes that warships and aircraft would likely be assigned to many other missions beyond direct support to the ground troops fighting on Taiwan. Thus, army artillery temporarily affixed to military and civilian transports could deliver suppressing fires while helping to ease the operational burdens placed on the PLA's air and naval services. Moreover, Dou observes, the army boasts enormous quantities of artillery that could be quickly modified to fire accurately from ships at relatively low costs.[12] It appears that Dou is reaching back to the earlier improvised efforts to arm vessels with army guns documented in this study.

These past island campaigns continue to cast a shadow over the PLA's thinking about a possible war against Taiwan. Chinese analysts are acutely aware of past failures and what they imply for a contemporary cross-strait conflict. They are eager to avoid the mistakes of the past and have discerned the ingredients to operational success from the offshore campaigns of 1949 and 1950. The PLA clearly wishes to avoid repeating the Jinmen fiasco even as it ardently hopes to reprise the success at Hainan. The Chinese writings identify material readiness, mass, and overwhelming firepower as particularly important ingredients for an effective operation against Taiwan. They also emphasize the importance of assessment, including realistic appraisals that eschew underestimating the enemy, as a precondition for campaign success. Intellect, then, must accompany brawn.

The offshore campaigns could also serve as models for future operations. The Zhoushan campaign points to a sequential strategy whereby the PLA would seize lesser territorial objectives on its way to the main prize. China could seize Taiwan's outlying islands in the South China Sea or Penghu as a prelude to a larger campaign. The Hainan campaign suggests that China would employ fifth-column elements on the island to cause maximum disruption to Taipei's defensive efforts. The Jinmen campaign represents a head-on assault that would seek to conquer Taiwan in a single move. Of course, these archetypes are not mutually exclusive. They could each play a part in a cross-strait campaign. These insights suggest that the CCP's earliest encounters with the seas can inform the PLA's judgments about future warfare. It behooves the West to study this history closely to make sense of the Chinese military trajectory in the coming years.

A BRIEF BUT IMPACTFUL HISTORY

China's strategic community has subjected the navy's founding and the early offshore campaigns to deep study. The PLA sees much in its past that it can be proud of. This brief but impactful history reinforces the Chinese military's self-image as a determined and resourceful organization. Mao's armies went to sea despite their technological inadequacies and prevailed on many occasions. The PLA's leaders proved remarkably adaptive and pragmatic at the institutional and operational levels of war. This nautical history further cements a long-standing belief, cultivated since the earliest days of Mao's revolutionary movement, that the moral factor is as important as the material dimension of strategy. The official histories and scholarly commentaries are also brutally honest about the failings of the various operations. They use detailed historical case studies as cautionary tales about the potential physical dangers and analytical traps that the Chinese military would likely confront in the twenty-first century. The PLA is eager to avoid reprising past tragedies. The literature surveyed in the preceding chapters demonstrates that China's strategists are attuned to the echoes of the past when they look to the future.

NOTES

1. 张晓林 班海滨 [Zhang Xiaolin and Ban Haibin], "渡江战役与人民海军的创建" [The Cross-River Campaign and the Founding of the People's Navy], 军事历史研究 [Military History Research], no. 2 (1989): 23.
2. 丁一平 李洛荣 龚连娣 [Ding Yiping, Li Luorong, and Gong Liandi], 世界海军史 [World Naval History] (Beijing: Haichao, 2000), 723. The lead author, Vice Adm. Ding Yiping, was formerly the commander of the North Sea Fleet (2000–2003), the deputy commander of the PLAN (2006–14), and the chief of staff of the PLAN (2006–8).
3. Frank Dikotter, *The Tragedy of Liberation: A History of the Chinese Revolution, 1945–57* (New York: Bloomsbury, 2013).
4. 王厚卿 主编 [Wang Houqing, ed.], 战役发展史 [The History of Campaign Development] (Beijing: National Defense University Press, 2008), 557–58.
5. 赵焕明 [Zhao Huanming], "金塘岛, 登步岛, 金门岛登陆作战的经验教训和启示" [The Lessons and Implications of the Jintang Island, Dengbu Island, and Jinmen Island Landing Operations], 军事历史 [Military History], no. 6 (2001): 3–7.
6. Zhao, 7.
7. 张连宋 王其云 主编 [Zhang Liansong and Wang Qiyun, eds.], 由海向陆的战争 生命线 中外重要登陆作战的后勤保障 [War's Lifeline from the Sea to the Land: Logistical Support in Important Landing Operations in China and Overseas] (Beijing: Haichao, 2005).
8. Zhang and Wang, *War's Lifeline from the Sea to the Land*, 182.
9. 刘兴 刘畅 李远星 [Liu Xing, Liu Chang, and Li Yuanxing], "金门战役民船保障存 在的问题及启示" [The Problems of Civilian Transport Support during the Jinmen Campaign and Their Implications], 军事交通学院学报 [Journal of Military Transportation University] 17, no. 2 (February 2015): 20–23.
10. 窦超 [Dou Chao], "让历史告诉我们—金门战斗之教训及对未来登陆战的启示 和思考" [Let History Tell the Future—The Lessons of Jinmen Combat and the Implications and Thoughts on Future Landing Operations], 舰载武器 [Shipborne Weapons], no. 4 (2008): 46–51.
11. Dou, 50.
12. Dou, 51.

EIGHT

Discerning Institutional Continuities

A newly established organization's formative experiences frequently exert a lasting and outsize influence on its values and outlook. The moment of creation and the circumstances surrounding that moment impart enduring lessons, deeply held beliefs, and habits of thought that are chiseled into an institution's identity. This identity finds expression in proclivities, assumptions, and patterns of behavior that tend be quite stable over time and lend a degree of predictability to how an institution thinks and acts.

Likewise, the seven-decades-old battles and bureaucratic decisions documented in this study likely left a deep imprint on the Chinese navy and on Chinese sea power. The founding era—spanning just eighteen months—shaped how the naval service understood its reason for being, organized itself, and thought about strategy and tactics. To the extent that the PLAN's earliest history baked in durable institutional traits, an understanding of this past could offer clues about how the naval service will evolve, think, and act in maritime Asia and beyond in the coming years.

To be sure, it is analytically difficult to draw a straight line between the PLAN's birth to the present and the future. It is hazardous at best to attribute a specific behavior today to some decades-old event. Yet, it is still possible to discern echoes of the past by identifying continuities in behavior and thought. These institutional legacies can be found in organizational behavior, personnel decisions, command structure, doctrine, force structure, budgeting priorities, core values, and so forth. Such historically rooted norms, preferences, and practices could also be adapted to meet future demands, especially as the Chinese navy prepares for global roles and missions. The following links the past to the present and engages in a forward-looking, speculative analytic exercise.

THE REGIONAL FLEET SYSTEM

The PLAN's regional fleets owed their existence to the Third and Fourth Field Armies, which provided the leaders, personnel, equipment, and resources to stand up the local navies. To secure their victory in the civil war, the field armies garrisoned the provinces and regions within their assigned theater of operations, becoming in effect occupying forces throughout China. Field army commanders and political commissars quickly assumed regional, provincial, and administrative leadership positions over their conquered territories as they transitioned to peacetime duties. For example, Chen Yi, commander of the Third Field Army, served as Shanghai's mayor for almost a decade. Ye Jianying, who co-commanded the operation to seize Guangzhou, became the city's mayor and the commander of the South China Military Region.

As the field armies settled into their respective geographic areas of control, they emerged as distinctive regional power centers. Political loyalties, personal networks, and patronage systems organized themselves around the field armies and their occupation zones.[1] According to one study, "a particular Communist version of 'warlordism' . . . became a fundamental element in the inter-regional distribution of economic and political power after 1950."[2] Indeed, after the Communists disbanded the field armies and replaced them with military regions in 1955, senior members and units of the field armies continued to dominate the military regions they had previously administered and garrisoned. Thus, the former elites of the Third and Fourth Field Armies largely led the Nanjing Military Region and the Guangzhou Military Region, respectively, and the associated regional naval commands well into the 1960s and beyond.

The Third Field Army's leadership dominated the East China Navy and its successor organization, the East Sea Fleet. Following Zhang Aiping's tenure, Yuan Yelie became the commander of the East China Navy in February 1951. During the Chinese Civil War, Yuan was deputy commander and chief of staff of the Shandong Military Region, which was later reorganized to help establish the East China Field Army, the predecessor to the Third Field Army. Tao Yong, Yuan's successor, was the commander of the 23rd Corps of the 7th Army under the Third Field Army. Tao led his forces in the cross-river campaign to take Zhenjiang and Jiangyin, which became a start-up hub for Zhang's East China Navy (see chapter 3). The 23rd Army would go on to participate in the Shanghai campaign and was one of the units destined for the Zhoushan campaign before the Nationalists withdrew.[3] After leading in the Korean War, Tao was appointed commander of the East China Navy in November 1952. He was then appointed commander of the East Sea Fleet in 1955 and remained in that post until 1967. Zhao Qimin was political commissar of the 34th Corps of the Third Field Army.[4] He was appointed the political commissar of the East China Navy in February 1951 and served in that position until November 1952. Yuan Yelie was moved laterally to serve as political commissar of the East China Navy when Tao Yong became the commander. Yuan's successor, Kang Zhiqiang, was political commissar of the 21st Corps under the Third Field Army.[5] Kang served as political commissar of the East China Navy until July 1962.

Similarly, the Fourth Field Army held sway over the southern naval command. Hong Xuezhi was deputy commander and chief of the staff of the 15th Army, the principal organization responsible for the Guangdong, Hainan, and Wanshan campaigns. After seizing Guangdong, Hong was appointed deputy commander of the Guangdong Military Region and commander of the Riverine Defense Command of the Guangdong Military Region. Hong's successor, Fang Qiang, was commander of the 44th Corps, which fought in the Guangdong and Wanshan campaigns.[6] Fang was appointed commander of the South Central Military Region Navy in October 1950 and held the post until 1953. Zhao Qimin was transferred from the East China Navy to succeed Fang and became commander of the South Sea Fleet in 1955. Zhao served as commander until December 1959 and was concurrently the political commissar from 1953 to 1956. Zhao's successor, Wu Ruilin, was commander of the Fourth Field Army's 42nd Corps, which fought in the Liao-Shen and Ping-Jin campaigns and in the Korean War.[7] Wu was commander of the South Sea Fleet from 1960 to 1968. Fang Zhengping, former director of the political department of the 22nd Army under the Fourth Field Army, was deputy political commissar and later political commissar of the South Sea Fleet from 1951 to 1956 and from 1956 to 1968, respectively. Except for Zhao, Fourth Field Army officers held the top regional naval posts from 1950 to the late 1960s.

Given the preeminence of the field army system, the Third Field Army and the Fourth Field Army likely exerted a significant influence on the East Sea Fleet and the South Sea Fleet, respectively. Importantly, the field armies had developed their own command relationships, warfighting styles, and politico-military thought—largely independent of each other—across diverse geographic settings and strategic circumstances over decades. Thus, each formed a unique institutional personality during the long revolutionary struggle. Future research could investigate how and to what extent the Third and Fourth Field Armies passed on their distinctive institutional DNAs to their respective regional naval descendants. Such an inquiry would require deep study of the histories, key leaders, and organizational cultures of the field armies. At the same time, intimate knowledge of the regional fleets would be necessary to discern how the field armies' institutional personalities manifest themselves in naval affairs.

It is noteworthy that the regional fleet system is not unique to the Communist era. The regionalization of naval power traces its origins to dynastic China.[8] In the late Qing period, for example, Manchu authorities paired neighboring provinces, such as Guangdong-Guangxi and Zhejiang-Fujian, as the jurisdictional basis for commanding local navies. Considerable autonomy characterized the Qing Empire's balkanized navy. Efforts to establish a national naval service failed repeatedly during imperial China's encounter with the West and Japan in the second half of the nineteenth century. Consequently, the utter absence of coordination between the regional fleets contributed to the disasters during the 1884–85 Sino-French War and the 1894–95 Sino-Japanese War.[9] The persistence of regional navies is thus deeply rooted in Chinese history and in early party-state formation.

The three fleets remain the principal organizations responsible for specific geographic areas of operations; surface, submarine, and aviation forces; naval bases and garrisons; and shipyards. Following the recent institutional reforms that established joint theater commands, the three fleets continue to serve as the naval components of their respective theaters, and the fleet commanders are concurrently the deputy commanders of the theater commands.[10] The regional fleet structure, then, will likely persist as the basis for enhancing the PLA's joint operations and future force building. It may be analytically fruitful to consider the extent to which the regional structures will likely endure and, if they do persist, how such organizations will adapt to new missions and requirements.

THE POLITICAL COMMISSAR SYSTEM

As the study makes clear, political control of the East China Navy and the PLAN was paramount during the founding period. Zhang Aiping and Xiao Jinguang, selected in part for their impeccable CCP credentials, were appointed to serve concurrently as commander and political commissar to oversee their respective organizations, including major educational institutions. During the recruitment drive to bring former Nationalists out of hiding, Zhang appointed political commissar Sun Kejin, director of the East China Navy's political department, to tap his underground network of operatives. At the level of warfighting, political commissars reached down to the regiment level, a practice that continues to this day.

The political commissars' duties extended well beyond instilling loyalty to the CCP. During the offshore campaigns of 1949 and 1950, political commissars fought at sea, stormed the beaches, and suffered casualties alongside their troops and also provided the education and training to reorient the mindset of ground pounders toward the sea. The commissars boosted morale and fighting spirit, which accounted in part for the impressive courage and near-suicidal actions of some PLA units, and rallied local communities to support the Communist forces. In addition, the commissars employed psychological warfare to encourage surrenders among the Nationalist island defenders during some of the offshore campaigns. In short, political commissars served as an important force multiplier.

The founding history of the PLAN shows that political commissars should be closely studied to understand contemporary Chinese naval operations. As one report argues persuasively, the dual-command structure will continue to play a decisive role in the command and control of the Chinese navy.[11] Unlike the Soviet system, the PLA's political commissars hold equal rank with their command and operational counterparts. Consensus and mutual consultations characterize the planning and decision-making processes from the highest levels of command down to tactical units. It should be expected that the CCP will continue to go to sea with its fleets. Outside observers should thus view China's behavior in the maritime domain as an expression of the party-navy system.

The dual-command system could make the PLAN particularly adept at using the naval instrument for political theater. Chinese commanders and political commissars could be quite skilled at conceiving and implementing plans designed to overawe friends and foes alike. They might be highly trained to employ three warfares—psychological, media, and legal operations—to disintegrate the enemy's will in peacetime and in conflict. Political commissars and their interpretations of intangible factors, such as morale, could also have an outsize influence on assessments of risk and opportunity. Material considerations alone, such as a tactical imbalance of capabilities, might not deter assertive or aggressive Chinese action at sea. The PLAN's early history of prevailing over a technologically superior adversary could reinforce the operational proclivity to lend great weight to the moral dimensions of strategy. The implications for deterrence signaling, misperceptions, and miscalculations in crisis or war could be quite profound.

LAND-BASED NAVAL POWER

The debates over strategy during the founding period reveal that Communist leaders were inclined to apply their terrestrial mindset to solve offshore problems. Lacking a navy and an air force, planners sought to use shore-based weaponry to influence events on the nearby seas. Xiao Jinguang memorably likened the Chinese mainland to a massive aircraft carrier from which land-based assets, such as coastal artillery, would project power in the maritime domain. Contemporary concepts and doctrines show that this continental habit of thought remains relevant to this day. The PLA's conception of the first island chain reflects in part a visual extension of China's territorial defensive perimeter in the seaward direction. The navy's offshore defense strategy is essentially a naval manifestation of Mao's active defense construct for land warfare.

While some have used this apparent terrestrial bias to dismiss China's prospects at sea, Beijing's impressive nautical ascent in recent years strongly suggests that a different prognosis may be more analytically productive.[12] Rather than viewing such a continentalist mindset as an impediment to naval development, it may be prudent to consider how China's landward notions of sea power might be adapted efficaciously to new circumstances and demands.

An important feature of the PLAN's land-based power is its naval aviation forces. As noted in the study, Xiao Jinguang and his lieutenants advocated for their own air arm because they could not trust the air force to protect their vulnerable surface combatants. The PLAN thus invested in independent shore-based airpower to defend China's maritime airspace and to support the surface fleet. Today, the naval aviation branch possesses hundreds of combat aircraft, including fixed-wing bombers and fighters. As China's surface combatants enhanced their organic air defenses in recent years, aviation units have increasingly reoriented their missions toward maritime strike. Ship-killing bombers along with a complement of reconnaissance aircraft have conducted sorties along the first island chain since 2013.[13]

How the introduction of carrier-based aviation will influence the future role of land-based aviation remains unclear. It seems unlikely that carrier air wings would completely displace their shore-based counterparts, which have enjoyed a storied history and long-standing institutional support. Constituents of the shore-based aviation community would also likely frustrate plans to eclipse the relevance of their subservice. It may be that as China's carrier aviators master fleet air defenses, land-based aircraft would further specialize in maritime strike and other niche missions. Moreover, the PLA Air Force's bomber fleet has begun to claim and play a more prominent role in maritime missions, thereby threatening the naval aviation's institutional prerogatives and share of resources. Such interservice rivalry could further push the PLAN's shore-based bombers to diversify their tactical specialties.[14] Looking ahead, a globalizing Chinese navy might find new uses for shore-based airpower. Naval air units and missile brigades could be deployed to forward bases along the Indian Ocean littorals to provide additional air coverage and maritime strike options for the PLAN's surface forces, creating in effect an expeditionary fortress fleet. The proclivity to use the land to control the seas could thus find new and creative expressions in faraway theaters.

THE CIVIL-MILITARY NEXUS

During the founding period, the party-army system tapped the civilian and commercial sectors to build the navy from scratch and to conduct island-seizing campaigns. The maritime industries and the associated human capital along coastal China provided the infrastructure, matériel, ships, expertise, and crew without which Communist efforts to build up sea power would have almost certainly foundered. The PLA's high degree of comfort in drawing from society for the war effort and for military modernization reflected its long-standing tradition of waging people's war. The Communists clearly saw the development of naval power as an all-of-nation effort.

Similarly, the civilian sector would likely be conscripted to support future PLA campaigns close to home and in theaters farther afield. Western scholars have begun to pay close attention to the potential roles of civilian shipping and infrastructure in a prospective cross-strait invasion. Conor Kennedy shows how China's merchant roll-on/roll-off ships could deliver troops, trucks, equipment, and amphibious assault vehicles ashore.[15] Thomas Shugart points to the sheer scale of Chinese civilian shipping that could be employed to transport PLA units to Taiwan.[16] In an in-depth study, Michael Dahm surveys military exercises and training to evaluate the capabilities of China's commercial fleet in a putative amphibious operation against Taiwan. He observes that "PLA authors uniformly assert that civilian ships, working closely with the military, will be an integral component of any major cross-sea logistics operation."[17] Notably, Dahm cites a PLA article that draws lessons from the October 1949 Jinmen campaign. He is skeptical about the ability of merchant ships to furnish logistical support to a major amphibious operation in a hostile environment, as least as of 2021. Nevertheless, he contends that "it would be a mistake to underestimate the ingenuity and tenacity of the PLA."[18]

This civil-military interrelationship is also discernible in recent far seas operations. The PLAN's antipiracy patrols in the Gulf of Aden rely on China's extensive overseas commercial network established by state-owned enterprises for logistical support. The massive shipping conglomerate China Ocean Shipping Company (COSCO) and its subsidiary based in the United Arab Emirates, COSCO West Asia, have provided access to the resupply infrastructure that feeds the crews and fuels, repairs, and maintains the ships involved in months-long deployments.[19] Like the founding period, the PLAN improvised and learned quickly on the job as it practiced the art and science of logistics for expeditionary operations. This commercial-military nexus—alongside China's permanent base in Djibouti—continues to sustain the Chinese navy in distant waters.

Looking ahead, it is worth examining how the civilian sector will further support expeditionary naval operations. Various civilian ports of friendly foreign countries in Asia, Africa, and Europe have already resupplied the PLAN's flotillas. In addition, COSCO-operated container terminals around the world, roll-on/roll-off vessels, container ships, tankers, passenger aircraft, and cargo planes could all be called upon to lend logistical assistance.[20] Notably, the Chinese navy has already experimented with underway replenishment using a COSCO container ship. China's dominant maritime industries are the backbone of these commercial assets and infrastructure.[21] These state-backed multinational corporations enjoy close ties with the military-industrial complex and advance China's initiative to fuse the civilian and military sectors. In the coming years, this global commercial-military nexus could serve as the foundation for an enlarged and entrenched Chinese naval presence along major sea-lanes connecting China to markets abroad. The PLAN's early history suggests that the naval service likely possesses the aptitude and the appetite for leveraging these overseas civilian networks.

NAVAL VALUES

This study contends that the Chinese navy's founding era left an indelible mark on its outlook, values, and institutions, offering clues about the PLAN's present and future. The first eighteen months of the naval service's existence had a particularly lasting influence on its identity. Just as John Paul Jones and the American Revolution continue to define how the US Navy sees itself, the Chinese navy's moment of conception remains a touchstone. Just as the US Navy's ceremonies and customs—rooted in its founding history—reveal much about its core values, the PLAN's discourse about its past offers hints about its self-appraisal.[22] One way to keep track of this lineage is to document how the institutional custodians of the Chinese navy retell—and retail—historical narratives that impart the service's highest values and treasured traditions.

Consider, for example, the writings of China's naval leaders. In a 2007 journal article articulating the Chinese navy's future missions, Adm. Wu Shengli, the former PLAN commander, harkens back to the past to inspire pride in the naval service. He refers explicitly to the founding period when "the People's Navy was created in gun smoke."[23] Among the 1,275 naval battles, the admiral lists 5 that "achieved glorious accomplishments." Notably, the Wanshan campaign detailed in this study makes the short list.

In a 2009 article commemorating the sixtieth anniversary of the PLAN's founding, Admiral Wu recalls how "the People's Navy grew up through baptism in the fires of war" by seizing offshore islands and breaking enemy blockades.[24] The PLAN commander again identifies the Wanshan operation as a standout in the Chinese navy's "splendid history book." Wu then recounts how specific units and individuals served as "heroic exemplars and models" that "illuminated the pages of the navy's history book."

In an article celebrating the seventieth anniversary of the PLAN's founding, Vice Adm. Shen Jinlong, Wu's successor, amplifies the significance of the Wanshan campaign. Shen extols the Chinese navy's "maritime pioneer spirit" that enabled a unit to "use small boats to fight big warships" and to "fight with bayonets at sea" during a naval engagement at Wanshan.[25] "*Pioneer*" (先锋 or *xianfeng*) is the namesake of the famous wood-hulled gunboat that fought a Nationalist warship at point-blank range. The encounter culminated in hand-to-hand combat after bayonet-wielding Communist troops leapt onto the enemy vessel (see chapter 6).

The PLAN's official handbook for officers and enlisted describes the amphibious operations to seize Wanshan as a key episode in the navy's "glorious history." According to the guidebook, the campaign reflects the naval service's "heroic spirit of using the small to fight the big, using the inferior to win over the superior, and daring to fight to secure victory."[26] The battle has been held up as a model for decades. In a 1987 article that surveys the navy's fine heritage, Adm. Liu Huaqing, the PLAN commander from 1982 to 1988, recalls the courage of those who fought at Wanshan. He too sees the PLAN's tradition of using weakness to defeat the strong as a core element of the navy's identity.[27]

Circumstances have certainly changed radically since the ragtag, improvised fleet helped the Communists prevail at Wanshan. The Chinese navy is already the largest in the world and boasts capabilities that rival the best at sea. Yet, the values embodied in Wanshan and in subsequent battles are likely to remain relevant today and into the future. Current Chinese doctrinal writings foresee great power rivalry and possibly war with the United States and its allies. China could well find itself isolated and outmatched against a formidable coalition. As the PLA looks ahead, it may have to plan for warfighting scenarios in which a Chinese expeditionary force finds itself cut off and surrounded in the Indian Ocean. The bottom line is that China's strategists must anticipate and prepare for fighting from a position of relative weakness. Time-tested concepts, such as applying tactical superiority within strategic inferiority, may find their uses in future combat at sea.

COMPARATIVE ASSESSMENTS

For future research, intraservice, interservice, and cross-national comparisons could yield valuable insights about the Chinese navy. By protocol order, the undersea force, the surface fleet, naval aviation, the marine corps, and coastal defense constitute the PLAN's five combat branches. Understanding the founding history and the evolution of each branch could reveal much about what the naval service values in terms of operational competencies and specialties. As observed earlier, Chinese naval leaders insisted on an aviation branch out of fear that the air force would provide inadequate or unreliable support. If this concern was deeply institutionalized, then it might indicate how hard constituents of naval aviation might fight to preserve the air branch's prerogatives and existence if they were ever threatened.

In-depth studies on the origins of the air force and the rocket force could illustrate variations in institutional traits among the services, bringing the PLAN's persona into sharper relief. As noted in this study, the Korean War vaulted the air force to the forefront as the Communist leadership prepared to contest American command of the air over the peninsula. The decision to prioritize airpower set back the PLAN's ambitious modernization plans for years. This turning point in the navy's early history may have had an outsize impact on its attitudes and perhaps insecurities about its place in the pecking order among the services. This trauma could in turn provide clues about how China's naval leadership perceives and justifies the PLAN's purpose, relevance, and mission in debates on strategy and resources.

Cross-national comparative studies could assess the institutional distinctions between the PLAN and the US Navy. The PLAN's dual-command structure, the primacy of the CCP, and consensus-based decision-making stand in contrast to the US Navy's cherished concept of independent command at sea and the absolute responsibilities vested in a single commanding officer. The US Navy continues to regard carrier-based fighter aviation as the apex branch of the organization, whereas the Chinese navy's emphasis on the submarine force is giving way to the surface fleet. The US Navy's land-based aviation is primarily concerned with maritime patrol and electronic warfare, whereas the PLAN's shore-based air arm includes maritime strike, air superiority, and land attack. It should be reemphasized that these differences between the two navies are rooted in their unique historical experiences.

Beyond these tactical and operational contrasts, the two services potentially differ on larger questions about sea power, strategy, and global operations. Many of the most important and iconic US regional commands and fleets were forged out of World War II and the subsequent Cold War struggle. Victory in the Pacific War, the liberation of the Philippines, the occupation of Japan, the Chinese Civil War, and the hot wars in Asia during the superpower rivalry form the essential historical context to understanding the US Seventh Fleet and its presence and operations in the western Pacific today.[28]

China's peacetime pathway toward a more robust naval presence in faraway theaters will likely look different from that of America's postwar model. For example, the PLAN's thinking about a forward-deployed fleet might be intermediated by the idiosyncrasies of the regional fleet system summarized above. At the same time, China's state-backed multinational companies and the commercial-military nexus could shape the PLAN's approach to peacetime access to shore facilities and wartime combat logistics at sea in ways that diverge markedly from the US Navy's long-standing practices. The future character of the Sino-American maritime competition could resemble that of the Anglo-Dutch rivalry during the second half of the seventeenth century, when commercial actors and interests played a prominent role in geopolitics.

It may be tempting to depict China's regional fleet system, dual-command structure, land-based airpower, reliance on commercial actors, and small-ship ethos as impediments to its global maritime ambitions. These elements of the PLAN's institutional personality might imply that China will struggle to overcome its political constraints, regional orientation, and landbound posture. But such a pessimistic diagnosis runs counter to the naval service's record thus far. The Chinese navy has demonstrated time and again its capacity to prove the naysayers wrong. The foregoing analysis suggests an alternative interpretation: Chinese leaders will adapt and formulate their own brand of sea power. It is incumbent upon observers to test this hypothesis, lest policy makers misread the Chinese navy's future trajectory.

NOTES

1. For a classic on this phenomenon, see William W. Whitson, *The Chinese High Command: A History of Communist Military Politics* (New York: Praeger, 1973).
2. William Whitson, "The Field Army in Chinese Communist Military Politics," *China Quarterly*, no. 37 (March 1969): 11.
3. 陈相灵 汪海波 张小明 宋慧 主编 [Chen Xiangling, Wang Haibo, Zhang Xiaoming, and Song Hui, eds.], 第三野战军的16个军 [The 16 Corps of the Third Field Army] (Beijing: National Defense University Press, 2015), 81–100.
4. Chen et al., 311–25.
5. Chen et al., 30–52.
6. 李力钢 池小泉 赵亚莉 主编 [Li Ligang, Chi Xiaochuan, and Zhao Yali, eds.], 第四野战军的16个军 [The 16 Corps of the Fourth Field Army] (Beijing: National Defense University Press, 2015), 154–76.
7. Li et al., 96–120.
8. Bruce Swanson, *Eighth Voyage of the Dragon: A History of China's Quest for Seapower* (Annapolis, MD: Naval Institute Press, 1982), 65–66.
9. John L. Rawlinson, *China's Struggle for Naval Development, 1839–1895* (Cambridge, MA: Harvard University Press, 1967).
10. Dennis J. Blasko, "A 'First' for the People's Liberation Army: A Navy Admiral Becomes a Joint, Regional, Commander," *China Brief* 17, no. 5 (March 2017), https://jamestown.org/program/first-peoples-liberation-army-navy-admiral-becomes-joint-regional-commander/. After the reorganization, the North, East, and South Sea Fleets also became known as the Northern, Eastern, and Southern Theater Navies, respectively.
11. Jeff W. Benson and Zi Yang, *Party on the Bridge: Political Commissars in the Chinese Navy* (Washington, DC: Center for Strategic and International Studies, June 2020), https://www.csis.org/analysis/party-bridge-political-commissars-chinese-navy.
12. Bernard D. Cole, *The Great Wall at Sea: China's Navy Enters the Twenty-First Century* (Annapolis, MD: Naval Institute Press, 2001), 177.
13. China Aerospace Studies Institute, *PLA Aerospace Power: A Primer on Trends in China's Military Air, Space, and Missile Forces*, 2nd ed. (Montgomery, AL: Air University Press, 2019), 36.
14. Ian Burns McCaslin and Andrew S. Erickson, *Selling a Maritime Air Force: The PLAAF's Campaign for a Bigger Maritime Role* (Washington, DC: China Aerospace Studies Institute, 2019), 42–43.

15. Conor Kennedy, "Ramping the Strait: Quick and Dirty Solutions to Boost Amphibious Lift," *China Brief* 21, no. 14, (July 2021), https://jamestown.org/program/ramping-the-strait-quick-and-dirty-solutions-to-boost-amphibious-lift/.

16. Thomas Shugart, "Mind the Gap: How China's Civilian Shipping Could Enable a Taiwan Invasion," *War on the Rocks*, August 16, 2021, https://warontherocks.com/2021/08/mind-the-gap-how-chinas-civilian-shipping-could-enable-a-taiwan-invasion/.

17. J. Michael Dahm, *Chinese Ferry Tales: The PLA's Use of Civilian Shipping in Support of Over-the Shore Logistics* (Newport, RI: China Maritime Studies Institute, Naval War College, 2021), 1, https://digital-commons.usnwc.edu/cmsi-maritime-reports/16/.

18. Dahm, 55.

19. Andrew Erickson and Austin M. Strange, *Six Years at Sea . . . and Counting: Gulf of Aden Anti-Piracy and China's Maritime Commons Presence* (Washington, DC: Jamestown Foundation, June 2015), 50.

20. Chad Peltier, *China's Logistics Capabilities for Expeditionary Operations*, report by Jane's prepared for the U.S.-China Economic and Security Review Commission, December 16, 2019, 54–58, https://www.uscc.gov/research/chinas-logistics-capabilities-expeditionary-operations.

21. Jude Blanchette, Jonathan E. Hillman, Maesea McCalpin, and Mingda Qiu, "Hidden Harbors: China's State-Backed Shipping Industry," *CSIS Brief*, July 2020, https://www.csis.org/analysis/hidden-harbors-chinas-state-backed-shipping-industry.

22. William P. Mack and Royal W. Connell, *Naval Ceremonies, Customs, and Traditions*, 5th ed. (Annapolis, MD: Naval Institute Press, 1980).

23. 吴胜利 胡彦林 [Wu Shengli and Hu Yanlin], "锻造适应我军历史使命要求的强大人民海军" [Building a Powerful People's Navy That Meets the Requirements of the Historical Mission for Our Military], 求是 [Qiushi], no. 14 (July 2007): 32.

24. 吴胜利 刘晓江 [Wu Shengli and Liu Xiaojiang], "建设一支与履行新世纪新阶段我军历史使命要求相适应的强大的人民海军" [Building a Powerful People's Navy Adapted to Requirements of Honoring New Historic Missions of the Chinese Military in the New Century and New Stage], 求是 [Qiushi], no. 9 (May 2009): 7.

25. 沈金龙 秦生祥 [Shen Jinlong and Qin Shengxiang], "人民海军: 杨帆奋进70年" [People's Navy: Sailing and Forging Ahead for 70 Years], 求是 [Qiushi], no. 8 (April 2019), http://www.qstheory.cn/dukan/qs/2019-04/16/c_1124364140.htm.

26. 杜景臣 主编 [Du Jingchen, ed.], 中国海军军人手册 [Handbook for Officers and Enlisted of the Chinese PLA Navy] (Beijing: Haichao, 2012), 570.

27. 刘华清 [Liu Huaqing], 刘华清军事文选 [Selected Military Writings of Liu Huaqing] (Beijing: Liberation Army Press, 2008), 588.

28. Edward J. Marolda, *Ready Seapower: A History of the U.S. Seventh Fleet* (Washington, DC: Naval History and Heritage Command, 2012).

NINE

Conclusion

The preceding chapters offer a more complete and balanced account of Maoist China's seaward turn than the existing Western literature. The foregoing shows that the CCP and the PLA were neither infallible nor incompetent at sea. China's maritime achievements from 1949 to 1950, while commendable, must be weighed against the difficulties and failures that the leadership encountered. But this study is by no means the final word on this understudied period. Future areas for research include the PLA's offshore campaigns that took place in subsequent years as well as Chinese assessments of foreign amphibious operations. There is also an opportunity to more fully engage the ROC literature that captures the Nationalist perspective about Communist China's earliest operations in the maritime domain. This study should further stimulate debate about how the PLA interprets its own past and how those historical narratives, in turn, should inform Western reappraisals of China's nautical ascent in the coming decades.

KEY FINDINGS

It is worth repeating that this origin story is not exclusively about the Chinese navy. Rather, it is about Chinese sea power, namely all the instruments of national power that can shape events at sea to serve China's interests. The various inputs of sea power, including Mao Zedong's armies, civilian shipping and seamen, commercial shipyards, coastal populations, and local insurgents, all played critical roles in achieving China's maritime goals. Indeed, the Qiongya Column on Hainan, which tied up significant Nationalist military power, may have been the difference between victory and failure for the amphibious operation.

From the beginning the Communists suffered from severe material shortcomings, inexperience, and inadequate human capital to support the initial naval buildup. The Nationalists took with them the best ships to Taiwan even as they sabotaged and destroyed what they had to leave behind. Faced with scarcity and international isolation, the victors thus had to make do with third-rate equipment and find workarounds that would have likely horrified their Western counterparts. The improvised hodgepodge fleet was laughably behind the modern navies of the day. There is, however, no denying the grit and ingenuity behind these efforts.

The naval leadership was all too aware of China's limitations in the naval sphere and, accordingly, set out modest and realistic objectives that were consonant with its constrained finances and limited industrial base. During the August 1950 naval conference, Xiao Jinguang and his lieutenants set a course for a coastal defense force that would comprise fast attack boats, submarines, and shore-based aircraft. This buildup plan was hardly grandiose. It was aligned with China's naval strategy of near-coast defense. Yet, even these humble goals were ultimately dashed due to the exigencies of the Korean War. Instead, scarce resources were redirected to the air force.

While the Communists sought help from their former enemies, suspicions and animosities ran deep on both sides. Naval leaders found it difficult to assimilate ex-Nationalists into their ranks. There was significant resistance among the Communist cadre, who viewed the Nationalists as potential ideological contaminants among the officers and troops. Disputes and bickering between the two camps even led to Nationalist desertions. Pragmatism did prevail over ideology to the extent that senior Nationalist officers were entrusted to advise the Communists. But the Communists did not bring in the Nationalists out of magnanimity; rather, it was out of necessity.

The PLA's operational performance was a mixed bag. To be sure, the conquest of Hainan was a significant feat. Yet, that victory must be measured against the blunders at Jinmen and Dengbu Islands that were the result of hubris, poor planning, and bad execution. The Communists failed to stop the Nationalist withdrawal of troops from Zhoushan and Hainan, numbering some 175,000 men, which helped to bolster Chiang Kai-shek's defense of Taiwan. The PLA literature, moreover, appears to have obfuscated the extent of losses during the successful Hainan and Wanshan campaigns. It is thus important to maintain a balanced view of Communist China's turn to the seas, neither exaggerating nor dismissing an important episode in the PLA's history.

AREAS FOR FUTURE RESEARCH

This initial inquiry into Communist China's first forays at sea provides a starting point for future research. First, many of the key sources cited in this study, including the official war histories, cover subsequent offshore operations that took place in the 1950s, 1960s, and 1970s. The 1955 Yijiangshan campaign, often touted as the PLA's first modern joint operation, is particularly promising. The local commander overseeing the operation was none other than

Zhang Aiping. In the so-called 86 Sea Battle in 1965, the PLAN conducted its first fleet-on-fleet engagement against the Nationalist navy from which the PLAN emerged victorious. The 1974 Paracels sea battle exhibited many of the tactical preferences that were at play a quarter century before.[1] A broader historical survey that seeks to connect the earliest encounters at sea to later campaigns would help Western analysts discern patterns and continuities in Chinese strategy, operations, and doctrine and would allow observers to assess the extent to which the formative experiences in 1949 and 1950 exerted a lasting influence on the PLA.

Second, the open-source literature suggests that the PLA has devoted substantial intellectual energy to learning from foreign amphibious operations. The writings include a multivolume PLA study on World War II that examines relevant campaigns in the European and Pacific theaters of operations.[2] Chinese strategists have pored over case studies from the bitter struggle over Guadalcanal to the bloody battles of Iwo Jima and Okinawa.[3] They have also paid close attention to postwar campaigns, including the Inchon landings during the Korean War and the fighting over the Falkland Islands. As the PLA continues its rapid modernization, which has increasingly focused on acquiring modern amphibious capabilities, these past operations involving high-end conventional combat between peer and near-peer adversaries will be ever more relevant to the Chinese military.

Third, scholars can further explore the trajectory of the PLA's intellectual development after 1950. As Xiaobing Li argues persuasively, the PLA underwent a massive doctrinal and force structure transformation during and after the Korean War. Following the conflict on the peninsula, PLA leaders argued among themselves about the extent to which the military should adhere to its own traditions or follow the Soviet model. The debates resembled those that took place within the PLAN in 1950. This later debate was personified by Liu Bocheng, who called for a Chinese way to developing the PLA, and by Peng Dehuai, who advocated for a wholesale adoption of Soviet military thought.[4] While Xiao sought to strike a balance between domestic and foreign ideas in 1950, the Soviet school championed by Peng won out in the post–Korean War era, enabling Peng to advance a puritanical program of Russianizing the PLA. Analysts can use this study as a baseline with which to determine the fate of the Nationalist intellectual influence in subsequent years. They can also discern to what extent the Cultural Revolution and other political upheavals disrupted or dismantled the former Nationalists' imprint on the PLAN.

Finally, this study is an admittedly one-sided story about the Communist experience. War is an intrinsically interactive encounter. Any account of it must consider all the combatants involved. While this study has referenced some ROC retrospectives of the island campaigns, a more complete history that incorporates the Nationalist perspective would add value to the literature. The KMT's local commanders almost certainly held different if not opposing views about the events that transpired in 1949 and 1950. The Nationalist side of the story may help to uncover biases or outright misrepresentations by the Communists. Documenting how the island defenders saw and interpreted the PLA's amphibious operations might help to fill gaps in the storylines that have been told and retold by the Communists. Such an account could help to better determine whether the Communists won by virtue of their operational brilliance or whether the Nationalists lost owing to incompetence and flagging morale.

As the select ROC and CIA accounts of the offshore campaigns show, the PLA literature likely exaggerates Communist gains and downplays their losses. Gen. Xue Yue's forces on Hainan inflicted significant harm on the Qiongya Column during its counterinsurgency operations in February and March 1950. One reason for the first wave of infiltrations across the Qiongzhou Strait was to shore up the besieged insurgents. Moreover, the urgent need to send reinforcements and supplies to the island indicates that the column's resources and manpower were not as abundant as the literature suggests. The Nationalist interdiction efforts against Communist shipping to and from Hainan were also likely far more costly than the writings let on. Similarly, US intelligence reports reveal that the ROCN dealt blows against the PLA's amphibious forces during the first phase of the Wanshan campaign. The literature is also tellingly silent on key events that were less than flattering of the PLA. The failure to preclude or at least disrupt the Nationalist evacuation of 125,000 troops from Zhoushan goes largely unmentioned. The PLA's inability to exploit its operational successes to prevent the KMT's withdrawal of 50,000 men from Hainan, despite the complete Nationalist collapse, is also unexplained. A more balanced narrative, drawing from ROC archives and secondary sources, thus awaits future scholars.

TIME TO REAPPRAISE THE PAST

For years, Western observers contended that the Chinese navy in its infancy was merely an army disguised as a naval service. They deprecated the role of Zhang Aiping and Xiao Jinguang, depicting them as ground pounders selected for their ideological credentials and for their loyalty to Mao and the CCP.[5] This study shows that such a dismissive portrayal is too sweeping. Mao's army went to sea and through the crucible of combat accumulated hard-earned experiences, developed its doctrine, and applied the PLA's unique operational style to the maritime domain. The PLA possessed independent agency, interacted intensively with the adversary and the warfighting environment, and climbed a steep learning curve. In short, 1949 and 1950 proved to be a remarkably productive period.

This origin story, as the Chinese tell it, casts Communist China's first encounters with the sea in a new light. The PLA was neither inert nor inept. It was a living force that acted on its will and, more frequently than not, imposed its will on the enemy. The writings surveyed in this study demonstrate that this formative history is a source of inspiration and pride and is a core component of the PLA's corporate identity. If the PLA's interpretation of its past can be likened to an individual's internal monologue, then it should be understood as positive self-talk. Thus, if outside observers misunderstand or miss this history, then they risk misdiagnosing the PLA's sense of itself as well as its purpose, its strengths, and its weaknesses.

This history should therefore prod PLA watchers to revise their understanding of the Chinese military's formative years in the maritime domain. China's earliest performance at sea must be judged against the enormous challenges the Communists faced and the crushing resource constraints on the PLA. By those standards, the PLA has much that it can be proud of. This history should also encourage US policy makers to place the Chinese navy's recent achievements in a proper historical context. As Dale Rielage persuasively argues, an "ahistorical hubris" has for too long colored the perceptions of US planners.[6] Such excessive self-confidence and the corresponding condescension toward China led the strategic community to persistently underestimate the PLA's ability to innovate and modernize into a formidable force. A deeper historical understanding of Communist China's first contact with the seas will better equip practitioners and scholars alike to evaluate Chinese sea power today.

NOTES

1. Toshi Yoshihara, "The Paracels Sea Battle: A Campaign Appraisal," *Naval War College Review* 69, no. 2 (Spring 2016): 41–65.
2. 军事科学院军事历史研究部 [Military History Research Department of the Academy of Military Science], 第二次世界大战史 1–5卷 [History of World War II, Vols. 1–5] (Beijing: Academy of Military Science, 2015).
3. 王文清 梁玉师 郁汉冲 [Wang Wenqing, Liang Yushi, and Yu Hanchong], 中外岛战 [Chinese and Foreign Island Wars] (Beijing: Liberation Army Press, 2009), 13–107; and 孙剑波 主编 [Sun Jianbo, ed.], 岛屿战争 [Island Warfare] (Beijing: NORINCO Press, 2003).
4. Xiaobing Li, *A History of the Modern Chinese Army* (Lexington: University of Kentucky Press, 2007), 119–29.
5. Bernard D. Cole, *The Great Wall at Sea: China's Navy Enters the Twenty-First Century*, 2nd ed. (Annapolis, MD: Naval Institute Press, 2001), 7–8.
6. Dale C. Rielage, "The Chinese Navy's Missing Years," *Naval History* 32, no. 6 (November–December 2018): 24, https://www.usni.org/magazines/naval-history-magazine/2018/december/chinese-navys-missing-years.

SELECTED BIBLIOGRAPHY

Blasko, Dennis J. *The Chinese Army Today: Tradition and Transformation for the 21st Century*. 2nd ed. London: Routledge, 2012.

陳明仁 [Chen Mingren]. "古寧頭戰役對我遂行島嶼登陸作戰之啟示" [The Guningtou Campaign and Its Lessons for Carrying Out Island Landing Operations]. 海軍學術雙月刊 [Navy Professional Journal] 54, no. 6 (December 2020): 122–138.

陳偉寬 [Chen Weikuan]. "古寧頭戰役: 海,空軍作戰研究" [The Guningtou Campaign: Research on Naval and Air Operations]. 海軍學術雙月刊 [Navy Professional Journal] 53, no. 6 (December 2019): 6–22.

陈伟忠 [Chen Weizhong]. "戡亂海南島戰役之研究" [Research on the Suppression Efforts in the Hainan Island Campaign]. 軍事評論史 [Military History Review], no. 27 (June 2020): 69–116.

陈新民 徐国成 罗峰 主编 [Chen Xinmin, Xu Guocheng, and Luo Feng, eds.]. 岛屿作战研究 [Research on Island Operations]. Beijing: Military Science Press [military circulation], 2002.

陈泽华 [Chen Zehua]. 解放战争海南敌后游击战纪实 [A Documentary of Guerilla Warfare behind Enemy Lines on Hainan during the War of Liberation]. Beijing: Liberation Army Press, 2011.

Cole, Bernard D. *The Great Wall at Sea: China's Navy Enters the Twenty-First Century*. 2nd ed. Annapolis, MD: Naval Institute Press, 2001.

邓礼峰 主编 [Deng Lifeng, ed.]. 中华人民共和国军事史要 [The Outline of the Military History of the People's Republic of China]. Beijing: Military Science Press, 2005.

丁一平 李洛荣 龚连娣 [Ding Yiping, Li Luorong, and Gong Liandi]. 世界海军史 [World Naval History]. Beijing: Haichao, 2000.

杜景臣 主编 [Du Jingchen, ed.]. 中国海军军人手册 [Handbook for Officers and Enlisted of the Chinese PLA Navy]. Beijing: Haichao, 2012.

中国海军百科全书编审委员会 [Editorial Committee of the Chinese Navy Encyclopedia]. 中国海军百科全书 [Chinese Navy Encyclopedia]. Beijing: Haichao, 1999.

海军史编委 [Editorial Committee of the History of the Navy]. 海军史 [History of the Navy]. Beijing: Liberation Army Press, 1989.

当代中国丛书编辑部 [Editorial Department of the Contemporary China Book Series]. 中国人民解放军 (下) [People's Liberation Army (Vol. 2)]. Beijing: Contemporary China Publisher, 1994.

南京军区编辑室 [Editorial Office of the Nanjing Military Region]. 中国人民解放军第三野战军战史 [War History of the Third Field Army of the People's Liberation Army]. Beijing: Liberation Army Press, 2008.

中国人民解放军军史编写组 [Editorial Team of the Chinese People's Liberation Army's Military History]. 中国人民解放军军史 第四卷 [Military History of the Chinese People's Liberation Army, Vol. 4]. Beijing: Academy of Military Science, 2011.

第四野战军战史编写组 [Editorial Team of the Fourth Field Army's War History]. 第四野战军战史 [War History of the Fourth Field Army of the People's Liberation Army]. Beijing: Liberation Army Press, 2008.

Elleman, Bruce. *A History of the Modern Chinese Navy*. London: Routledge, 2021.

房功利 杨学军 相伟 [Fang Gongli, Yang Xuejun, and Xiang Wei]. 中国人民解放军海军 60年 [60 Years of the Chinese People's Liberation Navy]. Qingdao: Qingdao Press, 2009.

房功利 杨学军 相伟 [Fang Gongli, Yang Xuejun, and Xiang Wei]. 解放军史鉴: 中国人民解放军海军史 [History of the Liberation Army: History of the People's Liberation Army Navy]. Qingdao: Qingdao Press, 2014.

郭德宏 主编 [Guo Dehong, ed.]. 解放军史鉴: 解放军史 (1945–1949) [The Annals of the Liberation Army: History of the Liberation Army (1945–1949)]. Qingdao: Qingdao Press, 2014.

胡士弘 [Hu Shihong]. 张爱萍与新中国海军 [Zhang Aiping and the New Chinese Navy]. Beijing: Renmin, 2015.

黄传会 周欲行 [Huang Chuanhui and Zhou Yuxing]. 中国海军 [The Chinese Navy]. Beijing: China Publishing Group, 2019.

黄胜天 魏慈航 朱晓辉 [Huang Shengtian, Wei Cihang, and Zhu Xiaohui]. "华东军区海军的创建" [The Founding of the East China Military Region Navy]. 军事历史研究 [Military History Research] 30, no. 1 (January 2016): 115–24.

霍小勇 主编 [Huo Xiaoyong, ed.]. 军种战略学 [The Science of Service Strategies]. Beijing: National Defense University, 2008.

Li, Xiaobing. *A History of the Modern Chinese Army*. Lexington: University of Kentucky Press, 2007.

梁芳 主编 [Liang Fang, ed.]. 海战史与未来海战研究 [The History of Sea Battles and Research on Future Sea Battles]. Beijing: Haiyang, 2007.

林福隆 [Lin Fulong]. "金門古寧頭之戰: 從戡亂到保臺" [The Battle of Jinmen-Guningtou: From Suppression to Securing Taiwan]. 軍事史評論 [Military History Review], no. 26 (June 2019): 5–44.

刘华清 [Liu Huaqing]. 刘华清回忆录 [Memoirs of Liu Huaqing]. Beijing: Liberation Army Press, 2004.

刘华清 [Liu Huaqing]. 刘华清军事文选 [Selected Military Writings of Liu Huaqing]. Beijing: Liberation Army Press, 2008.

刘统 [Liu Tong]. 跨海之战: 金门 海南 一江山 [Cross-Sea Battles: Jinmen, Hainan, and Yijiangshan]. Beijing: SDX Joint Publishing, 2010.

陆其明 [Lu Qiming]. 组建第一支人民海军部队的创始人 [The Founder of the People's Navy's First Fleet]. Beijing: Haichao, 2006.

陆儒德 [Lu Rude]. 江海客: 毛泽东 [A Maritime Advocate: Mao Zedong]. Beijing: Ocean Publisher, 2009.

陆儒德 [Lu Rude]. 中国海军之路 [The Path of the Chinese Navy]. Dalian: Dalian Press, 2007.

罗元生 [Luo Yuansheng]. 共和国首任海军司令员肖劲光大传 [Biography of First Navy Commander Xiao Jinguang]. Beijing: Great Wall Press, 2013.

军事科学院军事历史研究部 [Military History Research Department of the Academy of Military Science]. 第二次世界大战史 1–5卷 [History of World War II, Vol. 1–5]. Beijing: Academy of Military Science, 2015.

Muller, David G. *China as a Maritime Power*. Boulder, CO: Westview, 1983.

Office of Naval Intelligence. *China's Navy, 2007*. Suitland, MD: ONI, 2007.

Paine, S. C. M. *The Wars for Asia, 1911–1949*. Cambridge: Cambridge University Press, 2012.

Rielage, Dale C. "The Chinese Navy's Missing Years." *Naval History* 32, no. 6 (November–December 2018): 18–25. https://www.usni.org/magazines/naval-history-magazine/2018/december/chinese-navys-missing-years.

Ryan, Mark A., David M. Finkelstein, and Michael A. McDevitt, eds. *Chinese Warfighting: The PLA Experience since 1949*. Armonk, NY: M. E. Sharpe, 2003.

尚金锁 吴子欣 陈立旭 主编 [Shang Jinsuo, Wu Zixin, and Chen Lixu, eds.]. 毛泽东军事思想与高技术条件下局部战争 [Mao Zedong's Military Thought and Local Wars under High-Technology Conditions]. Beijing: Liberation Army Press, 2002.

沈金龙 秦生祥 [Shen Jinlong and Qin Shengxiang]. "人民海军: 杨帆奋进70年" [People's Navy: Sailing and Forging Ahead for 70 Years]. 求是 [Qiushi], no. 8, April 2019. http://www.qstheory.cn/dukan/qs/2019-04/16/c_1124364140.htm.

史滇生 [Shi Diansheng]. 世界海军军事概论 [Survey of World Naval Affairs]. Beijing: Haichao, 2003).

孙剑波 主编 [Sun Jianbo, ed.]. 岛屿战争 [Island Warfare]. Beijing: NORINCO, 2003.

孙祥恩 主編 [Sun Xiangen, ed.]. 登步島戰役70周年參戰官兵訪問記錄 [The 70th Anniversary of the Dengbu Island Campaign: A Record of Interviews with Veteran Officers and Troops]. Taipei: Administration Office of the ROC Ministry of National Defense, 2019.

Swanson, Bruce. *The Eighth Voyage of the Dragon: A History of China's Quest for Seapower*. Annapolis, MD: Naval Institute Press, 1982.

王厚卿 主编 [Wang Houqing, ed.]. 战役发展史 [The History of Campaign Development]. Beijing: National Defense University Press, 2008.

王懷慶 [Wang Huaiqing]. "析論1949年金門及登步兩島作戰對國共雙方的影響與啓示" [An Analysis of the 1949 Jinmen and Dengbu Island Operations and Their Influence and Lessons for the Nationalists and the Communists]. 陸軍學術雙月刊 [Army Bimonthly] 55, no. 567 (October 2019): 7–28.

王明瑞 主编 [Wang Mingrui, ed.]. 古寧頭戰役70周年紀念冊 [The Guningtou Campaign: 70th Anniversary Memorial Book]. Taipei: ROC Ministry of National Defense Administration Office, 2019.

汪庆广 主编 [Wang Qingguang, ed.]. 岛屿登陆战斗 [Island Landing Combat Operations]. Beijing: Military Science Press [military circulation], 2001.

王伟 张德彬 主编 [Wang Wei and Zhang Debin, eds.]. 渡海登岛: 战例与战法研究 [Cross-Sea Island Landings: Research on Case Studies and Tactics]. Beijing: Military Science Press [military circulation], 2002.

王文清 梁玉师 郁汉冲 [Wang Wenqing, Liang Yushi, and Yu Hanchong]. 中外岛战 [Chinese and Foreign Island Wars]. Beijing: Liberation Army Press, 2009.

Westad, Odd Arne. *Decisive Encounters: The Chinese Civil War, 1946–1950*. Stanford, CA: Stanford University Press, 2003.

吴殿卿 [Wu Dianqing]. 蓝色档案—新中国海军大事纪实 [Blue Files—A Documentary of the Main Events of New China's Navy]. Taiyuan: Shanxi People's Press, 2015.

吴殿卿 [Wu Dianqing]. 三十年海军司令萧劲光 [Thirty-Year Navy Commander Xiao Jinguang]. Taiyuan: Shanxi People's Press, 2013.

吴殿卿 袁永安 赵小平 主编 [Wu Dianqing, Yuan Yongan, and Zhao Xiaoping, eds.]. 毛泽东与海军将领 [Mao Zedong and His Navy Generals]. Beijing: People's Press, 2013.

吴胜利 胡彦林 [Wu Shengli and Hu Yanlin]. "锻造适应我军历史使命要求的强大人民海军" [Building a Powerful People's Navy That Meets the Requirements of the Historical Mission for Our Military]. 求是 [Qiushi], no. 14 (July 2007): 31–33.

吴胜利 刘晓江 [Wu Shengli and Liu Xiaojiang]. "建设一支与履行新世纪新阶段我军历史使命要求相适应的强大的人民海军" [Building a Powerful People's Navy Adapted to Requirements of Honoring New Historic Missions of the Chinese Military in the New Century and New Stage]. 求是 [Qiushi], no. 9 (May 2009): 7–9.

萧鸿鸣 萧南溪 萧江 [Xiao Hongming, Xiao Nanxi, and Xiao Jiang]. 金门战役: 记事本末 [The Jinmen Campaign: A Record of Events]. Beijing: China Youth Press, 2016.

萧劲光 [Xiao Jinguang]. 萧劲光回忆录 [Memoirs of Xiao Jinguang]. Beijing: Contemporary China Press, 2013.

萧劲光 吴宏博 [Xiao Jinguang and Wu Hongbo]. "组建新中国海军领导机关" [The Founding of the New Chinese Navy's Leading Institutions]. 军事历史研究 [Military History Research], no. 6 (November 2016): 117–22.

杨迪 [Yang Di]. 创造渡海作战的奇迹—解放海南岛战役决策指挥的真实记叙 [Creating the Miraculous Cross-Sea Operations—The True Story behind the Campaign Command Decisions in Liberating Hainan Island]. Beijing: Liberation Army Press, 2008.

杨贵华 主编 [Yang Guihua, ed.]. 中国人民解放军战史教程 [Course Materials on the Chinese People's Liberation Army's War History]. Beijing: Military Science Press, 2013.

杨国宇 主编 [Yang Guoyu, ed.]. 当代中国海军 [Contemporary Chinese Navy]. Beijing: China Social Science Press, 1987.

叶飞 [Ye Fei]. 叶飞回忆录 [Memoirs of Ye Fei]. Beijing: Liberation Army Press, 2007.

Yu, Miles Maochun. "The Battle of Quemoy: The Amphibious Assault That Held the Postwar Military Balance in the Taiwan Strait." *Naval War College Review* 69, no. 2 (Spring 2016): 91–107.

张连宋 王其云 主编 [Zhang Liansong and Wang Qiyun, eds.]. 由海向陆的战争生命线 中外重要登陆作战的后勤保障 [War's Lifeline from the Sea to the Land: Logistical Support in Important Landing Operations in China and Overseas]. Beijing: Haichao, 2005.

鄭維中 王懷慶 [Zheng Weizhong and Wang Huaiqing]. "1950年國軍舟山轉進作戰情報作爲與得失啓示" [The 1950 Nationalist Information Operations during the Zhoushan Withdrawal and the Lessons from the Gains and Losses]. 陸軍學術雙月刊 [Army Bimonthly] 56, no. 574 (December 2020): 82–102.

朱冬生 主编 [Zhu Dongsheng, ed.]. 江河海岛作战卷 [Volume on Riverine and Island Combat]. Beijing: Liberation Army Press, 2010.

INDEX

People's Liberation Army Navy (PLAN)
(*continued*)
warfare at sea" doctrine of, 5; salvaging of the *Changzhi*, 34; sources and methods used in the study of, 13–16; Soviet role in, 118; Staff Management Department of, 54; values of, 137–38; Western historiography of, 10–11. *See also* East China Navy
People's Republic of China (PRC), 13, 15, 77
Ping-Jin campaign, 18, 24, 53, 92, 132
Pingtan Island, 66, 119
Pishan campaign (1950), 46–50, 48*map*, 119–20
PLA. *See* People's Liberation Army
PLAN. *See* People's Liberation Army Navy
PRC. *See* People's Republic of China

Qingdao, 30, 50
Qingdao naval base, 19, 55
Qingdao Press, 14
Qing Empire, 38, 132
Qiongya Column, 92–93, 96, 97, 98, 100, 101–2, 103–4, 111n10, 122, 126, 142, 145
Qiongzhou Strait, 91, 95
Qiqu Islands, 45
Quanzhou, 67

Republic of China (ROC), 74, 100, 145; professional military journals of, 16; ROC Air Force, 31, 83, 101, 120; ROC Navy, 101
Republic of China Navy (ROCN), 24, 27, 33, 44, 101, 104, 116, 145; fall of the ROCN's infrastructure, force structure, and personnel into Communist hands, 30
Rielage, Dale, 11
ROC. *See* Republic of China
ROCN. *See* Republic of China Navy

Sanman Island, 109
sea power, 3, 4, 7. *See also* Chinese sea power, key concepts concerning
Second Field Army, 18, 29; 11th Army of, 55; formation of, 17–18
Second Sino-Japanese War (1945), 17
Seventh Fleet (US), 50
Shandong Military Region, 131
Shandong Peninsula, 33
Shandong Province, 50, 66
Shanghai, 25, 44, 45, 79, 85; damage to major shipyards in, 30, 31; fall of, 30, 33
Shaoxing, 123–24
Shengsi Islands, 45
Sichuan, seizure of, 18
Song Weishi, 112n32
South Central Military Region China Navy, 55, 131, 132
South China Sea, 3, 7, 109
South Sea Fleet, 19, 55, 132
Soviet Union/Soviets, 58–59, 118
Stalin, Joseph, 61
Sun Keji, 29
Su Yu, 85
Swanson, Bruce, 10

Taihe, 107
Taikang, 102
Taiwan, 1, 2, 7, 57, 67, 68, 86, 119, 142; as the highest priority of the PLA and Mao, 16–17, 19
Taiwan Strait Crises (1954, 1958), 4, 7
Taizhou Bay, 46, 50
Tanxushan Island, 45
Taohua Island, 82, 83, 84
Third Field Army, 2, 13, 15, 19, 42n45, 43, 66, 77, 79, 85, 86, 92, 95, 110, 120, 130–31, 132; 21st Corps of, 131; command headquarters of in Baimamiao, 26; follow-on operations of in southern China, 25–26; formation of, 17–18; leadership of, 131; official war history of, 88n58; reorganization of

ABOUT THE AUTHOR

TOSHI YOSHIHARA is a senior fellow at the Center for Strategic and Budgetary Assessments. He previously held the inaugural John A. van Beuren Chair of Asia-Pacific Studies at the US Naval War College. Yoshihara is the author of *Dragon against the Sun: Chinese Views of Japanese Seapower* (2020), for which he won the 2021 Kokkiken Japan Study Award. He also coauthored *Red Star over the Pacific: China's Rise and the Challenge to U.S. Maritime Strategy* (first edition 2010, second edition 2018) and coedited *Strategy in the Second Nuclear Age: Power, Ambition, and the Ultimate Weapon* (2012).